UNIVERSAL CITIZENSHIP

BORDER HISPANISMS

Jon Beasley-Murray, Alberto Moreiras, and
Gareth Williams, *series editors*

UNIVERSAL CITIZENSHIP

LATINA/O STUDIES AT
THE LIMITS OF IDENTITY

———

R. ANDRÉS GUZMÁN

University of Texas Press

AUSTIN

Requests for permission to reproduce material
from this work should be sent to:

Permissions
University of Texas Press
P.O. Box 7819
Austin, TX 78713-7819
utpress.utexas.edu/rp-form

This work was partially funded by the Office of the Vice Provost of Research
at Indiana University Bloomington through the Grant-in-Aid Program.

All images courtesy of the author.

♾ The paper used in this book meets the minimum requirements
of ANSI/NISO Z39.48-1992 (R1997) (Permanence of Paper).

Library of Congress Cataloging-in-Publication Data

Names: Guzmán, R. Andrés (Ricardo Andrés), author.
Title: Universal citizenship : Latina/o studies at the limits of identity / R. Andrés
    Guzmán.
Other titles: Border Hispanisms.
Description: First edition. | Austin : University of Texas Press, 2019. | Series:
    Border Hispanisms | Includes bibliographical references and index.
Identifiers: LCCN 2018012489 | ISBN 978-1-4773-1762-4 (cloth : alk. paper) |
    ISBN 978-1-4773-1763-1 (pbk. : alk. paper) | ISBN 978-1-4773-1764-8
    (library e-book) | ISBN 978-1-4773-1765-5 (nonlibrary e-book)
Subjects: LCSH: World citizenship. | Group identity. | Identity politics. |
    Immigration enforcement.
Classification: LCC JZ1320.4 .G89 2019 | DDC 323.6—dc23
LC record available at https://lccn.loc.gov/2018012489

doi:10.7560/317624

FOR MICHAEL THOR, THE REAL SUPERHERO

CONTENTS

ACKNOWLEDGMENTS

THE JOURNEY TOWARD completing this book has been a long one, and I have gladly accumulated many debts along the way. First and foremost, I would like to thank Bram Acosta for his encouragement, mentorship, and friendship. From my time as a graduate student until now, Bram has been a constant source of guidance and support, not to mention the fact that this project would have been unimaginable to me without his own teaching and work. Javier Durán, Laura Gutiérrez, and Carlos Gallego helped me through the first phase of this project, when it was still a dissertation, and I would like to thank them for being exemplary teachers and scholars whose great impact continues to persist. Seminars I took with Malcolm Compitello, Miranda Joseph, and Spike Peterson also had a significant influence on my thinking and my research. From my time at Arizona, I would also like to thank Sara Beaudrie, Armando Chávez Rivera, Juliana Freire, Isela González, Rosario Hall, Miluska Martínez, Guillermo Martínez-Sotelo, Araceli Masterson, Roberto Mendoza, Maribel Moreno, Mary Portillo, Andy Rajca, Eva Romero, Cory Schott, Beatriz Urrea, and Mercy Valente. A special thanks to the borderólogos Ale Barajas, Willie Costley, Bea Jiménez, Daniela Johannes, and Jamie Wilson.

At Indiana University, I have had the fortune of having Patrick Dove as a mentor, colleague, and friend. I cannot thank Patrick enough for all of his professional and personal support and generosity. Abdul Aijaz, Anke Birkenmaier, Purnima Bose, Deborah Cohn, Manuel Díaz-Campos, Melissa Dinverno, Hamid Ekbia, Ryan Giles, Shane Greene, Nick Greven, Edgar Illas, Gaëlle Le Calvez, Mintzi Martínez-Rivera, Alejandro Mejías-López, Kate Myers, Luciana Namorato, John Nieto-Phillips, Jonathan

Risner, Micol Seigel, John Trevathan, Alberto Varon, Estela Vieira, Reyes Vila-Belda, Shane Vogel, and Steve Wagschal have made IU an excellent place to work, think, and grow. Thanks especially to Kim Geeslin for finding a way for me to get a research leave during a crucial time. I have also benefited enormously from the intense intellectual engagement and true friendship of the gang: Majed Akhter, Ishan Ashutosh, Akwasi Owusu-Bempah, Olimpia Rosenthal, and Jessie Speer; with you all, the borders between work and play become pleasantly blurred.

Gareth Williams, Bruno Bosteels, and David E. Johnson read all or parts of the manuscript and provided valuable feedback. Thanks especially to Gareth for all the ways he has supported my work and me, and to Bruno for his generosity. Thank you to the participants of the Mellon Dissertation Seminar at Cornell, the Comparative Subalternities Workshop in Gurgaon, India, and the Race, Place, Capital Workshop at Ohio State for their feedback as well. The India workshop was supported by an International Workshop Award from the Antipode Foundation. At the University of Texas Press, I would like to thank the series editors, Jon Beasley-Murray, Alberto Moreiras, and Gareth Williams, and the two anonymous reviewers. A heartfelt thanks to Kerry Webb for believing in this project and for being a wonderful editor with whom to work. Angelica Lopez-Torres was also incredibly helpful at every stage of preparing the manuscript.

My family has supported and encouraged me all along. Infinite thanks to my parents, Francisco and María Eugenia, my siblings, Francisco, Cristina, and Paulina, my nieces and nephews, Tatiana, Sofía, Gabriel, Alek, Kai, and Marco Andrés, and my cuñados, Christian and Rudy. Many thanks to the Rosenthal and Dawson families as well.

Lastly, thank you to my best friend, colleague, and partner, Olimpia Rosenthal, for allowing me to share every aspect of my life with you.

AN EARLIER VERSION OF CHAPTER 3 was published as "Criminalization at the Edge of the Evental Site: Undocumented Immigration, Mass Incarceration, and Universal Citizenship," *Theory and Event* 19, no. 2 (April 2016). A previous version of chapter 4 originally appeared in *CR: The New Centennial Review* 16, no. 3 (Winter 2016): 173–209, © 2016 Michigan State University. I would like to thank these journals for their permission to reprint this material.

UNIVERSAL CITIZENSHIP

Introduction

Universal Citizenship at the Limits of Nature and Culture

The More-and-Less-Than-Human-Animal in Us

In the closing pages of the first session of his seminar *The Beast and the Sovereign*—a seminar devoted to analyzing the various overlapping figurations of sovereignty and animality, as well as the unstable distinctions between humans and animals more generally—Derrida turns to Freud's ruminations in *Civilization and Its Discontents* on the differences between human and animal "societies." "The animals are related to us, they are even our brothers, . . . they are our kin, and there are even animal states, but we humans would not be happy in them. . . . Why?" asks Derrida, repeating Freud's line of inquiry; because "these states are arrested in their history . . . and the reason for this arrest, this stabilization, this stasis (and in this sense animal states seem more stable and therefore more statelike than human states), the reason for their relatively a-historical stasis is a relative equilibrium between the environment and their drives."[1] While it may be that other animal species have been able to achieve a balance "between the influences of their environment and the mutually contending instincts within them. . . . It may [also] be that in primitive man a fresh access of libido kindled a renewed burst of activity on the part of the destructive instinct," Freud states, with Derrida noting that "an excess or relaunching of libido might have provoked a new rebellion on the part of the destructive drive . . . and therefore a relaunching (be it finite or infinite) of history."[2] After this brief speculation on the difference between humans and animals, however, Freud immediately shifts his attention to a concern he considers more near: "What means does civilization employ in order to inhibit the aggressiveness which opposes it, to make it harmless, to get rid of it, perhaps?"[3] Freud's concern thus shifts toward the repressive mechanisms that may prevent or inhibit the sources of social instability. Yet a central theme of *Civilization and Its Discontents* is that this very aggression that must be controlled for the stability and continuation of civilization always finds other channels for its expression, hence the proliferation and increasing destructiveness of war. Repression thus appears as a condition of both the *possibility* and the *impossibility* of civilization. It is a necessary mechanism for the development of human societies at the same time that its failure both endangers the existence of such societies *and* constitutes the basis of their historicity—after all, it is animal societies that, though they have achieved highly complex forms of social organization, are nevertheless "arrested in their history" due to their effectiveness in establishing an equilibrium within themselves and in their relation with their environment. In the above formulation, it is animal societies that have evolved to such a degree that they have achieved the end of history.

What is striking both in Freud's speculation and in his immediate shift toward the necessity of repression is that animal societies come off as being more "civilized" than human ones. Alternatively, it is human societies, plagued by an excess of aggression and destructive drive that hinders the stability of ordered relations, that appear as more "barbarous." To the extent that animals, according to Freud, have attained a level of harmony both within their species and in their relationship to their environment—which is to say, insofar as they have eliminated antagonism in the relationships among themselves and between themselves and their environment—they exhibit a more "civil" form of sociality. In being subject to an excess that disrupts this balance, then, it is humans that are less civil(ized) than animal societies—essentially suggesting a lack in/ of a relationship among humans and between humans and their environment. This libidinal revolt, this rebellion of the destructive drive, thus appears as a barbarous element that, paradoxically, is also what makes us more than the human animals we are. It enables us to carry out a torsion against our very animality in a way that turns a natural situation into a historical one. Indeed, one of Lacan's main insights after Freud is locating human subjectivity in "the radical maladaptation between the human subject and its environment."[4] It is our condition as faulty animals that constitutes the basis of our freedom; it is our "less than" that allows us to be "more than."

Frank Ruda reconfigures the disjunction between humans and "nature" within the human animal itself. "There is no relation between the human and the animal . . . but there is such a thing as a human animal, which is an embodiment of this non-relation," Ruda posits: "And embodiment means: there is a material incarnation of this without-relation, of a non-relation. And this embodiment of non-relation is an embodiment of freedom, a natural incorporation of something a-natural."[5] Humans are thus the animals that embody the gap immanent to nature itself. Nature is not-whole, and humans are the animals that attest to this. Humans embody the anatural proper to nature. Ruda's proposition can be formulated in terms of the logic that Lacan attributes to the female side of his formulas of sexuation: there does not exist a living being that is not natural, though not-all living beings are natural.[6] A human is a natural being, though not-all of her is so. To the extent that the anatural escapes determination by nature, as an excess that is immanent to nature itself, it marks the place of freedom.

The burst of the "destructive instinct" to which Freud alludes, and which Derrida figures as a kind of rebellion, registers this anatural excess that makes possible our freedom. Along these lines, Mladen Dolar theorizes the political implications of the drive: "The drive is not just what preserves a certain institutional order, it is at the same time the reason that this order cannot stabilize itself and close upon itself, that it can never be reduced to the best arrangement of the existing subjects and institutions, but presents an excess which subverts it."[7] Hence Dolar proposes the possibility of "turning into an agent of the (death) drive, untying the glue of social bonds, in the hope of establishing the possibility of another kind of relation in the social non-relation."[8] The drive according to Dolar is thus not simply destructive; rather, in undoing the social bonds that exist, it creates an opening for the novel and creative rearticulation of social relations. The drive itself is not politics, but it makes manifest a gap in which a political subjectivation can make its thought/practice consist in transforming an old order into a new one.[9]

Emanating from the nonrelation between humans and animals—which is to say, emanating from the site of nature's excess over itself as embodied in the human animal—this subjectivizing torsion may also be read as registering a break with the limitations of human finitude, as an instance when infinity imposes itself upon finite presentation. Alenka Zupančič's theorization of comedy can help schematize this. Challenging figurations of the subject in terms of irony or tragedy, Zupančič makes the case for comedy, insisting similarly on comedy's own rupture with finitude. Zupančič argues against the idea that comedy's function is to present us with our own limitations in a way that compels us to confront and then accept our natural finitude.[10] "Is not the very existence of comedy and of the comical telling us most clearly that a man is never just a man, and that his finitude is very much corroded by a passion which is precisely not cut to the measure of man and his finitude?" she asks. "'[M]an,' a human being, interests comedy at the very point where the human coincides with the inhuman," she continues, "where the inhuman 'falls' into the human (into man), where the infinite falls into the finite."[11]

Infinity finds its expression as the errancy proper to finite presentation, at the limits of our natural animality. This incursion of the infinite into the finite jolts the parameters of the possible by introducing something that was previously deemed impossible; it makes of the impossible something actual. In the social field, equality is precisely the "impossible" proper to inegalitarian forms of social organization. Egalitarian politics evince the ability of people to think and act beyond identitarian boundaries that, even if intersectional, function to restrict our thought to our social location and our self-interested "human nature." The ability to think beyond these limitations registers our actual capacity for (infinite) thought in its break with our human finitude. With every advent of egalitarian politics, history has demonstrated that "the impossible happens." Yet the impossible "cannot be reached by a gradual extension of the possible," just like infinity cannot be reached by the gradual extension of the finite, and equality cannot be reached through the gradual extension of, and inclusion into, the parameters of an unequal order.[12] A subjective torsion is needed through the very place of their nonrelation.

Arendt and the Empty Foundations of Rights

In "The Decline of the Nation-State and the End of the Rights of Man," Hannah Arendt notes a contradiction that became evident in the twentieth century with the rise of large numbers of stateless people, one that voided the supposedly natural foundations of human rights. "The conception of human rights, based upon the assumed existence of a human being as such," notes Arendt, "broke down at the very moment when those who professed to believe in it were for the first time confronted with people who had indeed lost all other qualities and specific relationships—except that they were still human."[13] Indeed, "it turned out that the moment human beings lacked their own government and had to fall back upon their minimum rights, no authority was left to protect them and no institution was willing to guarantee them."[14] In this way, the "Rights of Man . . . proved to be unenforceable . . . whenever people appeared who were no longer citizens of any sovereign state."[15] Without a nation-state to recognize their belonging, the stateless were rendered rightless in the eyes of all other nation-states as well. What this demonstrated was that human rights in general are premised upon an initial right that had heretofore been unacknowledged: the *right* to have rights. With their expulsion from the nation-states to which they had belonged, the stateless lost this initial right. As a result, the right to have rights was shown to be an implicit right premised upon the recognition of one's belonging to a juridico-political community.[16]

Arendt's argument demonstrates that with regard to human rights, "humanity"—like the "state of nature" in social contract theory—has never been anything other than a political fiction created *within* the political community to ideologically provide human rights' empty foundations with substantive ground. Among the consequences of this insight is the acknowledgment that there is no "Other of the Other": there is no external, prepolitical, or transcendental source that can guarantee rights beyond the symbolic/legal order proper to a given juridico-political community. The "right" to have rights is an initial right that can only be retroactively posited as such once one's belonging has been established. As a necessary condition that can only be assumed after the fact, it indexes the real of juridico-political community. It also marks the limits of deduction: it is a right that cannot be deduced either from other rights or from nature or humanity.

Given the positioning of this right at the limits of deduction, I argue that we can benefit from shifting the emphasis from the requirement that one's belonging be recognized (which places its stress on the function of a gatekeeper), to thinking the function of a prescriptive enactment of belonging by the excluded themselves, and thus of an axiomatic affirmation of the right to have rights. The present book contributes to such a line of thought from the perspective of undocumented people in the United States. It endeavors to theorize a mode of subjectivation that obtains not from recognition and inclusion, but from a forceful intervention into the political from the very place of its real, from the place of its empty foundations. Thus, rather than simply being an assertion of the right to belong, the prescriptive affirmation of the right to have rights, I hold, shows our first human right to be the axiomatic right to *revolt*.

Universality at the Limits of Cultural Citizenship

Of the many theorizations of citizenship in Latina/o, ethnic, and area studies, the concept of "cultural citizenship" has gained much traction due to its attention to expressions of citizenship outside formal political channels and its focus on the cultural dimensions of formal citizenship.[17] Renato Rosaldo, who coined the term, describes the work of cultural citizenship in the following terms:

> Cultural citizenship operates in an uneven field of structural inequalities where the dominant claims of universal citizenship assume a propertied white male subject and usually blind themselves to their exclusions and marginalizations of people who differ in gender, race, sexuality, and age. Cultural citizenship attends, not only to dominant exclusions and marginalizations, but also to subordinate aspirations for and definitions of enfranchisement.[18]

Cultural citizenship operates at the level of universal citizenship's disavowed underside, where the pillars of universal citizenship are shown to support a particular and exclusionary figure of the subject—a propertied white (and heterosexual) male subject—projected onto the very structure of the political. It seeks to diversify these foundations by forcing the recognition and inclusion of difference. It thus challenges the liberal notion of formal equality by distinguishing "the formal level of theoretical universality from the substantive level of exclusionary and marginalizing practices," while demonstrating the efficacy of oppositional cultural practices in not simply enabling the marginalized to lay claims to existing rights, but in creating new rights that aspire to make a more inclusive society.[19] In this manner, cultural citizenship exhibits a subjective, interventionist character made possible by the fact that citizenship is always "contested and incomplete."[20] It is capable of performing the very rights it demands through cultural practices that are constitutive of new subjects.[21]

Despite its interventionist character and its claim to adopt the perspective of the marginalized, cultural citizenship is grounded on an identitarian logic, I argue, that undermines its political objectives and compels it to reproduce some of the very exclusions against which it agitates. This can be gauged in William V. Flores's account of cultural citizenship in the context of organizational campaigns around undocumented immigration. "Cultural citizenship can be thought of as a broad range of activities of everyday life through which Latinos and other groups claim space in society, define their communities, and claim rights," Flores asserts: "It involves the right to retain difference, while also attaining membership in society. It also involves self-definition, affirmation, and empowerment."[22] At the heart of cultural citizenship, and in this case specifically *Latino* cultural citizenship, is the assertion of a distinct group identity. This identitarian affirmation is an act of communitarian self-definition that is simultaneously the basis upon which rights claims are made. Against the homogenizing abstraction of formal citizenship, cultural citizenship functions on the declaration of substantive difference. It is a political act through which a community affirms its difference and demands to be included through the recognition of this very difference.

The shortfalls of this conception are evinced precisely with regard to undocumented people, since not only are they excluded from legal citizenship, but they are also at the margins of the Latino community seeking to assert its own identity. In Flores's account, the prerogative of self-definition continues to fall on the side of legal citizens. In the cases that he uses as examples, it is Chicano/Latino citizens who defy the government and choose to protect and include undocumented people in their various organizations and campaigns. "By defending the undocumented," Flores argues, "the Chicano activists asserted their right to determine who is and who is not part of their community."[23] "Community" in these cases, continues Flores, "is self-defined, not imposed by government officials."[24] Yet in "draw[ing] clear boundaries between who is and who is not part of the community," a move that is exclusionary by definition and is implicit in the very act of *self-definition*, it seems that cultural citizenship merely shifts the right to include/exclude from the state to the community.[25]

Although it is laudable that the community has chosen to include the undocumented, it by no means follows from the notion of cultural citizenship that this need be the case—indeed, the agency of cultural citizenship rests on the *communitarian decision* on its own limits, which means that its degree of inclusivity and exclusivity cannot be determined beforehand. In fact, given that Latino cultural citizenship "involves the creation of a distinct Latino sensibility, a social and political discourse, and a Latino aesthetic, all of which flow out of the unique reality of being Latino in the United States and the desire to express that uniqueness," one also wonders whether the community would have made the same decision if the undocumented did not share a similar ethnic background as the Chicano/Latino community described by Flores.[26] After all, one of the reasons for providing the undocumented with protection, according to an activist cited by Flores, was that "[w]e felt we had to protect them. . . . That's what being Chicano is all about, *protecting your own, protecting your community.*"[27] Framed in this way, the difference between Latino cultural citizenship and the discriminatory identitarian discourse against which Rosaldo developed the concept of cultural citizenship in the first place becomes less certain.

Noncitizens, moreover, are only attributed a derivative form of agency in Flores's account. "[B]y their actions to include both undocumented and legal residents in their social movements, *Latinos* create social space for immigrants to emerge as subjects joining with U.S.-born Latinos to fight for common interests," Flores argues.[28] The subjectivation of noncitizens is in this way dependent on the action of Latino *citizens*—even if the latter are themselves often treated as second-class citizens. It is the Latino citizen ally who creates a space for noncitizens to emerge as subjects. While the distinction between citizens and noncitizens may blur as they engage in collective struggle, the initial decision on belonging that creates space for subjectivation still falls on the side of the citizen as gatekeeper.[29] The subjectivation of noncitizens continues to rely on the kindness of citizens to provide them with an initial degree of belonging. Thus, far from approaching citizenship from the perspective of the excluded, Flores's account of cultural citizenship continues to take the legally recognized citizen as its point of departure and reifies the exclusion and subjection of noncitizens by denying them an autonomous capacity for political action. Further, if the objective of cultural citizenship is to fight against the exclusions of universal citizenship by developing a cultural practice that enables the excluded to claim and enact rights, it becomes evident that it can only do so by producing and disavowing its own identitarian exclusions—that is, whoever does not have the ethnocultural background that enables him or her to participate in producing a "distinct Latino quality of life."[30]

It is at the limits of identity, I claim, that universal citizenship must be (re)thought and (re)affirmed. Yet this is not a simple return to the abstract universality of formal equality, nor does it disregard the situatedness of those upon whose exclusion the political is founded. Cutting through the opposition between abstract universality and substantive particularity, we must shift our focus onto the "universalizability of the place of enunciation itself," a place that I hold is politically universalizable when it is situated at the constitutive, nonidentitarian limits of the political.[31] Rather than restricting ourselves to pointing out the substantive exclusions and limitations of formal equality's purported universality, we must endorse "these limits by transforming them into the very points of the infinite and generic power of the universal."[32] If "citizenship," at its most radical, names a politics that aims to transform social and economic order, then "universal" citizenship begins precisely with the subjective affirmation of this politics—indeed, with an autonomous enactment of the right to *revolt*—from the location of said order's foundational exclusions, and names a process that inheres in the gap that makes "not-all" of both nature and culture. Alain Badiou's philosophy provides the conceptual tools to think the consistency of this process, and specifically with regard to the way in which it remains subtracted from identitarian capture. In order to explain in more detail what a Badiouan approach can contribute to postidentity theory, I situate my discussion in the wake of debates around subalternity and posthegemony in the field of Latin American studies.

The Critique of Identity Politics, or,
Toward a Nonidentitarian Theory of the Subject

My engagement with the theorists that follow is meant to provide an overview of some of the theoretical and philosophical undercurrents that inform recent critiques of identity politics—what I refer to as postidentity theory—and to specify the contribution that a rethinking of universal citizenship informed by Badiou's philosophy can make to these discussions. What follows is by no means exhaustive of debates around identity politics, seeking rather to situate my argument in the wake of a number of critical positions that emerged in the field of Latin American studies around the theorization of subalternity. It demonstrates the extent to which my rethinking of universal citizenship is informed and made possible by these debates, while also outlining how it may allow one to cut through what I see as some of their impasses.

In *The Exhaustion of Difference*, Alberto Moreiras draws on the resources of subaltern studies to find a way out of the deadlocks around the concepts of identity and difference.[33] Moreiras's work is central to the formulation of a "deconstructive and philosophico-theoretical" strand of Latin American subaltern studies that strives to think the subaltern beyond the realm of identitarian self-consciousness.[34] For him, "[s]ubalternity is the site, not just *of* negated identity, but also *for* a constant negation of identity positions [since] identities are always the product of the hegemonic relation, always the result of an interpellation and, therefore, not an autonomous site for politics."[35] Identitarian subject positions are always already the outcome of ideological interpellation, and are hence a product of structural capture.[36] Since the positive systematicity of structure depends upon the determination of an exclusionary limit (subalternity), the latter marks a site both constitutive and in excess of it. This subaltern excess is then capable of having a disruptive effect back upon the hegemonic order from which it is constitutively expelled. Since the hegemonic field demarcates the limits of meaningful intelligibility, however, subalternity is situated beyond such intelligibility and thus can only be thought negatively.[37]

This constitutive negativity is the astructural condition for the possibility of a form of causality beyond hegemony. Thought along these lines, subalternity emerges not only as the negative side of identity formation, as the nonidentitarian limit necessary for the intelligibility of any identitarian position, but as the persistent remainder that impinges upon the latter's stable reproduction; a remainder that, insofar as it inhabits a site "within and beyond all hegemonic closures," is also "beyond all difference and beyond all identity."[38] This deconstructive theorization of subalternity thus opens the way toward a mode of "posthegemonic" thought and practice that, in the words of Gareth Williams, is capable of "resist[ing] appropriation by interrupting hegemony's signifying processes; and it does not coincide with hegemony even when it converges with it."[39] Posthegemony seeks to forgo the logic of subaltern inclusion in order to target the very determinations constitutive of the political field itself. Refusing to submit to the terms established by the political logics of hegemony or counterhegemony, posthegemony ventures to open up the political field to the liberating effects of unintelligibility.[40]

John Beverley, however, is critical of the effectiveness of this line of theory for thinking about (and supporting) actual political events in Latin America, like the coming into power of the various leftist governments grouped under the banner of the "marea rosada," or "pink tide." Against thinking the subaltern as a negative remainder, Beverley insists on conceptualizing the subaltern as a specific identity, from which he concludes that "the politics of the subaltern must be, at least in some measure, 'identity' politics."[41] For a subaltern politics to be "real politics," he stresses, it must necessarily entail a struggle for hegemony. Thus, for a viable "subaltern-popular" politics to succeed—that is, one that seeks to advance a change from the perspective of the subaltern—it must hegemonically interpellate and reterritorialize a range of identities within the nation-state in a form of radical multiculturalism.[42]

For the theorists of posthegemony, a "subaltern hegemony" can only ever be a contradiction in terms, a logical impossibility inasmuch as any hegemony must by necessity constitute itself on the production of subalternity as immanent negation. Meanwhile, for Beverley, the failure not only to affirm this as a theoretical possibility but to acknowledge that this is effectively what has happened in some places across Latin America is a deeply depoliticizing stance. A critique of hegemony directed at its formal logics at the expense of a proper consideration of differences in content—the failure to consider the differences in content between the hegemonic articulations of Nazism and that of the Movimiento al Socialismo in Bolivia, for example—can only lead to "a *renunciation* of actual politics," Beverley maintains, "which means that despite their claim to be 'transformative,' they remain complicit with the existing order of things."[43] Indeed, Beverley's charge echoes Bruno Bosteels's warning that

> there remains the tangible risk that the increasing self-reflexivity about the inevitable presence of a subaltern remainder would become in turn the irrefutable guarantee of radicalism in the purest sense. . . . What remains problematic about this otherwise acute insight is that any specific change will inevitably become liable to the criticism that it misrecognizes its own conditions of possibility, insofar as these are also at the same time conditions of impossibility. . . . A heightened metacritical awareness of this liability, nevertheless, should neither serve as an alibi for radical quietism nor allow the critical thinker to hide behind the mask of the beautiful soul, free of all worldly guilt.[44]

It is precisely this deadlock between a radical critique of statist and identitarian logics, on the one hand, and the necessary commitment to real politics, on the other, that the conception of universal citizenship that I propose seeks to cut through. Universal citizenship as I formulate it bypasses the pitfalls that Bosteels identifies, moreover, by thinking a mode of politics of the not-all, one that inheres in and proceeds from the place of subalternity while remaining subtracted from the identitarian logics of recognition and inclusion—thus signaling a politics that remains at the margins of statist intelligibility.

Indeed, despite their significant differences, the positions put forth by both Beverley and posthegemonic theorists like Williams and Moreiras are united by a consensus on the assumption that any actual political sequence, and any conception of such a sequence that maintains a figure of the subject, can only ever be identitarian.[45] I posit that this need not be the case. I seek to demonstrate that the coupling of identity and real politics is not a necessary one. We *can* think real politics that elude identitarian capture, that remain at the margins of state intelligibility, and we need not relegate such thinking to a form of politics-to-come. In fact, we can find evidence of this in the thought produced by revolutionary sequences throughout history. At least since the French Revolution, moreover, this kind of politics has been linked to the thought of universal citizenship in its most radical form.

Badiou's philosophy is central to my theorization of a nonidentitarian mode of politics, providing an ontological account of what I term universal citizenship. In *Chicana/o Subjectivity and the Politics of Identity*, Carlos Gallego also advances a critique of identity politics that draws on Badiou and serves as a major point of reference for bringing Badiou's philosophy to bear upon the field of Chicana/o and Latina/o studies.[46] In this work, Gallego traces a "literary-philosophical genealogy of Chicano/a subjectivity" to demonstrate the ways in which an identitarian paradigm based on Hegel's dialectic of recognition has functioned as a persistent conceptual reference point for the formulation of oppositional subjectivities.[47] To the extent that social justice is made to depend on recognition (whether of sameness or of difference), Gallego argues that it relies on an ideologically laden conception of the subject that bolsters the reproduction of existing social order. "[T]he search for social justice through recognition . . . inevitably results in a reinforcement of the state of the situation, deferring true revolutionary change in favor of an ideological fantasy that only solidifies a predisposition for narcissism and self-interest," he maintains.[48]

One of the advantages that Gallego sees in Badiou's philosophy is its ability to conceive of the subject neither as "simply a structural given as it is for Althusser and Lacan," nor as an entity whose agency is founded on identitarian recognition or self-consciousness.[49] Against a conception of the subject as a purely ideological formation that is both a product of and complicit with existing configurations of power/knowledge, Badiou wagers his philosophy on the need to maintain the category of the subject for thinking the advent of truths. In the particular way in which he links subject and truth, however, Badiou also distances himself from Lacan, for whom "the subject must be maintained in the pure void of its subtraction if one wishes to save truth," signaling a tendency in Lacan to identify the subject wholly with the void or empty place in the signifying structure.[50] Badiou's project, on the other hand, is to think the subject in the form of a productivity that traverses a given order. It goes against a conception that in its attempt to evacuate the subject of identitarian particularities situates it wholly in the place of structural lack, even while Badiou's subject is founded on this very lack—which is to say, it is founded on a given order's lack of foundation. It is this lack of foundation, signaling the failure of structural totalization, that makes possible a form of thought/practice that exceeds structural determination and identitarian capture.

What Badiou contributes to postidentity theory is a formulation of a nonidentitarian subject and a systematic account of a subjective process that remains illegible to the administrative reason of the state. The mode of this subjective traversal is what Badiou refers to as a "generic procedure," which includes an account of the generic multiple or nonidentitarian collective constituted through this very process. The generic procedure is conditioned by an event that registers the intrasituational inherence of the void (i.e., of being as "not-one," as inconsistent multiplicity—precisely the inconsistency that must be prohibited for the constitution and maintenance of order as such). An event, in other words, is made possible by, and so registers, the fact that a situation's structure is incomplete and can never rid itself of immanent errancy—of the void as its condition of (im)possibility. An event can thus open a situation up to a possibility previously deemed impossible (an affirmation of universal equality, for example), and the generic multiple is the collective brought together around a process that tests and transforms the situation on the basis of this new possibility—a possibility addressed to all, and thus universalizable, due to the universalizability of the void (of the not-one/not-all). Insofar as this universalizability allows the generic procedure to cut across the social groups that compose a given order, and to gather together multiples from each group, both the procedure and the collective it forms remain subtracted from identitarian determination. The universality at stake here is thus not another identitarian particularity passing itself off as neutral standard.

The generic collective is and remains indiscernible.[51] Accordingly, a generic set "is rightfully declared *generic*, because, if one wishes to qualify it, all one can say is that its elements *are*. The part thus belongs to the supreme genre, the genre of the being of the situation as such."[52] This is also why the generic collective is linked to the truth of a given situation: "for what the faithful [i.e., generic] procedure thus rejoins is none other than the truth *of the entire situation*, insofar as the sense of the indiscernible is that of exhibiting as one-multiple the very being of what belongs insofar as it belongs."[53] Hence a truth is never ready-made, but is instead *produced* as a generic multiple through a subjective fidelity to an event.[54] Since "[a] truth is a subset of the situation but one whose components cannot be totalized by means of a predicate of the [situation's] language," Badiou asserts, "a truth is an indistinct subset; so nondescript in the way it gathers together its components that no trait shared by the latter would allow the subset to be identified by knowledge."[55] The commonality of the elements that make up the generic set is reduced to the bare minimum of indistinct belonging as such; to the fact that they *are* in a given situation. What holds these elements together, moreover, is a process oriented by a subjective fidelity to, or a wager without guarantee on, the possibility opened up by the void's evental incursion. Badiou's concept of truth, like his conception of the subject, thus pushes through the formalization of foundational lack, incompleteness, or indeterminacy and toward the formalization of a process that, while remaining subtracted from identitarian predicates, is capable of transforming a situation through its real productivity and temporal duration.

Given the traversal function of a generic procedure, beginning from the universalizability of the consequences of the void's evental intrusion, I posit that the transformative nonidentitarian trajectory of the generic procedure in politics be designated "universal citizenship," stressing the formulation of universality from the perspective of the impossibility of full representation, from the limits in relation to which meaning is constituted. To these ends, I examine various sequences of generic politics—across multiple contexts ranging from the Chicano Movement and the immigrant rights protests in the United States in 2006 to Frantz Fanon's account of anticolonial struggle in Algeria—that escape identitarian capture and serve as points of reference for a renewed understanding of universal citizenship. I define the citizen as a collective subject brought into being by *anyone* who in a given juridico-political situation endeavors to transform the latter on the basis of an evental affirmation of equality. The advent of the "citizen" and "citizenship," moreover, does not depend upon prior identitarian or legal recognition since they stem from the exclusions upon which legally recognized citizenship and "legitimate" political belonging are founded. In a way that seeks to unsettle the terms of the current immigration debate in the United States, I further propose that universal citizenship, insofar as it aims to transform the basic organizational politico-economic coordinates of society, is itself on the border of legality and illegality. Universal citizenship is the collective process through which a situation is radically transformed, of which the citizen-subject is the formal designation of its productivity. Drawing on both the revolutionary conception of nation in the French Revolution and on Frantz Fanon's writings on the Algerian Revolution, moreover, I argue that the generic collective itself *is* a revolutionary nation in action.

Badiou, Capitalism, and Latina/o and Ethnic Studies

Because Badiou's philosophy is central to my theorization of universal citizenship, a few words are in order with regard to the limitations of his framework and what they may mean for its intersection with Latina/o and ethnic studies. One can approach this through the status of capitalism in his work. Badiou's engagement with the Marxist critique of political economy, for example, has long been a point of contention, in large part because of statements such as the following from *Theory of the Subject*, where he declares that "Marxism, seized from any point that is not its effective operation which is entirely of the order of politics within the masses, does not deserve one hour of our troubles."[56] Even if one allows for a degree of polemical overstatement, Badiou has remained consistent on the idea that if Marxism has any political function it is only in its capacity to sustain a politics heterogeneous to the economic, one that is not transitive to economic analysis.[57] This is so because to the extent that an event and the politics it makes possible break with "objective" conditions—with what within a situation is deemed to be historically necessary or objectively possible—they precisely cannot be deduced from these conditions.[58]

Yet the impossibility made possible by an event is specific to a particular situation; it is the making possible of an impossibility constitutive of *that* situation. Likewise, the trajectory of a generic sequence also develops in its transformation of the specific situation in which it unfolds. Despite some formal invariants, politics occurs in a particular place and time, and a sequence is shaped by its ability or inability to transform the conditions it confronts. Its trajectory is shaped by the friction between a set of prescriptions and the context it tries to transform on the basis of those prescriptions. Thus Badiou clarifies that "[j]ust as we cannot maintain that the determination of political singularity is transitive to the global analysis, it isn't simply transitive to axioms of the will [either]," which means that while politics breaks with existing conditions, it nevertheless does not imply pure voluntarism.[59]

The level of abstraction in Badiou's philosophy, on the other hand, necessarily results in erasing much of the richness and complexity of context. It tells us very little about strategic points of intervention, for which we still need historical and politico-economic analyses. An affirmation of equality does not by itself tell us enough about where we should concentrate our energies. In determining this, we must diagnose the points of tension, convergence, and systemic contradiction of the context in which politics takes place, even if a political sequence will also force a transformation back upon the analytical frameworks we use. The logic of equality tells us nothing about how money functions, for example, and thus nothing about how we can imagine alternative forms of exchange that impede the private accumulation of social wealth.[60] For this we require not only political invention but a sustained engagement with the Marxist critique of political economy. Economic analysis can help in generating a vision of how capitalism works in order precisely to be better equipped to dismantle it. To remain blind to this can only limit political effectiveness.[61]

This also brings up the question of what Badiou's philosophy can imply for other sociohistorical factors, such as race, ethnicity, and gender. To the extent that he insists that a generic politics is "indifferent to difference," due to the universality of the event's address and to the sameness implied by our universal capacity to think and act beyond the specificity of our differences, his framework severely minimizes attention to the historical and contemporary function of these categories in structuring social relations, and especially in their codetermination with capitalism—even as his philosophy should not be confused with the race-blind discourse promoted by many conservatives (paradoxically, in the name of liberalism).[62] While Badiou makes plain not only that identitarian differences need not be erased in politics, but indeed that the various perspectives made possible by such differences are in fact essential to politics, he nevertheless stops short of addressing the systemic role that such differences play in configuring inequality.[63] Accordingly, Badiou has very little to tell us about them.

Just as with the critique of political economy, however, Badiou's philosophy is not necessarily incompatible with the consideration of these questions, as I attempt to demonstrate throughout the course of this book. In fact, I argue that it is the same erasure caused by formalist abstraction that allows Badiou's framework to be deployed in considering all these issues. It is its very lack of substantive detail and specificity that enables one to put his thought to work in a range of different contexts and with regard to a variety of different factors. In sum, it is this aspect of Badiou's philosophy that allows it to speak to issues central to the fields of Latina/o and ethnic studies—not to mention the more direct connection of Badiou's philosophy and political practice to the issue of undocumented workers, which is also important to Latina/o studies.

Far from arguing that the insights gleaned from political economy and ethnic studies should be ignored, much less replaced by his framework, the present study seeks to *supplement* Badiou's framework with these insights, even as I argue that universal citizenship as generic politics entails a process that breaks with and exceeds "objective" determinations, existing knowledge, and identitarian constraints. If knowledge functions through the logic of identity, then a politics that punctures a hole in knowledge must also constitute a break with identitarian thinking. Like the shift from the finite to the infinite, this cannot simply happen by expansion (which supposes a transitivity), but by prescription.[64] Similar to the way in which economic analysis does not necessarily lead to radical politics, neither does the analysis of race, ethnicity, gender, or sexuality. On the other hand, any radical egalitarian politics must carry out a sustained engagement with the analysis of such factors, among others, as it transforms and exceeds them via a subjective torsion.

Chapters

The trajectory of the ensuing pages is organized around a general progression in focus, from the structural function of "lack," to the theorization of moments of revolt, to the question of the consistency of politics as process. With this in mind, the logical progression of the chapters is conceptual and thematic, and not chronological. The first and last chapters, moreover, function as theoretical bookends, the specific content of which is restricted neither to the United States nor to Latina/o studies but which are important in setting up and extending the book's theoretical argument.

Chapter 1 begins by theorizing universal citizenship through the concept of the "democratic act," one that indexes the subjective and forceful advent of antagonistic causality from the real of a juridico-political order. Insofar as such an act entails a struggle over the field of struggle, it cannot be contained within communicative models of democracy and blurs the lines between "democracy" and "dictatorship." It is this zero point of politics that some theorists of democracy disavow, effectively doing away with antagonistic causality as a condition for more profound political transformations. The chapter then shifts focus from the question of causality to that of consistency. It analyzes the relationship between "citizenship" and "nation," noting the transformations in the conception and function of the latter around the time of the French Revolution. "Nation," it maintains, is one of the main categories through which modern political community has attained its ideological consistency via nation's function as both "quilting point" and fantasy. With respect to the French Revolution, however, it finds in the work of Jürgen Habermas and Eric Hobsbawm the identification of two competing conceptions of the relationship between citizenship and nation: (1) a conception that, drawing on this word's previous association with ethnic and linguistic communities, took nation to designate the ground that made possible and determined the values and actions of citizens, and (2) a conception that held nation to be the product of the concerted action of anyone who chose to participate in revolutionary politics. While in the first conception the particularities of the national character and national belonging determine and authorize the actions of citizens, in the latter conception it is citizenship itself, as an active participation in politics, that is constitutive of nation. The latter is consistent with the radical idea of universal citizenship in disregarding identitarian predicates as conditions for political participation and national belonging. Turning to the late nineteenth-century context of the United States, the chapter ends by reading historian Frederick Jackson Turner's "frontier thesis" as an example of an identitarian, liberal construction of nation. Through his writings, Turner constructs a fantasy of the origins of American national identity that hinges on the paradoxical figure of the Indian as its condition of (im)possibility.

The second chapter argues for a reconceptualization of the subject in Latina/o and ethnic studies through the figure of the "alien" and the structural fact of alienation. It begins by analyzing the passage in 2010 of HB 2281, a law that sought to ban Mexican American studies from public high schools in Tucson, Arizona. Accusing Mexican American studies of promoting the overthrow of the US government, proponents of the law revived Cold War rhetoric that constructed the program as a foreign-inspired national security threat. Defenders of the program, on the other hand, pointed to the academic success of students who participated in it, and identified as a source of this success the recognition that students obtained by means of the subject matter. In doing so, the program's supporters deployed a discourse that drew on the tenets of ego psychology by stressing the way in which Mexican American studies helps students overcome feelings of alienation by developing a stronger sense of self. In dialogue with Antonio Viego, the chapter argues for the critical advantages of a Lacanian psychoanalytic perspective that highlights the political drawbacks of the assimilationism presupposed by ego psychology and holds alienation as a structural constant. It develops this argument by tracing the way in which the figure of the "alien" has been deployed throughout US history—beginning with the Alien and Sedition Acts of 1798, though focusing mainly on the twentieth century—as the embodiment of the threat of radical politics and the figure against which racialized conceptions of nation and citizenship have been (re)articulated.

The "alien" appears as the symptomatic figure that betrays the fact that political community is always already alienated from itself. In this way, the very fact that different ethnic/racial groups have historically been designated as the embodiment of the "inassimilable" with regard to the national political community actually points to the inassimilable (real) as a structural site in excess of identitarian particularities. This site, which indexes a breach immanent to political community, is also coupled with the threat of radical antagonism. The chapter follows by analyzing moments of alienation, and tracing the political implications of such moments, in the life of labor organizer Luisa Moreno and in the testimony of Bertolt Brecht—the famous theorist of alienation—before the House Un-American Activities Committee. It closes by returning to Viego's suggestion that the radical potential of Latina/o studies could be better served by employing what Lacan calls the "hysteric's discourse," to the extent that it is a discourse articulated from the perspective of the persistent structural function of lack. Arguing that a mere acknowledgment of or exposure to lack does not go far enough in thinking the conditions for structural change, the chapter finds an alternative theory of the subject in Julia de Burgos's poem "To Julia de Burgos." In this poem, Burgos links the gap of self-alienation to the antagonism that splits society from itself, and figures a process of subjectivation in which the political intervention of the masses will condition a torsion of the alienated individual back upon herself as she participates in a collective revolt that, proceeding from the place of the inherent incompleteness of the self and of society, is in excess of identitarian constraints and self-interest.

Chapter 3 analyzes the governmental production of illegality/criminality through the criminalization of (un)documented immigration and the phenomenon of mass incarceration in the United States. Linking such processes to the state's attempt to preempt social disturbance and the advent of radical politics in a context characterized by the systemic overproduction of a surplus population, it formulates the concept of universal citizenship as a politics initiated and developed from the perspective of figures (like the "undocumented" and the "criminal") upon whose exclusion legally recognized citizenship and the state's demarcation of the political are constituted. The chapter argues that as a form of "unlicensed" citizenship that aims to transform society's basic organizational premises, universal citizenship is always on the border of legality and illegality. The previous chapter's theorization of the alien and alienation is reconfigured in this chapter through Badiou's concept of the "evental site": a site that belongs without inclusion but which, given its location at the limits of structure, holds the potential for an evental disruption. The chapter analyzes the 2006 immigration marches as an example of such a disruption and of the actualization of universal citizenship.

Chapter 4 shifts focus to the Chicano Movement and to the legal and literary work of Oscar "Zeta" Acosta. Acosta's literature has often been read through the prism of identity politics. This chapter argues for a more nuanced understanding of Acosta's work by analyzing his literary production in relation to his experience as a militant lawyer. It argues that Acosta's grand jury discrimination challenge—in defense of Chicano militants indicted for conspiracy and other charges in the aftermath of the 1968 East Los Angeles high school walkouts—compelled an identitarian stance that ultimately fed into developing notions of Chicano nationalism by requiring the defense to prove the existence of Mexican Americans as a distinct social group. In his semiautobiographical novel, *The Revolt of the Cockroach People*, however, Acosta reflects on the political limitations of his legal work. In doing so, he proposes a generic conception of the political collective and figures a mode of politics subtracted from the law and representation. In the novel, Cockroach comes to name a generic collective—one that, rather than being held together by a common identity, is held together by a subjective wager on an egalitarian possibility without guarantees.

The fifth and final chapter returns to the general problematic with which the book begins but expands on the theorization of a nonidentitarian, generic collective by focusing on the question of fantasy, the social bond, and ideology. Sigmund Freud's work on group psychology and Ernesto Laclau's theory of populism posit the identitarian self-conception of a group qua group and a subsequent libidinally constituted social bond as necessary sources of a group's consistency. In doing so, both employ a logic homologous to Lacanian fantasy ($ \$ \lozenge a $). Badiou, however, suggests that a "genuinely political organisation . . . is the least bound place of all," asserting the existence of a generic political collective that does not proceed on the basis of a common identity or a social bond between members.[65] The chapter finds in Fanon's account of revolutionary nation (as opposed to its chauvinistic identitarian counterpart) a similar conception, where anyone who fights for Algerian independence is "Algerian," and where the revolutionary process itself proceeds through a rearticulation of social relations "unbound" from their prior configurations. The revolutionary Algerian nation is thus a collective the consistency of which is not provided by identitarian definition, but rather by a political logic

developed on the basis of anticolonial struggle. Given that Badiou designates the generic set with the mark of ♀, the chapter ends by theorizing
the ontological status of such a collective through Lacan's formulas of
sexuation. Beginning from the site where the structure is "not-all" (the
female side), revolutionary politics can only maintain itself via a process
and discourse that "goes through the fantasy" and "punches a hole in
knowledge" (i.e., that reconfigures the male side) without attempting to
close itself off from its own real—which is to say, without disavowing its
own lack and re-creating its own counterfantasy.

Cause and Consistency

The Democratic Act, Universal Citizenship, and Nation

The citizen is unthinkable as an "isolated" individual, for it is
his active participation in politics that makes him exist.

ÉTIENNE BALIBAR, *Citizen Subject*

———

IN THIS CHAPTER, I begin to make the case for a universalist and non-identitarian conception of the political subject and of political action. By way of doing so, I combine a historical perspective—that of the French Revolution and the declaration of the universal "right to politics"—with a theoretical reflection on some of the deadlocks found in contemporary political and cultural theory. In *Metapolitics*, Alain Badiou points out that in today's world, "[i]t is forbidden, as it were, not to be a democrat," adding that "any subjectivity suspected of not being democratic is regarded as pathological."[1] As a signifier the adherence to which is seemingly beyond question, "democracy" today is a primary category in a statist conception of politics that limits the latter to the sphere of the modern parliamentary state and its legal designation of citizenship. Yet this conception runs up against the increasing evidence that no profound egalitarian reorganization of society can occur from within the official democratic political system itself. Without abandoning the notion of democracy, however, I draw from a series of contemporary theorists and philosophers in order to advance a different and more radical notion of democracy that both distinguishes it from legalistic and identitarian determinations and reactivates its transformative force.

By "democracy" I refer to the transformative effects upon the political, economic, and social field of a process founded on the affirmation of the equality of social elements whose inferiority or illegitimacy is taken for granted in the quotidian reproduction of social order. This egalitarian affirmation, moreover, is manifested in the fact of the democratic act itself. To the extent that democracy constitutes the forceful entrance into the political field by those upon whose exclusion this field is founded, it entails the subjective actualization of universal citizenship. It affirms the right of anyone to participate in the process of political change.

I propose that the democratic act itself entails the forceful creation of the possibility of a new social order and that its consequences implicate everyone within said order. The statements and actions constitutive of the democratic act can orient a process that transforms a situation on the basis of an egalitarian principle. Given today's general suspicion of revolutionary politics, and the anxiety of revolutionary violence, however, it is no surprise that this forceful manifestation of politics is often downplayed or disavowed by political theories that try to contain politics within the realm of consensual discourse and official legality. Against such theories, I hold that the possibility of profound social change today depends on embracing a more radical notion of democracy as a subjective act, one that is irreducible to the determinations of objective social conditions. Yet at the same time it is necessary to emphasize that the notion of force that I propose cannot simply be reduced to violence. Though it can certainly manifest itself as violence, force is also evident in mass protests and acts of civil disobedience, in actions that challenge the parameters within which political decisions are usually made and whose effectivity relies on widespread support and organization.

After theorizing the question of political causality, I turn toward the question of consistency, looking specifically into the relationship between "nation" and "citizenship" with regard to the consistency of political community. "Nation," I maintain, is one of the main categories through which modern political community has attained its ideological consistency via nation's function as both "quilting point" and fantasy. With respect to the French Revolution, however, one finds in the work of Habermas and Hobsbawm the identification of two competing conceptions of "nation": on the one hand, a conception that, drawing on this word's previous association with ethnic and linguistic communities, took it to designate the ground that made possible and determined the values and actions of citizens, and, on the other hand, a conception that took nation to be the product of the concerted action of anyone who chose to participate in revolutionary politics.[2] While in the first conception the particularities of the national character and national belonging determine and authorize the actions of citizens, in the latter conception it is citizenship itself, as an active participation in politics, that is constitutive of nation. This latter conception, moreover, is consistent with the radical idea of universal citizenship in disregarding identitarian predicates as conditions for political participation and national belonging.

Evident in the identitarian concerns that structure contemporary debates about the meaning and function of nation and nationalism—especially in light of the effects of transnational capital, intensified international migration, and the power of supranational institutions and politico-economic regional blocks—is the fact that the former, more substantive conception of nation is the one that predominates today.[3] To the extent that the social configuration of a nation-state is secured via the function of nation-as-fantasy, it is this fantasy that must be traversed if society is to be transformed. Yet psychoanalysis and much scholarship on nation are reticent toward the severe disruption of fantasy due to the fear that if such a disruption were to occur, it would result in catastrophe; for psychoanalysis, the fear is that it would result in the annihilation of the analysand's psychic universe, and for political theory, the fear is that it would result in the dissolution of the social bond and the dispersal of the political community.[4] This reticence implies a certain conservatism that has resulted in a tendency in contemporary theory to avoid thinking the possibility of a process of structural change initiated via a sustained torsion from the site where a structure is incomplete, an incompleteness that is precisely covered over by fantasy.[5]

Since social fantasy is constitutive of the affective relations that create the social bond, politics, as the disruption of social fantasy, entails a process of unbinding necessary for the reorganization of social relations. The political collective that emerges through such a process of unbinding, moreover, cuts across established social groups and identities in a way that allows it to remain subtracted from identitarian capture. Politics as unbinding is in this way linked to the affirmation of the equality of anyone with anyone else as regards the ability to think and act beyond the determinations particular to one's social position and identity. The collective that is constituted through this process, I argue, thus tends to coincide with the more radical conception of nation identified by Hobsbawm and Habermas, to which Badiou himself gestures through the axiom "[W]hoever practices the politics of revolution, has the rights that are attached to being a member of the nation."[6]

Badiou and Lacan

In *Theory of the Subject*, his first major philosophical work, Badiou identifies an important shift in the thought of Jacques Lacan, from an early Lacan whose dominant term is the symbolic, to a late Lacan whose thinking revolves around the real that resists symbolization. It is a change of perspective from "the lack of being" to "the ontology of the hole . . . and, consequently, [to] the being of lack," or, stated otherwise, "from the primacy of the symbolic to the consistency of the real."[7] The importance of this shift for Badiou lies in the manner in which it can point to a way out of the impasses of the structural dialectic and allow for the thinking of change beyond repetition or a mere change of places, even if Lacan himself failed to do so. The drawback with the first Lacan, as Badiou sees it, is that his emphasis on the symbolic—as a chain of signifiers set forth by the real as vanishing cause[8]—ultimately shifts his focus away from thinking the possibilities through which the structure of the totality of the series can itself be changed. "[T]he problem with this doctrine," Bosteels explains, "is precisely that, while never ceasing to be dialectical in pinpointing the absent cause and its divisive effects on the whole, it nevertheless remains tied to the structure of this totality itself and is thus unable to account for the latter's possible transformation . . . which means that there is no temporal advent of novelty."[9] It is thus in effectively "denying the divisibility of the existing law of things," in that the structure itself is assumed unchangeable despite its internal divisions, that Badiou accuses Lacan of idealism.[10]

In his later work Lacan tempers this tendency by shifting his emphasis from the symbolic to the real, and thus dialectically confronts his own
"idealist" emphasis on structure with a "materialist" and historical out-
look. Badiou explains, "Beginning in the 1970s, which one can mark by
the primacy of the knot over the chain, or of consistency over causality,
it is the historical aspect that gains the upper hand over the structural
one."[11] Focusing on Lacan's conception of the real as a nonrelation in
his theorization of sexual difference, Badiou translates this into political
terms: "[I]f the real of psychoanalysis is the impossibility of the sexual
qua relation, the real of Marxism can be stated as follows: 'There are no
such things as class relations.' What does it mean to say that there are no
class relations? . . . antagonism."[12] Rather than naming a conflict between
two preexisting terms, "class struggle," as the antagonism thought by
Marxism, is the name of the confrontation between the structure and its
inherent limit, its immanent incompleteness: its real.[13]

Indeed, one can conceptualize antagonism, and in the process distinguish between the structural logic of the symbolic and the disruptive
force of the real, in terms of the distinction between "weak" and "strong"
difference. Weak difference refers to the kind of difference found between
terms that make up a series, the latter itself being the effect of an absent
cause. Far from constituting a threat to the structure, this type of difference actually works to maintain the latter's internal coherence since it is
a product of the structure's logic of places.[14] As I will argue throughout,
this is the problem with discourses of identitarian inclusion, since even
demands to be included as *different* are compatible with the structural
logics of capitalism and the state.[15] Once recognized and included as different, an identity also becomes the same; it becomes one more identity
among others. Weak difference thus tends to fall on the structural and
"algebraic" side of the dialectic. Strong difference, on the other hand, is
only ever indexed by the effects whereby the coming-into-existence of
one term entails the simultaneous destruction of the second term—the
second term being the Law, which *is* the structure—as well as the first's
self-annihilation:

> Relative to the conflictual field, the major difference is that in which
> one of the terms affirms itself only by destroying the other, not only
> in its manifestation (in which a true discourse destroys a false dis-
> course), but in its support (in the way the proletariat destroys the

bourgeoisie, all the while destroying itself, by the way . . .). This is
what Mao calls antagonistic contradiction.[16]

The sustained effects of strong difference as antagonistic contradiction thus
index the force of the real in affecting the structure itself—that is, the very
basis upon which the terms are organized. Since the real is also the absent
cause of the initial chain of signifiers, Badiou asserts that Lacan advances
two concepts of the real: one as vanishing cause for the serial chain, and
another that links the real to a consistency that makes a knot out of this
chain—that makes a topology out of the algebra through a form of torsion.[17]
Yet while Badiou clearly sees in this second conception the possibility
to transform the structure itself through a torsion that establishes a heterogeneous consistency, he critiques Lacan for threatening to continue to
draw the cause of this torsion from the very structure.[18] "[T]he Lacanian
concept of consistency is too restrictive," Badiou objects: "By failing to
oppose and conjoin explicitly the algebra and the topology, he exposes
himself to the risk of thinking of consistency only as an attribute of algebra."[19] In other words, the topology risks being reduced to an outcome of
the algebra, and thus torsion, to an outcome of the structure. Lacan risks
turning a strong difference into a weak one, and figuring all torsion in
continuity with the logic of existing order.[20] Consequently, Badiou faults
Lacan for ultimately turning away from thinking change from the perspective of antagonistic contradiction. For real change to happen, torsion
must occur by means of a heterogeneous cause that conditions its ability
to bring into being a new consistency.
At this point I move to demonstrate that tensions similar to the ones
that Badiou identifies in Lacan can also be found in some of the impasses
of political thought as regards the question of cause and consistency in
politics. Bringing this to bear on the thinking of citizenship, I argue that
universal citizenship is initiated in the form of the (real/antagonistic)
democratic act that brings forth the possibility of a new social order irreducible to the previous one.

The Real as Cause (and Consistency): On Politics and Law

I begin with the question of causality as it pertains to the creation of a
new social and legal order. As regards the problem of identifying the
foundations of the modern rights of the citizen, Étienne Balibar points

to several unresolved tensions between contending perspectives.[21] One of the tensions that he mentions results from the fact that the very manner in which a democratic order is constituted points to a foundational contradiction inasmuch as the advent of democracy is carried out via a forceful, nondemocratic, and thus "dictatorial," act. According to Balibar, this stems from "the fact that not only the idea but also the very process of 'foundation' is essentially and irreducibly *antinomical*—that is, destined to contradict itself, to turn around into the *negation of the principle* that it institutes."[22] Now this should not be interpreted as a mere repetition of the view that all revolutionary-democratic politics always deteriorate into their authoritarian opposite. Rather, what Balibar refers to here is a paradox inherent in the notion of constituent power that "makes the ultimate point of institution of law or order necessarily also represent a point of *dissolution* of all order and all legality, a point of *exception* with respect to its universality and of *liberation* with respect to its legal constraint."[23]

In *In Defense of Lost Causes*, Slavoj Žižek provides an instructive account of this tension.[24] "This strange coupling of democracy and dictatorship is grounded in the tension that pertains to the very notion of democracy," he argues: "There are two elementary and irreducible sides to democracy: violent egalitarian imposition by those who are 'supernumerary'; and the regulated (more or less) universal procedure of choosing those who will exert power."[25] In this way, Žižek situates the split between dictatorship and democracy *within* the notion of democracy itself, with "dictatorship" referring to the forceful interruption of the previously existing order by those whom said order disregards as worthy of participation, and "democracy" referring to the regulated process by which people participate in electing political representatives—thus essentially siding dictatorship with the question of *causality* and democracy with the question of *consistency*. Yet this is not the extent of their coincidence, since Žižek shows that each side is itself split by the same division. Indeed, he demonstrates that the very conception of the "dictatorship of the proletariat," which he uses mainly to illustrate the "dictatorial" side of democracy with regard to causality—and which I figure as the democratic act par excellence—must also operate on the side of consistency (i.e., on the side of a new democratic order) if it is to bring into lasting existence the egalitarian consequences of the initial intervention.[26]

But I begin with Žižek's assertion that "*the 'dictatorship of the proletariat' is another name for the violence of the democratic explosion itself.*"[27] Clearly making reference to the question of causality, he continues: "The 'dictatorship of the proletariat' is thus the zero-level at which the difference between legitimate and illegitimate state power is suspended, in other words, when state power as such is illegitimate."[28] Since the state is the entity that traditionally reserves for itself a monopoly on the legitimate use of violence, one can see here, in a manner closely mirroring Balibar's point, that in its very foundational act in the form of the democratic intervention, the dictatorship of the proletariat entails the dissolution of all legality capable of distinguishing between "legitimate" and "illegitimate" forms of power. That this democratic outburst can be referred to as "dictatorial" results from two factors: (1) because it entails the suspension of existing law, and (2) because it implies a kind of confrontation where *force*, rather than dialogue, is the only means by which it can be carried out. Both of these factors, in turn, follow from the fact that since this struggle is at bottom "the struggle about the field of struggle itself," there exists no "common ground" in the form of a legal or social framework through which the confrontation can occur by any other means.[29] Indeed, communication as an alternative to force is precluded to the extent that the democratic irruption as radical antagonism obtains from the lack of *relationality* itself; it irrupts from the place of the social nonrelation.[30]

With that said, one is perhaps left wondering why one can continue to refer to this initial "dictatorial" act as "democratic" at all. This is due to the universalizability of the place from which it originates. Drawing from the conceptual vocabulary of Jacques Rancière, Žižek explains:

> [W]hat is democracy at its most elementary? A phenomenon which, for the first time, appeared in ancient Greece when the members of the *demos* (those with no firmly determined place in the hierarchical social structure) not only demanded that their voice be heard against those in power . . . on an equal footing with the ruling oligarchy and aristocracy; even more, they, the excluded, presented themselves as the embodiment of the Whole of Society, of true Universality: "we—the 'nothing,' not counted in the order—are the people, we are All against others who stand only for their particular privileged interest."[31]

The reason one can call the dictatorship of the proletariat "democratic" is thus because the proletariat is the embodiment of the demos, of those heretofore excluded from the legitimate exercise of power and upon whose exclusion rests the legitimacy of those in positions of power. The universality of their action is a consequence of their anonymity and nonstatus, of the fact that "they lack the particular features that would legitimate their place within the social body."[32] Thus their action is not that of a particular group vying for its own particular interests, but is an action justified merely by the fact that they, like everyone else, exist in the juridico-political space in which they intervene. On the other hand, their universality also results from the fact that, as the "part of no part" whose immanent exclusion is constitutive of the existing order as it is, their intrusion into said order, in the form of the radically antagonistic "democratic explosion," can affect this order in its entirety.[33] Furthermore, democracy here is thus not "government by all" in the usual sense. Rather, to the extent that "the rule of the demos" is the universal effect of the intrusion of the part of no part, whose very manifestation registers the inherent incompleteness of the established order, democracy can perhaps be more accurately conceived as "the rule of the not-all."[34]

It is this coincidence of dictatorship/force with democracy that many political theorists are unable to come to terms with and try to disavow. Balibar notes this in his critique of the way in which Habermas deals with the constitutive tensions that Balibar identifies. Habermas's strategy as regards these tensions is to introduce the notion of the "communicational" sphere as a way "to remain precisely at the level of the constitution of rights."[35] For Habermas, this communicational sphere is important to the extent that "the illocutionary binding forces of a use of language oriented to mutual understanding serve to bring reason and will together, [and] as participants in rational discourses, consociates under law must be able to examine whether a contested norm meets with, or could meet with, the agreement of all those possibly affected."[36] Hence the sphere of communication allows Habermas to resolve the question of the foundation of rights in a way that avoids reliance either on an extrapolitical moral sphere or on the imposition of rights by popular force. Balibar, however, notices a problem and wonders "whether this 'solution' is not in fact circular, since the communicative procedure is quite likely to be the *effect rather than the source* of 'consensus' or mutual recognition."[37] This is so because for communication to occur one must already assume the existence of a kind of "consensus" on the terms and parameters of the speech situation itself. Yet it is precisely in the struggle over the determinations of this "common ground," including the struggle over what counts as speech and what is relegated to mere noise, that the initial democratic act can only be an expression of force. That this act is incompatible with the realm of communication and consensus is the reason that Rancière defines politics as "disagreement," where the disagreement "generally bears on the very *situation* in which speaking parties find themselves."[38] In this way, Habermas's logic glosses over the initial determination of a common framework and thus simultaneously disavows the question of foundational force.

Iris Marion Young makes a similar move when developing her notion of "differentiated citizenship," which she articulates in her famous essay "Polity and Group Difference: A Critique of the Ideal of Universal Citizenship." In this essay, Young aims to resolve the contradiction present in the fact that despite the legal recognition of formal equality among citizens, inequality, exclusion, and marginalization nevertheless persist both at the level of the political process and at the level of its results. She refers to this phenomenon as the "paradox of democracy," which results from the fact that "social power makes some citizens more equal than others, and equality of citizenship makes some people more powerful citizens."[39] Young's "paradox" can be distilled in the following way: (1) socioeconomic inequality among citizens (re)produces differences of power and prestige among them; (2) the formal political equality of citizens overlooks differences of power and prestige that result from socioeconomic inequalities; (3) since formal equality overlooks the existence of inequalities in terms of power and prestige that result from socioeconomic inequalities, these inequalities continue to structure the greater influence of some citizens over the determination of citizens' collective action, to the former's advantage—for example, in the creation and enactment of policies deemed to be representative of the "general interest" but that actually serve to reproduce the initial socioeconomic inequalities. Though stated this way, however, the "paradox" no longer seems to be a paradox at all, since formal equality is seen to simply be an inadequate and superficial form of equality in that, by not addressing the existence of effective inequalities of resources, power, and prestige among citizens, it allows such inequalities to continue to reproduce themselves at the cost of the systematic political and socioeconomic disadvantage of some of its members. In light of this, Young concludes that the solution to this problem lies in the creation of "differentiated citizenship" as a means of promoting socioeconomic equality by "providing institutionalized means for the explicit recognition and representation of oppressed groups" at the political level.[40]

Significantly, however, Young glosses over the question of antagonistic causality to the degree that she reduces politics to a regulated decision-making process where social groups—the prior "legitimate" existence of which she takes as a given, and whose members are already endowed with citizenship—can vie for their own interests. Indeed, Linda Bosniak points out that Young ignores groups excluded from citizenship, which, as such, lack a recognized basis for their political participation in the first place.[41] This can be gauged when Young, ignoring the existence of undocumented people, states as a basic premise at the beginning of her argument that "[n]ow in the late twentieth century . . . citizenship rights have been formally extended to *all groups* in liberal capitalist societies."[42] In other words, everyone in Young's conception is *already* a counted member of the polity. Much as with Habermas, Young's conception takes as its implicit starting point the existence of an already-established consensus on a general framework upon which contending political demands can be evaluated by means of rational and free communication.[43]

By staying within existing legality, Young fails to question whether its very foundations are adequate to the task of creating socioeconomic equality. In other words, while she identifies the depoliticization of social and economic life as a reason for the persistent oppression and exclusion of social groups even after they have been granted full citizenship status, she stops short of considering whether the economic logic promoted by the foundational rights of liberal democracy is itself an obstacle.[44] In the long run, furthermore, it seems that Young falls prey to the very logic that she aims to critique, in that her emphasis on identitarian groups also ironically tends to eliminate *her* recognition of the possible influence of persistent socioeconomic inequality *within* any given social group in determining a representative "general interest" of its own. As a consequence, this strategy by which a more complete form of representation is sought merely displaces, from the general group of citizens to the various subgroups of citizens, the problem of the way in which any general position would still tend to be disproportionally influenced by the particular interests of the most powerful. That is, in a conceptual framework like Young's, where politics is reduced to furthering particular interests, it must be assumed that even at the level of particular groups, the most powerful within said groups would continue to advocate for and have a significant impact over the determination of the group's collective position in a way that would benefit and reproduce their privilege.

At the same time, and given that one of the main targets of her critique is the notion of formal equality, it is not clear if there remains room in her conception for any concept of equality at all. In fact, in the move through which differentiated citizenship replaces the notion of formal equality, the idea of equality is replaced with the imperative of *differentiated representation* in a way that sidelines the former in favor of the administrative management of inequality and privilege in the name of "fairness."[45] Moreover, in trying to meet the "requirement that all experiences, needs, and perspectives on social events have a voice and are respected,"[46] she reduces all forms of conflict to "weak" difference, and thus, in a manner perhaps not unrelated to her disregard for universality, disavows the element of antagonism upon whose exclusion exist things as they are and upon whose interruption hinges the possibility of things to be radically otherwise—an antagonism that is universal in two ways: (1) in the fact that as a constitutive exclusion of the system, its intrusion into the system can affect the latter in its entirety, and (2) in the fact that its consequences cannot be contained within the particular interests of any preexisting social group. Thus the urgent question of how a novel form of equality can be made to exist in a context organized around inequality is still left unanswered by Young, and with it the thought of the possibility of a struggle over the field of struggle itself.

It is thus the very thought of the revolutionary outburst as the irruption of the real that both Young and Habermas attempt to foreclose. It is in this sense that I also suggest that one may refer to their positions as "idealist." As demonstrated above with Badiou's critique of Lacan's idealism, a defining characteristic of idealism is its denial of the divisibility of existing law. "The indivisibility of the law of the place excepts it from the real," argues Badiou: "[This] amounts to stipulating the radical anteriority of the rule."[47] In taking for granted as preexisting a common framework upon which all forms of conflict can be resolved, it is indeed on the radical anteriority of the rule that their conceptions implicitly rely. By being blind to the ideological retroaction by which the law is established as radically anterior to any form of political confrontation, both of these theorists cannot but fall back on a legalist conception in which the law itself constitutes the only ground upon which any political confrontation can take place. Therefore, in their liberal democratic conceptions,

Habermas and Young fail to acknowledge the nondemocratic "dictatorial" aspect inherent in their *own* delimitation of such ground, which forecloses the thought of the democratic outburst as the real that makes evident that the law is "not-all"—that it is incomplete and that this incompleteness can serve as a site for the advent of a torsion that can further divide the law between a before and an after. Having established this, I now move to the question of politics in its temporal duration, with specific focus on the sources of its consistency.

The Real as Consistency (and Cause): On Citizenship and Nation

Once the numerical succession is engendered in the efficacy
of the vanishing term, we must still know what it is
that makes all these numbers hold together.

ALAIN BADIOU, *Theory of the Subject*

———

If the modern contribution to the history of citizenship lies in the effort to universalize the latter and create a nonidentitarian basis for political participation, it is nevertheless evident that modern conceptions of citizenship are plagued by a bind where political community, membership, and the citizen itself acquire restrictive definitions through their very institutionalization and expression in legally and culturally meaningful terms. Ideas of nation have been pivotal in this. Most theorists of nation agree that "nation" and "nationality" are juridico-political and imaginary constructs that give meaning to and help reproduce group relations. Eric Hobsbawm, for example, stresses the "element of artifact, invention and social engineering which enters into the making of nations," adding that "[t]he 'national question' . . . is situated at the point of intersection of politics, technology and social transformation."[48] Benedict Anderson points to the role of print capitalism in facilitating the development of nations as imagined communities.[49] Similarly, David Miller concedes that "many things now regarded as primordial features of the nation in question are in fact artificial inventions—indeed very often deliberate inventions made to serve a political purpose."[50] The imaginary status of nation and the fact that different nations privilege different criteria as constitutive of themselves suggest that "nation" is perhaps nothing but an empty category, the importance of which lies not in its particular meaning but in its functional role in *the production of meaning as such* as it pertains to political community.[51] It is in this sense that I suggest that one can characterize its role as an ideological one.

Besides its particular production by means of techno-cultural inventions that shaped the development and extension of ideas of nation and national belonging, what makes modern nation different from previous conceptions is its *politicization*, which includes its role in linking political community to the modern territorial state, thereafter transformed into a *nation*-state.[52] Thus, Hobsbawm argues that "in its modern and basically political sense the concept *nation* is historically very young."[53] The articulation of nation in political terms is intricately related to modern conceptions of citizenship and the state: "The 'nation' so considered, was the body of citizens whose collective sovereignty constituted them a state which was their political expression. . . . [T]he element of citizenship, and mass participation or choice was never absent from it."[54] Indeed, one can begin to see the way in which "nation" knots together the relationship between citizens and a new political order by suturing the gap between popular political action and its institutionalization. Along these lines, David Miller notes the political articulation of nation as a factor that differentiates the signifier from its earlier usage as referring to "kin groups" and "people of common stock and customs," yet dates this change much earlier than does Hobsbawm, for whom the modern concept of nation begins to emerge at the end of the eighteenth century with the American and French Revolutions.[55]

According to Habermas, "[n]ationalism is the term for a specifically modern phenomenon of cultural integration."[56] That the specificity of this kind of cultural integration results in part from its relationship to politics is evinced when he explains:

> This type of national consciousness is formed in social movements and emerges from modernization processes at a time when people are at once both mobilized and isolated as individuals. Nationalism is a form of collective consciousness which both presupposes a reflexive appropriation of cultural traditions that have been filtered through historiography and which spreads only via the channels of modern mass communication. Both elements lend to nationalism

the artificial traits of something that is to a certain extent a construct, thus rendering it by definition susceptible to manipulative
misuse by political elites.[57]

One can thus find in Habermas an account of the way in which nationalism—
developed through a reflexive appropriation of cultural traditions and dis-
seminated through the technologies of mass communication—also serves
as a mechanism to bring together and give meaningful consistency to people who are both politically mobilized and yet still "isolated as individuals."
Nationalism is that through which such individuals come together into a
political community; it is that through which a social bond develops.

NATION AS QUILTING POINT

With that said, one must look more closely at the construction of "community" and the question of how it attains systemic consistency. Since
a culturally intelligible community is discursively constructed, it is useful to begin by looking at the formal characteristics of language itself.
After Saussure, we know that meaning is the result of a system of differences wherein each signifier receives its identity or value retroactively,
through its differential relationship with other signifiers. Each act of
signification thus presupposes the involvement of the totality of signifiers within the system. "The problem," Ernesto Laclau points out, "is that
the very possibility of signification is the system, and the very possibility of the system is the possibility of its limits."[58] These limits, however,
precisely as the *limits* of the signifying system, cannot themselves be
signified in the same way as other terms, since if they could they would
remain wholly *within* the field of signification, a fact that would preclude
them from actually being limits. Hence, such limits can only exist as
the immanent interruption of the process of signification itself. In this
way, concludes Laclau, "we are left with the paradoxical situation that
what constitutes the condition of possibility of a signifying system—its
limits—is also what constitutes its condition of impossibility—a block-
age of the continuous expansion of the process of signification."[59] Furthermore, the limit of a system cannot simply be neutral, for if it were,
the limit would actually be "continuous with what is at its two sides,
and the two sides [would] simply [be] different from each other. As
a signifying totality is, however, precisely a system of differences, this

means that both are part of the same system and that the limits between the two cannot be the limits of the system."[60] Consequently, the notion of limit must presuppose an *exclusion*—a nonneutral limit, which Laclau also likens to the Lacanian real,[61] whose nonneutrality lies in the fact that "the actualization of what is beyond the limit of exclusion would involve the impossibility of what is this side of the limit."[62] What lies beyond the nonneutral (real) limit, then, is none other than the threat of strong difference, or antagonism.[63]

But this exclusion is also the necessary condition for a system to become and remain a system—it founds the very *systematicity* of the system; it is what must remain "impossible" for the system to be constituted and remain as such. Indicating a further consequence of the necessity of such a constitutive exclusion, and one that has strong implications for our thinking of community, Laclau affirms: "Now, if the systematicity of the system is a direct result of the exclusionary limit, it is only that exclusion that grounds the system as such. This point is essential because it results from it that the system cannot have a positive ground and that, as a result, it cannot signify itself in terms of any positive signified."[64] In the case of a community, this means that its coherence as a system of relations cannot be founded on any positive characteristic or natural ground, and thus that there is no positive element that can ensure its "natural" consistency. Yet, as with any other system, a community cannot signify itself in a manner that establishes the semblance of full consistency without finding a way to account for its empty foundation. Since the absence that is its constitutive exclusion cannot be signified as one more difference among others, it can only be indexed through a term emptied of its content: an empty signifier. In Laclau's conception, an empty signifier is thus necessary for the establishment and signification of positive order.[65] Without the empty signifier and the resulting order, the differential relation of signifiers would be anarchic.

Since the function of the empty signifier as Laclau describes it in "Why Do Empty Signifiers Matter in Politics?" is similar to that which he and Chantal Mouffe attribute to the "nodal point" in their earlier work, *Hegemony and Socialist Strategy*, and which they adapt from Lacan's *point de capiton*, I turn more directly to a Lacanian perspective, since in the long run it will also allow me to include the role of fantasy and affect in the analysis of ideology. According to Lacan, the *point de capiton*, or "quilting point," is that "by which the signifier stops the otherwise indefinite sliding of signification."[66] Like the empty signifier, the quilting point is also an empty category that helps establish systemic consistency. The quilting point "is not a point of supreme density of Meaning. . . . On the contrary . . . [i]n itself it is nothing but a 'pure difference': its role is purely structural. . . . [I]n short, it is a 'signifier without the signified.'"[67] While the quilting point's structural role as a kind of empty signifier is clear, however, within the field of ideological meaning, this same element "is perceived as a point of extreme saturation of Meaning, as the point which 'gives meaning' to all the others and thus totalizes the field of (ideological) meaning."[68] In this way, what the notion of the quilting point reveals is that it is precisely this empty category that is taken to be the bearer of meaning itself within the field of ideology, and that the very attribution of this quality indirectly acknowledges its structural role as a condition for the production of meaning as such.

To exemplify the logic of the quilting process, Žižek refers to the relationship between the famous Marlboro cowboy advertisement and American national identity. While it is obvious that Marlboro did not invent the myth of the western cowboy and that the advertisement merely activates a series of preexisting associations related to this figure, there is nevertheless a particular inversion that occurs that is essential to the quilting process. "The effect of 'quilting,'" explains Žižek, only occurs when "'real' Americans start to identify themselves (in their ideological self-experience) with the image created by the Marlboro advertisement—until America itself is experienced as 'Marlboro country.'"[69] In other words, quilting occurs not because Marlboro connotes something that already coincides with a preexisting image of America, but when a certain experience of America attains ideological coherence through people's identification with the Marlboro image. Likewise, Žižek gives the example of Coca-Cola: "the point is not that Coca-Cola 'connotes' a certain ideological experience-vision of America (the freshness of its sharp, cold taste, and so on); the point is that this vision of America itself achieves its identity by identifying itself with 'Coke.'"[70] The important point, however, is that while one could then affirm "America, this is Coke!" or "America, it is Marlboro country!" these phrases could not be inverted to say "Coke, this is America!" The reason for this is that in the move whereby the ideological experience of America is constituted through its identification with Marlboro or Coke, the latter two signifiers become the site of "the unattainable X, the object-cause of desire."[71]

Bearing in mind the acknowledgment by theorists of nationalism of the role of cultural referents in the creation of particular national identities, it is clear that such referents serve a double function: (1) as quilting points that fix the sliding of signification via a process of identification, and (2) as paradoxical empty signifiers that, while establishing the semblance of systemic closure, are in themselves the *emptiness* that is perceived as the very site of *fullness.*

While this gives insight into the ways in which national identities are constituted, the aim of my current analysis is to demonstrate the ways in which "nation" itself also comes to serve as a quilting point for the consistency of the modern political community. I thus argue that the politicization of the concept of nation (which is what tends to distinguish the modern concept of nation from its earlier uses), far from entailing a mere change in its meaning, actually registers a change in the *function* of this category into a quilting point for political community. This change is perceived in Habermas's account of the history of the term. As he indicates, the concept of nation has a much longer history that predates the first modern revolutions. In Roman times, the term *natio* referred to "people of the same descent, who [were] integrated geographically . . . and culturally by their common language, customs, and traditions, but who [were] not yet politically integrated in the form of state organization."[72] This meaning persisted until early modern times. From the middle of the eighteenth century, however, the difference between "nation" and "politically organized people" began to disappear, to the extent that with the French Revolution the nation became the source of state sovereignty and national self-determination, a guiding political principle.[73]

The tendency described by Habermas, whereby "nation" is used to lend coherence to a political collective, may be facilitated precisely by the term's previous association with prepolitical community.[74] This brings back the tension between historical continuity and rupture, with the idea of nation often being mobilized to establish historical continuity. Emphasis on continuity, moreover, is carried out via a retroaction that functions to account for the antagonistic rupture of a political sequence by attributing causality to certain preexisting, and often prepolitical, factors. This kind of retroaction is acknowledged by Terry Eagleton as part of the logic of what he calls the "metaphysics of nationalism," through which the self-realization of a people as a subject "must somehow curiously preexist its own process of materialization—must be equipped . . . with certain highly determinate needs and desires, on the model of the autonomous human personality."[75] Balibar echoes this at the beginning of "The Nation Form" when he calls attention to the way in which national histories tend to narrativize the nation in a manner that gives it the continuity of a subject coming into self-awareness.[76] Similarly, Benedict Anderson notes from early in the development of European nationalisms the prevalent trope of "awakening from sleep," whereby the initial novelty of a historical rupture was reintegrated into "an historical tradition of serial continuity."[77] Resonating with Badiou's critique of Lacan discussed previously, this trope folds the break of the awakening back into the causality of the chain. In this way, the "awakening," rather than signaling a break, was instead interpreted as "a guaranteed return to an aboriginal essence."[78] One of the functions of this retroaction is to account for a political sequence by designating a particular "national" essence as the reason for its occurrence (i.e., as its "object(ive)" cause). "Nation" is thus made to bring consistency to political community by becoming the signifier within which the prepolitical object-cause of desire, that unattainable X, resides. Besides attenuating the sense of historical rupture, making nation into a supposedly substantive cause—one that covers over the contingency of the democratic act and with it the real of antagonism—also traps citizenship within an identitarian net.

A NATION OF CITIZENS

But Habermas also identifies another tendency in the conception of the modern relationship between "citizen" and "nation" that reverses the relation of causality, from one that takes citizenship to be an expression of the nation, to one that takes nation to be the product of citizenship as collective action. This reversal is evident in the conception of a nation as a "nation of citizens," and is one that moves toward affirming universal citizenship by eliminating substantive characteristics and prepolitical belonging as prerequisites or supposed ground for political action. According to Habermas:

> The nation of citizens does not derive its identity from some common ethnic and cultural properties, but rather from the *praxis* of citizens who actively exercise their civil rights. At this juncture, the republican strand of "citizenship" completely parts company with the idea

of belonging to a prepolitical community integrated on the basis of descent, a shared tradition and a common language.[79]

This reversal, which underlines politics' creative potential, shifts the conception of nation from a set of particular ethnic, cultural, or linguistic traits that motivates and maintains political action, to nation understood as the outcome of a collective praxis constituted in and through itself. In the first conception, the nation and national belonging both motivate and sustain political mobilization by providing the "ground" and "glue" for this kind of action, while in the second conception, politics takes a leading role to the extent that the nation is no longer the source but the outcome of a political sequence.[80] In this way too, politics is no longer an expression of national desires or national destiny. As an autolegislating process whose reason lies in the praxis of citizenship itself, politics creates nation in and through its very action. This latter conception opens toward universality in that national belonging is no longer a condition but a *result* of citizens' action in a way that points toward a breach between politics and identitarian determinations.

This conception of nation is also identified by Hobsbawm in reference to the French Revolution. For the revolutionaries, he explains,

> there was no logical connection between the body of citizens of a territorial state on the one hand, and the identification of a "nation" on ethnic, linguistic or other grounds or of other characteristics which allowed collective recognition of group membership. Indeed, it has been argued that the French Revolution "was completely foreign to the principle or feeling of nationality; it was even hostile to it" for this reason.[81]

Consequently, continues Hobsbawm, "French experts were to fight stubbornly against any attempt to make the spoken language a criterion of nationality which, they argued, was determined purely by French citizenship."[82] It is thus that the connection of the citizenry to an ethnic or linguistic conception of nationality was not taken for granted by the revolutionaries as constituting a logical necessity; in fact, such a connection was opposed. Signaling a truly "generic" mode of politics, it was only the exercise of citizenship that determined nationality and not the other way around. In this broadly Jacobin conception, argues Peter

Hallward, the nation is simply that which is "made up of all those who, whatever their cultural origin or 'way of being,' collectively *decide* to assert (or re-assert) the right of self-determination."[83] In this manner, I argue that another factor that distinguishes this term from its earlier usage is its coupling with the political affirmation of universal citizenship. This generic and revolutionary nation is the logical consequence of the sustained actualization of the universal right to revolt, and thus of the universal right to politics.

It is important to keep in mind, however, that both conceptions (nation-as-cause and nation-as-result) continued to coexist in tension with one another, with each proposing a contending vision of community corresponding to conflicting political tendencies.[84] Hobsbawm refers to these contending visions as nationalist and revolutionary-democratic, respectively. "The equation state = nation = people applied to both," he stresses, "but for nationalists the creation of the political entities which would contain it derived from the prior existence of some community distinguishing itself from foreigners, while from the revolutionary-democratic point of view the central concept was the sovereign citizen-people = state which, in relation to the remainder of the human race, constituted a 'nation.'"[85] In the latter revolutionary-democratic view, then, what constituted a nation was the concerted political action (i.e., citizenship) of the people; nation was nothing but the generic name for the collective of citizens. Against the revolutionary-democratic insistence on breaking from identitarian determinations is a reactionary tendency implicit in the nationalist disavowal of rupture in favor of substantive causality and continuity. Hobsbawm argues that this reactionary form of nationalism became dominant after the 1880s, after which "ethnicity and language became the central, increasingly the decisive or even the only criteria of potential nationhood," a change that was accompanied by "a sharp shift to the political right of nation and flag, for which the term 'nationalism' was actually invented in the last decade(s) of the nineteenth century."[86]

NATION AS FANTASY

Notwithstanding the quilting function of nation, Yannis Stavrakakis has called attention to the fact that "[t]he force of national identity . . . is not wholly attributable to the structural position of the nation as a nodal [i.e., quilting] point."[87] What is still missing from this analysis, and what a Lacanian perspective enables one to see, is the *affective* dimension of nation beyond its function as quilting point and through its articulation in the form of collective fantasy. Part of the function of fantasy is to account for and contain the inconsistencies and contradictions immanent to political community, which obtain from the fact that community is not-whole. Fantasy operates beyond the level of the purely discursive, beyond the level of meaning, precisely as it tries to capture that which escapes symbolic and imaginary identification.[88] A Lacanian theory of ideology therefore points to the nonsensical element of enjoyment that works as ideology's last support and accounts for its stubborn hold.[89] As a consequence, the critique of ideology must supplement a basic analysis focusing on the quilting points that organize the ideological field with an analysis that extracts the element around which ideological fantasy structures our enjoyment.

In order to describe the constitution and function of fantasy in more detail, it is necessary to take a step back to the quilting process's inability to fully interpellate the subject—that is, its inability to fully integrate it into the socio-symbolic field through the interplay of imaginary and symbolic identification. As Žižek explains: "After every 'quilting' of the signifier's chain which retroactively fixes its meaning, there always remains a certain gap, an opening which is rendered . . . by the famous '*Che vuoi?*— 'You're telling me that, but what do you want with it, what are you aiming at?' "[90] The gap presented here is the gap between "utterance" and "enunciation," where the former refers to the actual content of the message, to its meaning, and the latter to the secret or unconscious aim hidden behind the fact of the address itself.[91] It is precisely above the level of the utterance, above the accessible meaning, that Lacan places the indeterminate desire hidden behind the enunciation.[92] It is here, then, that one finds an initial function of fantasy as an answer to the unanswerable question of what the Other wants. Rather than meaningfully articulating what the Other wants, however, the function of fantasy is to bypass the deadlock of the Other's desire by instead giving consistency to the desire of the subject, by helping it "learn 'how to desire,'" by providing it the "frame co-ordinating our desire, [which is] at the same time a defense against '*Che vuoi?* "[93]

Symbolic inconsistency also results from the fact that the symbolic order is itself pierced by a "pre-symbolic (real) stream of enjoyment," (i.e., jouissance) whose "presence in the field of the signifier can be detected only through the holes and inconsistencies of this field."[94] The role of fantasy "is to serve as a screen concealing this inconsistency . . . [and to constitute] the frame through which we experience the world as consistent and meaningful."[95] Fantasy thus plays a double role in that it both covers up the "hole" in the Other, thereby covering the source of the inconsistency that results from the fact that the Other is barred, $S(\cancel{A})$, and does so at the same time by structuring the subject's desire via a fantasy-scenario that makes a particular element the object-cause of our enjoyment, $\$ \lozenge a$.[96] In this way, fantasy does not merely help to establish the semblance of coherence and closure, but endows it with a psychic investment rooted in enjoyment.[97] It is precisely at this level of enjoyment and its role in constituting affective libidinal bonds that Stavrakakis situates the source of the hold that national identity has had as "one of the forms, in fact the dominant one, that the social bond acquires within modernity."[98]

Inconsistency abounds even after the semblance of completeness has been established, however, and this is actually accounted for by the fantasy itself by means of the paradoxical function of the *objet a*, both as the object-cause of our enjoyment and as the reason that our enjoyment falls short of what it promises to be. Its function is to integrate the failure of totalization into the very attempt to construct such a totality. Fantasy creates the semblance of consistency while simultaneously (and, indeed, *by* simultaneously) offering the answer to why things went wrong or why they are not as they should be—that is, it offers an answer as to why consistency has been undermined.[99] It is thus no surprise that ideological fantasy accounts for inconsistencies by means of symptomatic figures deemed to be the embodied source of disorder.

In its strongest form, it is the threat of social antagonism that fantasy tries to account for and contain through the fetishized figures of the Indian, the Jew, the alien, the criminal, and the "illegal" immigrant, among others. Upon being identified as the supposed cause of the failure of harmonious totalization, the object becomes the surface upon which are condensed various antagonisms (e.g., economic, political, and moral) and the figure against which collective aggression is directed in the very process through which social bonds within the collective are established.[100] Keeping in mind that the target of such aggression is at the same time the object-cause of our desire as structured by ideological fantasy, the truly paradoxical status of such an element reveals itself as a condition for the establishment of group identity. In this way, any criticism of ideology must entail the detection within the ideological construction of the element that represents its condition of (im)possibility.[101]

Frederick Jackson Turner and the Fantasy of the Frontier

In order to illustrate the role of nationalist ideology in producing the consistency of a particular liberal political community, I turn to the work of Frederick Jackson Turner and analyze the ways in which his "frontier thesis" helped to do this in the context of the United States. In doing so, I also demonstrate that the fantasy-scenario of the frontier upon which Turner's thesis stands is indeed predicated on the disavowed production of the figure of the Indian as both what is necessary for the making of the frontiersman and what must be exterminated for the advent of American national identity. As a historian writing at the end of the nineteenth century, Turner posited the frontier as a central factor in the development of American national identity, American national values, and the political subjectivity of American citizens. He declared the frontier to be the source of a particular American "character" by insisting that it provided the specific conditions for the development of a unique kind of national political subjectivity. David Weber underscores Turner's influence on subsequent generations by pointing out that "[f]or much of [the twentieth] century, Frederick Jackson Turner's frontier thesis has been regarded as a most useful, if not the most useful, concept for understanding the distinctive features of American civilization."[102] Likewise, other scholars have stressed the influence of Turner's frontier thesis on popular conceptions of American nationalism through the manner in which it links the frontier to an idea of American expansionism as destined, and to specific conceptions of freedom, self-sufficiency, individualism, and democracy that today continue to form part of the dominant articulations of the meaning and values of the American "people" and nation-state.[103]

Turner's influence is due to the role the frontier thesis played in helping to articulate and define certain characteristics of national identity that were linked to a specifically liberal form of subjectivity at a time when the US nation-state was coming into its own. Indeed, Popper, Lang, and Popper point out that Turner's thesis constitutes a founding myth elaborated during a pivotal time in US history after the Civil War. Guided by the work of Michael Kammen, the authors view the period between 1870 and

1910 "as an era when Americans agreed to link their identity to their past; they elevated collective memory into national self-conception," emphasizing that "Turner's myth was a key part of the transformation."[104] The authors argue that Turner's writings went beyond the purely academic realm by helping a large population define itself through the articulation of a collective identity taken to be the result of a shared history. They argue that Turner "broadened the frontier myth by creating a more flexible, inclusive version of it: the frontier thesis that permanently changed academic and popular thought."[105] As the authors allude in this remark, by the time Turner delivered his famous essay, "The Significance of the Frontier in American History," to the American Historical Association in 1893, notions of the frontier and the American West were already present in the popular imaginary. Turner's contribution consisted in rearticulating the frontier as an original and "natural" source of American identity.

It is significant that Turner's thesis was presented in 1893, three years after officials of the US census had declared that the frontier had ceased to exist and thus would no longer constitute a statistical category.[106] With regard to a situation that no longer existed in an empirical sense, the time of Turner's writing marked both a closure of a historical period and an opening for the retroactive determination of what that period meant. Thus, as Tiziano Bonazzi also suggests, the text's "meaning, then, does not simply lie in a new interpretation of the past, but in a new use of the past for the present. This implied building a theory whose very structure would change man's understanding of himself."[107] As I will demonstrate, the theory's structure is that of a fantasy.

The frontier thesis did not merely posit a new understanding of history in order to show how things really were at a certain point in the past, but was instead influential to the extent that it helped people understand the present as a direct—and, I would argue, *inevitable*—result of particular historical and natural conditions. Bonazzi points out that Turner was heavily influenced by evolutionary theories of human development and suggests that "[t]he champions of neo-Lamarckian evolutionism taught him that the process of identification is one of differentiation and of growing inner cohesion depending on the organism's response to its environment."[108] The relationship between an organism and its environment is important for Turner insofar as he believed that the physical environment of the frontier came to fundamentally determine the character of the American people. Yet, as I will show, Turner's frontier thesis actually collapses the figure of the Indian *into* nature and thus presents what is in fact a (non)relationship between frontiersman and native as a relationship between human and nature. Symptomatic is the way the environment covers antagonism as it is made to function as the "natural ground" for American identity. Consequently, regardless of the lack of scientific validity of Turner's framework, what is important is the role that his frontier thesis played both in its historical moment and after by providing a version of American national identity—along with supposed American values—with a *solid* and *natural* ground.

Thus, Turner outlines the way the frontier creates in Americans a specific liberal disposition:

> [T]he frontier is productive of individualism. Complex society is precipitated by the wilderness into a kind of primitive organization based on the family. The tendency is anti-social. It produces antipathy to control, and particularly to any direct control. The tax-gatherer is viewed as a representative of oppression. . . . The frontier individualism has from the beginning promoted democracy.[109]

Despite the contradiction in claiming both the production of individualism *and* the precipitation of society into a "primitive" clan-like organization, a striking aspect of Turner's assertion is the way in which it activates many of liberalism's central motifs by constructing as interrelated the development of radical individualism, an aversion toward the state's intervention in economic and private affairs, and democracy, at the same time that it attributes causality to the frontier. Implicit is a notion of freedom as both freedom from the state and freedom to do what one would like with one's property. As regards the liberal notion of freedom, Marx demonstrates that in its particular conception as the right of liberty—that is, as "the power which man has to do everything which does not harm the rights of others"[110]—it is closely articulated with the right of property: the right "which belongs to every citizen of enjoying and disposing as he will of his goods and revenues, of the fruits of his work and industry."[111] "The right of property," Marx points out, "is, therefore, the right to enjoy one's fortune and to dispose of it as one will; without regard to other men and independently of society. It is the *right of self-interest*."[112] Along these lines, Turner exalts the frontier's role in producing democracy, yet it is a version of democracy reduced to liberal (economic) freedom.[113] It is thus that the frontier also produces a form of individualism that seems antithetical to the development of a political community in that it is, by definition, "antisocial."

In describing the characteristics of Jacksonian democracy as an example of frontier democracy, however, Turner asserts:

> It was based on the good fellowship and the genuine social feeling of the frontier, in which classes and inequalities of fortune played little part. But it did not demand equality of condition, for there was abundance of natural resources and the belief that the self-made man had a right to his success in the free competition which western life afforded, was as prominent in their thoughts as was the love for democracy. On the other hand, they viewed governmental restraints with suspicion as a limitation on their right to work out their own individuality.[114]

At a first glance, this remark reproduces the same liberal tenets outlined previously, but with a more direct acknowledgment of the right of property, a justification of the resulting social inequality—that is, the "right" of the wealthy to their wealth and the triumph of *economic* man in free competition—and a view of the state as a threat to individual freedom. In addition, though, one also sees the recognition of a social bond— "good fellowship" and "genuine social feeling"—that creates community by precisely covering over class inequalities. The frontier is that which bridges the lack of a class relation through an affective bond. If the frontier in its constant expansion returns society to its formative moments of primitive accumulation and class stratification, the experience of mutual affect bridges the gap of antisocial individualism. This affect, moreover, also creates an attachment to the very principles presupposed by liberal democracy. At this point it becomes evident that Turner's frontier thesis is at bottom a reworking of a foundational liberal myth that positions the frontier itself as the natural source of liberal principles. Since these principles arise from frontier living conditions, there is no need for them to be affirmed through a political act, nor do they require the state or any other entity to secure them; it is frontier life itself that does so. It is the frontier that both gives rise to (causes) and maintains (gives consistency to) a certain character and set of values. Being integral to American identity, any politics antithetical to these principles cannot but appear "alien."[115]

An account of Turner's frontier thesis is still incomplete if one fails to analyze the way in which the Indian serves as the paradoxical limit figure through which the collective fantasy of the American nation is established and the social bond secured. Before doing this, however, one must acknowledge that the function of the Indian as the embodiment of the limits of the US nation-state and its people has a much longer history. Legal scholar Robert A. Williams Jr. has analyzed the historical construction of the figure of the Indian in US legal discourse, where the Indian is precisely figured as that which has to be excluded and even exterminated for the consolidation of the American nation-state.[116] That the foundation of the American nation-state depended on the exclusion of the figure of the Indian for its internal consistency is no exaggeration, since it can be found in the first US legal document, the Declaration of Independence, where among the list of grievances against King George III is the claim that "he has endeavored to bring on the inhabitants of our frontiers, the merciless Indian Savages, whose known rule of warfare, is an undistinguished destruction of all ages, sexes and conditions."[117] The continued function of the Indian as the embodiment of radical alterity, inassimilability, and antagonism, the exclusion of which gives consistency to instances of legal reasoning, is recognized by Williams when he asserts: "A long-established language of racism that speaks of the American Indian as an uncivilized, lawless, and warlike savage can be found at work through the leading Indian Law decisions of the nineteenth-century U.S. Supreme Court."[118] American Indians are conceived as a destructive force that must be excluded to secure the survival of the nation-state itself. The constitutive and persistent function of such notions are evinced when Williams stresses that "[t]he racist, organizing iconography of the Indian as *irreconcilable* and *inassimilable* savage other continued after the Revolution as one of the core organizing beliefs inspiring the Founders' vision of America's growth and potentiality as a new form of expansionary white racial dictatorship in the world."[119] Thus, Williams paraphrases George Washington's blueprint of what would be the United States' first Indian policy as recommending that "[t]he United States should continue to regulate the trade with the Indians but should keep them on the other side of that line, until the forces of civilization achieved the Indians' certain extinction as a doomed race of savages."[120]

With these precedents established, I now turn back to Turner, where he outlines the constitutive function of the US frontier in greater detail:

The frontier is the line of most rapid and effective Americanization. The wilderness masters the colonist. It finds him a European in dress, industries, tools, modes of travel, and thought. It takes him from the railroad car and puts him in the birch canoe. It strips off the garments of civilization and arrays him in the hunting shirt and the moccasin. It puts him in the log cabin of the Cherokee and Iroquois and runs an Indian palisade around him. Before long he has gone to planting Indian corn and plowing with a sharp stick; he shouts the war cry and takes the scalp in orthodox Indian fashion. In short, at the frontier the environment is at first too strong for the man. He must accept the conditions which it furnishes, or perish, and so he fits himself into the Indian clearings and follows the Indian trails. Little by little he transforms the wilderness, but the outcome is not the old Europe. . . . The fact is, that here is a new product that is American.[121]

As Turner insists once again, it is only through contact with the frontier that a truly American identity is formed. He begins by personifying the wilderness and giving it a sense of agency, since it is the wilderness itself that transforms the European colonist into an American. It is quickly apparent, however, that the transformation of the colonist consists in the colonist adopting the dress, home, tools, and methods of war and cultivation of indigenous peoples, who are here mostly reduced to mere adjectives and are present only through their objects. Quite literally, American Indians function as the absent cause of Turner's account in that they are present only through their effects in the form of a series of objects—the canoe, the hunting shirt and the moccasin, the cabin, the palisade, the corn and the stick, and the trails and the clearings—and in the colonist's disavowed learning process, the way he learns to plant, plow, and scalp using the techniques of the natives. The actual agency of the Indian as absent cause, however, is accounted for by attributing causality once again to the natural environment of the frontier. The representation of the wilderness as agent and of the frontiersman as passive proves to be a rhetorical move that attempts to hide the fact that there is, in actuality, a learning process involved whereby the frontiersman only survives by learning from the natives. The colonist must subject himself to the environment's/native's power in order to assure his survival since "the environment is at first too strong for the man." It is only after the frontiersman has appropriated the wilderness's/native's knowledge and can produce his own sustenance—the "before long" in the preceding excerpt—that he ceases to be dependent on the wilderness/native and, through an attack evidenced in the war cry and in taking the scalp of an unspecified enemy, he asserts his dominance, being thereby transformed into a "new product": the *American* subject.

Significantly, Turner is unable to maintain his erasure of the Indian all the way through his account. In describing the very moment when the colonist violently affirms his independence, Turner is compelled to use the scalp as synecdoche for that upon the domination of which his independence rests, in this way demonstrating that nature has been the Indian all along. Once one recognizes that the form of agency and knowledge belonging to the wilderness is actually the dislocated effect of a spectral indigenous population, and that the same population is also the target against which the frontiersman levies his war cry, one reaches the following conclusion: the Indian is both the necessary *and* impossible condition for the constitution of American national identity and subjectivity, a paradoxical function that Turner disavows by covering it over with the "frontier" as natural determination. The affective attachments constitutive of the social bond among Americans are themselves structured around the collective identification with this fantasy of national identity. This fantasy, moreover, obfuscates the degree to which the constitution of the American nation-state and national identity relies on the supposedly necessary exclusion of, and acceptable violence against, native peoples.

While Williams makes a strong case for the persistence of the Indian as limit figure, it is also certain that other limit figures besides the Indian have also served, and some continue to serve, a similar function—for example, the African American, the black slave, the Asian, the Mexican, the communist, the homosexual, the criminal, and the "illegal" immigrant, among others.[122] With that said, I suspect that both the frontier as fantasy-scenario and the figure of the Indian served a strategic function at the time of Turner's writing nearly thirty years after the end of the Civil War. The Indian seems to be a particularly adequate figure for the ideological production of an encompassing national identity since this figure enabled people with attachments to either side of the conflict to forge a collective identity against the same signifier of the outsider. Likewise, by creating a fantasy-scenario that could extend into the distant past precisely at the time that the frontier ceased to officially exist, the frontier was ripe for its resignification as the mythical site of national identitarian origins. The popularity of Turner's thesis, moreover, can be said to result from its success in fostering affective social bonds through a simultaneous attachment to liberal principles.

Conclusion

At this point, I once again return to Badiou's initial critique of Lacan, but from another perspective: that of the symptom. Psychoanalysis teaches that it is in a system's contradictions that the real can be indexed, with the symptom betraying the fact that an antagonistic contradiction has been repressed as a condition for the constitution of the system as it is. The notion of the symptom, however, is not a single one in Lacanian psychoanalysis, and Žižek tracks its different formulations. In an initial conception, the symptom was understood to be "a symbolic, signifying formation . . . a kind of cipher, a coded message."[123] It was the result of a repression that reemerged in a coded form. The function of psychoanalysis was then to "re-establish the broken network of communication by allowing the patient to verbalize the meaning of his symptom," after which the symptom was supposed to automatically dissolve.[124] The problem, however, was that even after interpretation, the symptom continued to persist. The reason for this, concluded Lacan, was that the symptom also serves as "a way for the subject to organize his enjoyment."[125]

In attempting to isolate this aspect of enjoyment in the symptom, Lacan proceeded by distinguishing and then opposing the notions of "symptom" and "fantasy," situating the dimension of enjoyment in the latter. The symptom then continued to denote a signifying formation that could be analyzed, while fantasy was a construction that, in contrast, resisted interpretation and hence could not be resolved by analysis. This distinction implies two stages of the psychoanalytic process: (1) an initial interpretation of the symptom up to the fantasy, and (2) a process of "going through" the fantasy. As Žižek describes:

> When we are confronted with the patient's symptoms, we must first interpret them and penetrate through them to the fundamental fantasy as the kernel of enjoyment which is blocking the further movement of interpretation; then we must accomplish the crucial step of

going through the fantasy, of obtaining distance from it, of experiencing how the fantasy-formation just masks, fills out a certain void, lack, empty place in the Other.[126]

Yet even at this point the question arose of how to explain the persistence of the symptom in patients who had, without a doubt, gone through the fantasy.

It is in response to this question that Lacan develops the concept of "sinthome," defined as "a certain signifying formation penetrated with enjoyment: it is a signifier as a bearer of *jouis-sense*, enjoyment-in-sense," which also implies a certain "synthesis between symptom and fantasy."[127] The sinthome is attributed an ontological status as "the only positive support of our being, the only point that gives consistency to the subject," and enables us to avoid madness "through the binding of our enjoyment to a certain signifying, symbolic formation which assures a minimum of consistency to our being-in-the-world."[128] Yet to the extent that we encounter jouissance in the sinthome, and remembering that jouissance is radically incompatible with the symbolic order, it would seem that in going through the fantasy we would also come up against the possibility of an emancipatory escape from symbolic determination—a kind of zero point where the limit between the real (radical antagonism) and the symbolic would be most directly encountered, and thus the possible point from where a process radically transformative of the coordinates of the symbolic could begin.

Nevertheless, already evident in the preceding explanation of the symptom as sinthome is that, according to psychoanalysis, "[t]he only alternative to the symptom is nothing: pure autism, a psychic suicide, surrender to the death drive, even to the total destruction of the symbolic universe."[129] This is why, for the final Lacan, the end of the psychoanalytic process requires that the patient *identify* with the symptom rather than achieve its complete dissolution. "So what happens with desire after we 'traverse' fantasy?" asks Žižek: "Lacan's answer . . . is *drive*, ultimately the death drive . . . its pulsation around the *sinthome*."[130] This is why, according to Žižek, the very formalization of the sinthome should be that of the drive ($ \$ \lozenge D $).[131] The problem, Hallward points out, is that while "the drive is truly independent of the Other, [its] independence is trapped within the effectively thoughtless pursuit of inarticulate *jouissance*."[132]

In this manner, the potential for emancipatory *praxis* is precluded by the mindless pulsation of the drive. One thus returns once again to the fact that Lacan seems to fall back on the side of structure. We are limited to identifying and living with a symptom whose role is to maintain the consistency of the structure, with no possibility of the coming into existence of something upon which a new consistency can be made to exist.[133] "For this reason," argues Bosteels, "even [Lacan's] uncompromising insistence on the real, which otherwise would seem to hold the greatest political potential, threatens to become contemplative and idealist."[134]

In other words, it is not enough that in passing through the fantasy we simply experience that there is nothing behind it, that the fantasy precisely hides this nothing.[135] For the possibility of a new consistency to emerge from such an encounter, something else must come into existence onto which a new process can latch. The possibility of true change depends upon the emergence of something in excess of lack precisely in instances where such a lack is encountered.[136] "Something else has to happen, beyond the mere occupation of an empty place," explains Bosteels: "Otherwise the structure of what is given would merely open itself up to a flickering alternation between the false appearance of plenitude and the vanishing act of the real of lack," leaving the structure essentially unchanged.[137] This "something" is what Badiou formulates as an event and the "implicative remnant of the encounter," or the trace it leaves behind upon its disappearance.[138]

This means that we need a theory of the subject beyond that of Lacanian psychoanalysis.[139] Badiou's step in formulating such a theory is to "map a subjective process onto the rare emergence of a new consistency . . . in which a subject not only occupies but exceeds the empty place in the old structure, which as a result becomes obsolete."[140] It is no exaggeration to say that almost all of Badiou's philosophical work is dedicated to formulating the existence of such a subject in thought. What he proposes is the "liberation of truth from the drive" by turning the work of the subject into a sustained and disciplined procedure that, by following the trajectory of consequences made possible by the novelty of an event, can make it consist in a fundamental transformation of the coordinates that organize a situation.[141]

Thus, while the specific trajectories of particular political sequences vary, my concern centers on the way in which all sequences confront and transform the ideological underpinnings of existing social order. Since the social bond is established by fantasy, to the extent that politics works upon and displaces such fantasy, it also affects the social bond in a way that can facilitate a process of unbinding. This unbinding makes manifest the equality of thought, the equal ability of anyone to think and act beyond determinations established by one's social status.[142] Since the correlation of social status with corresponding interests is (re)produced (and naturalized) via the experience of identity as produced by fantasy, politics as unbinding is thus at bottom also a procedure that exceeds the bounds of identity. Moreover, to the extent that "nation" functions today as the primary quilting point and fantasy-scenario for the stability of political community, it is precisely a category that must be displaced, yet not abandoned. As I have argued, political modernity produced another conception of nation: nation as the product of universal citizenship. It is toward such a conception of the political collective that the following chapters aim to contribute, beginning from instances of revolt that actualize, in their particular places and times, the universal right to politics.

Ethnics of the Real

HB 2281 and the Alien(ated) Subject

Let foreigners teach us at least to become foreign to ourselves.

ALAIN BADIOU, *The Meaning of Sarkozy*

———

IN MAY 2010, Arizona governor Jan Brewer signed into law House Bill 2281, a measure meant to regulate the content and outcomes of public school instruction by prohibiting Arizona school districts from offering courses that (1) promote the overthrow of the US government; (2) promote resentment toward any race or class of people; (3) are designed primarily for pupils of a particular ethnic group; and (4) advocate ethnic solidarity instead of the treatment of pupils as individuals. As was clear from previous attempts by the state legislature to pass similar legislation, the main target of the bill was the Tucson Unified School District's Mexican American/Raza studies program, which the state superintendent of public instruction, Tom Horne, had been trying to eliminate since the renowned labor organizer Dolores Huerta told an assembly of Tucson High School students in 2006 that "Republicans hate Latinos."[1] Coming on the heels of SB 1070, the infamous "show me your papers" immigration enforcement law that Brewer had signed a few weeks before, and that many rightly feared would subject people of color to racial profiling, HB 2281 seemed to be just the latest in a spree of anti–Mexican/Mexican American legislation. While the attack against Mexican American studies was also motivated by conservative attempts to roll back the vestiges of the civil rights era—a general project that claims to address the problem of racial discrimination by trying to eliminate race from our critical vocabulary altogether, and that frequently does so by appropriating the very discourse of civil rights[2]—what these interpretations overlooked was another of the law's implicit objectives: the preemption of the threat of radical politics associated with the program, the potential for which advocates of the law saw in the program's purported focus on collectivism over individualism and in its rereading of US history and literature from the perspective of race and ethnicity. Considering texts by the Brazilian radical educator Paulo Freire, Mexican American historians, and critical race theorists as evidence of the program's promotion of the overthrow of the US government, proponents of the law further attempted to ground the specter of radical politics by reviving Cold War rhetoric that constructed the program as a foreign-inspired national security threat, if not an outright communist conspiracy.[3]

The conflict that arose around the law's passage, however, also requires consideration of the discourse of Mexican American studies, and of ethnic studies more generally. Given their status as fields of study whose origins lie in the revolutionary and civil rights struggles of the last century, and whose political imaginary was nurtured by the international decolonization and national liberation movements from which they drew inspiration, one must once again raise the question of their political potential. Abraham Acosta, for example, has drawn attention to the way in which the very determination of the parties in conflict around HB 2281, as a conflict between an Anglo majority and a Mexican American minority, was premised upon the latter's adoption of a subhegemonic logic through which its status as the *largest* minority enabled it to appropriate for itself the minority position altogether.[4] This has led to a lack of analysis of the law's implications for other minority groups. Acosta's insistence that we "account for the fact that this community will not be the only one affected" was indeed borne out by the subsequent finding by John Huppenthal, who succeeded Horne as the state's superintendent of public instruction, that "classes taught from the African American perspective" similarly violated the law's prohibitions against promoting the overthrow of the US government, advocating ethnic solidarity, and promoting resentment, because they used texts and songs by Rage Against the Machine and KRS-One.[5]

By analyzing the arguments that arose for and against ethnic studies, I seek to demonstrate that what is at stake is also a conflict over contending, but sometimes surprisingly similar, conceptions of the political subject. The uneasy relationship between nation, race, ethnicity, and abstract individualism in the legal and public discourse in support of HB 2281 betrays the fact that liberal formalism has itself been made meaningful through its articulation in nationalist terms—an articulation that depends on the simultaneous production of the "foreigner" or "alien" as both ethnic/racial other *and* as the threat of nonliberal radical politics. While those in favor of HB 2281 claim the primacy of the individual against a supposedly divisive focus on ethnic difference, the very terms upon which proponents of the law construct the liberal individual are premised on narrow identitarian conceptions of citizenship and national belonging with a much longer history. Indeed, it is precisely this history that ethnic studies takes as one of its main objects of analysis. Yet, while ethnic studies' frequent focus on inclusion, recognition, and disalienation may have pedagogical value, I claim that such notions still depend on an assimilationist logic—even when affirming a group's difference— with depoliticizing implications. The radical potential of ethnic studies as a field, I claim, rests on its ability to rethink nonassimilation—a form of nonassimilation that, rather than giving way to a counteridentitarian retrenchment (as in the form of various ethnocultural nationalisms), would make its thought consist at the very limits of the "national," at the limits of both the individual and the community, from the point of view of the "alien" as limit figure and of "alienation" as a structural constant.

HB 2281 and the Trauma of Alienation

The initial attempt to build a case against ethnic studies in Tucson can be dated to 2007, three years before HB 2281 was passed, when Tom Horne wrote an open letter to Tucson citizens warning them about the Mexican

American/Raza studies program in the Tucson Unified School District (TUSD). The letter begins with the claim that "[t]he citizens of Tucson, of all *mainstream* political ideologies, would call for the elimination of the Tucson Unified School District's ethnic studies program if they knew what was happening there."[6] This appeal, by directing itself to adherents of "mainstream" political ideologies, thus opens by implicitly suggesting that whatever was happening in the ethnic studies program was in violation of a widely held consensus on acceptable political ideas. After outlining his belief that "people are individuals, not exemplars of racial groups," and that "students should be taught that this *is* the land of opportunity, and that if they work hard they can achieve their goals," Horne condemns the Mexican American studies program for teaching "destructive ethnic chauvinism."[7] This chauvinism, according to Horne, stems from the program's focus on race, its critical portrayal of US history, and its use of "oppression" as an analytical category.

In delineating the consequences of this course of study, Horne again resorts to thinly veiled references to the threat of radical politics and communism. Drawing upon the testimony of anonymous sources—in a way that hearkens back to the Cold War use of secret evidence against suspected subversives[8]—Horne mentions the "horrors" that TUSD employees had witnessed. He justifies his reliance on anonymous sources by claiming that the "totalitarian climate of fear" has "ke[pt] them from being quoted."[9] Suggesting the existence of a kind of popular revolutionary tribunal run amok, he cites local conservative reporter Doug MacEachern's warning that "[t]eachers and counselors are being called before their school principals and even the district school board and accused of being racists. And with a cadre of self-acknowledged 'progressive' political activists in the ethnic-studies department on the *hunt*, the race transgressors are multiplying."[10] Indeed, as Horne's successor, John Huppenthal, later declared in an interview, what was at stake in the conflict over ethnic studies was the "eternal battle . . . of collectivism against the forces of individual liberty," and the forces of collectivism were winning.[11]

The response of ethnic studies teachers, students, and supporters, on the other hand, was to point out the logical flaw in suggesting that the use of race as an analytical category is enough to make one a racist or ethnic chauvinist, and to challenge the allegation that the purpose of acknowledging and studying structural inequality is to breed "resentment."[12] The program's critical stance toward the notion of liberal individualism, moreover, is at the heart of the historical development of the field itself. "In the new ethnic model [that emerged in the 1960s]," Juan Poblete points out, "the unit became the community [and] a new group-based platform emerged from which to claim rights in a direct challenge to the traditional liberal focus on individual rights."[13] The focus on group rights was itself tied to the denunciation by ethnic minorities of the persistence of discrimination despite formal equality. This, in turn, led to the investigation of structural factors that undermined the fiction of abstract equality and maintained the marginal position of ethnic minorities with respect to citizenship rights and national belonging.

The most cogent defense of TUSD's Mexican American studies program, however, pointed to the program's effectiveness in stimulating academic performance, reducing the achievement gap between Latina/o and Anglo students, and obtaining higher graduation rates and standardized test scores.[14] Supporters have maintained that the main source of this success is the recognition that students are able to obtain through a curriculum in which they see themselves reflected and that allows them to learn a more complete version of history that accounts for the contributions of Mexican Americans.[15] Such a curriculum is said to help students overcome both the social alienation they experience outside the classroom and the alienation they experience inside the classroom from a lack of representation in the materials of mainstream courses. It is this reinforced sense of self and of community that is identified as the cause of students' improved performance. While its success in achieving important educational outcomes is unquestionable, fidelity to the radical political impulse of ethnic studies also requires one to turn a critical eye toward the political implications of the assumptions that support this discourse. To be clear, my point is not to dismiss the program's educational achievements, which should be lauded. Given ethnic studies' political origins, my point, rather, is to resist the reduction of ethnic studies' political efficacy to these outcomes, and to lay out what I consider to be both the limits and potential of the oppositional subjectivities the field seeks to foment.

I posit that what underpins many of the arguments in defense of the program—especially around questions of recognition, disalienation, and the affirmation of national belonging—is a logic of inclusion and, ultimately, of assimilation. As Catherine Ramírez points out, some of the program's defenders sought to counter accusations that Mexican American studies is un- or anti-American by reasserting its "American" credentials.[16]

This was the response of Arizona congressman Raúl Grijalva, who defended the program by claiming that it was doing "a very American thing [in teaching] students to value themselves, to value their families, to value who they are, to know who they are."[17] If beyond the pedagogical objectives of producing students with a developed sense of self and community, whose identity as anchor allows them to better navigate the various hurdles of racism and structural inequality, one analyzes the political implications of the figure of the subject presupposed by the program, I suggest that such a figure proves to work against its own political intentions. Furthermore, if we take seriously the form of civic engagement that the program promoted and the impressive political capacity that the students demonstrated in the aftermath of HB 2281's passage, critical engagement becomes our duty.

I thus argue that an assimilationist logic undergirds the very desire for an unalienated subject. Disalienation hinges on the recognition students obtain from curricular material. This material in which the student sees herself or himself reflected "completes" the student as it interpellates her/him as an identitarian citizen-subject. The political and social horizon that the program identified for itself was premised on transforming the signifier "Mexican American" (or "Raza," "Chicano," etc.) into an object through which the subject could overcome his alienation.[18] The relationship between the alienated subject and the object through which the subject fills in the gap of his division precisely reproduces Lacan's formula for fantasy ($ \$ \lozenge a $). This fantasy that articulates the subject's desire is the identitarian fantasy of self, community, and liberal citizenship.

In its attempt to produce an unalienated identitarian subject better equipped to operate in a racist social and institutional context, I suggest that the program grounded itself conceptually in the tenets of ego psychology. Indeed, Antonio Viego makes the case that much of the discourse of Latina/o studies, and ethnic studies more broadly, has unwittingly relied on the premises of ego and social psychology. He argues that in its search for the unalienated, whole, self-evident, and fully knowable subject of ego psychology, Latina/o studies, "against its best intentions, provide[s] precisely the image of ethnic-racialized subjectivity . . . upon which racist discourse thrives and against which [it] imagine[s] doing battle."[19] Significantly, Viego, following Lacan, attributes as a cause for the development of ego psychology in the United States the "North American coercive assimilatory imperatives working on ethnic-racialized

subjects—. . . Jewish immigrant psychoanalysts who fled Nazi Europe—
that demand[ed] of them a certain mandatory adjustment and adaptation
to North American 'reality.' "[20] Keeping in mind the nascent Cold War context of that immigration, such assimilatory pressures, it must be pointed
out, also included the rejection of radical and communist politics.[21] Since
much of Lacan's work consisted precisely in challenging the development
of ego psychology, which tended to minimize the role of the unconscious
and ignore the structural role of language in creating the barred subject—
essentially conflating the ego with the subject—Viego argues that it is
imperative for Latina/o and ethnic studies to engage with the insights
of Lacanian psychoanalysis.[22] Indeed, given that teachers and students
themselves adopted the language of therapy in describing the effects of
the program—by emphasizing, for example, Mexican American studies' "power of healing academic and personal trauma"—it is evident that
bringing psychoanalysis into the discussion is far from irrelevant.[23]

Yet the following objection could immediately be made: is the "border subject" in Chicana/o and Latina/o studies (a subject crossed by or
inhabiting a space in between languages, cultures, nationalities, sexuali-
ties, genders, etc.) not another name for Lacan's barred subject? And, in
light of Frances Aparicio's claim that the border subject "has been the
most important concept that Latino studies has contributed to cultural
studies in the United States, Europe, and Latin America," does this turn
to Lacan not turn out to be unnecessary after all?[24] Viego's response is
that the various figurations of the border subject—be it Gloria Anzaldúa's
"mestiza consciousness," Chela Sandoval's "differential consciousness,"
or José Esteban Muñoz's concept of "disidentification," for example—
continue to rest on a conception of the subject founded on identitarian
self-consciousness, no matter their more hybrid, flexible, or fluid articulations. They continue to ignore the divided (or alienated) subject as the
irreparable outcome of the function of language as structure.[25] In Lacan's
words, alienation results from "the fact that the subject depends on the
signifier and that the signifier is first of all in the field of the Other."[26] As
a consequence, what psychoanalysis teaches is that "[t]here is no utopic
resolution to alienation . . . since alienation is the inevitable condition of
existence" for human beings as such.[27]

I argue that a similar dynamic plays out at the collective level, with
regard to any given community. Community is never a coherent "whole."
It is always already alienated from itself. This immanent breach, moreover,

is the condition of possibility for radical politics since it marks the site from where strong difference, or antagonism, can emerge. The state's function as the guarantor of social order, on the other hand, is to do all that it can to keep such antagonism at bay. In fact, the attempt to close this gap through the "exclusion of something alien, of a radical other- ness" is the foundational gesture of juridico-political order in the first place.[28] It is thus no surprise that the "alien" has historically functioned as a marker of the threat of inconsistency and disorder endangering the stability of juridico-political community. One may even say that the figure of the alien comes to occupy the gap of alienation. Consequently, before delving into what Lacanian psychoanalysis can or cannot contribute to a rethinking of the subject in Latina/o studies, I will take a historical detour, both to provide a genealogy of the discourses from which propo- nents of HB 2281 drew to couch their arguments within the purview of national security, and to trace the historical function of the figure of the "alien," and of foreignness in general, in various articulations of Ameri- can citizenship, nation, and politics.

Alien Politics, Alien Races

In *Democracy and the Foreigner*, Bonnie Honig notes a persistent undecid- ability attached to the figure of the foreigner, one that makes foreignness function "as an undecidable supplement in national democratic imagina- tions."[29] The figure of the foreigner is thus inserted into conflicting nar- ratives that range from its representation as a necessary figure for the revitalization, and even (re)foundation, of political community, to its repre- sentation as the cause of corruption, disorder, and the breakdown of politi- cal community. This undecidability, however, suggests the function of the figure of the foreigner as something akin to Lacan's *objet a*: it is variously construed both as the figure through which the community can be made whole (once again)—that is, the figure through which the community can overcome the discord or inconsistencies that hound it and undermine its cohesion—and as the very source of the community's gravest problems. In both of these contending formulations, then, the "foreigner" marks the real of political community as the latter's condition of (im)possibility.

In what follows, I analyze the ways in which the figure of the racialized and/or politically radical foreigner (the "alien," to put it in the lexicon of immigration law) has served throughout US history—and particularly in times of war or social, economic, and political anxiety—as the embodiment of potential threat and thus as what must be kept out, deported, or stripped of legal protections for the preservation of US social and political order. In this section, I aim to demonstrate not just the way in which the "alien" has been associated with the threat of radical politics but that radical politics has itself been recurrently figured as "alien." My objective in critically analyzing the persistent figuration of the racial and political "foreigner" as a necessary exclusion is not to limit myself to the liberal argument that true democracy depends on the inclusion of foreigners in their diversity, but rather to make the case that this figure actually marks the place of the real that is always already *immanent* to social and political order. It is symptomatic of the fact that the real, as the very figure of the inassimilable, is the immanent and paradoxical condition of a given order. More than a figure that may bring a new law from the outside, the alien betrays the fact that existing law is itself "not-all"—that it is split, that it is alienated from itself, and that this alienation is a necessary (though not sufficient) condition for radical politics.

In the United States, the association of radical politics with the foreign can be traced back at least to the short-lived Alien and Sedition Acts of 1798. During this time, as tensions between federalists and republicans ran high, "[i]t suffice[d] for a man . . . to believe that human affairs [were] susceptible of improvement, and to look forward, rather than back to the Gothic ages, for perfection, to mark him as an anarchist, disorganizer, atheist, and enemy of the government," noted republican Thomas Jefferson.[30] At a time when the republican principle of popular government was joined in the imagination of many to the Terror of the French Revolution, "fears that the 'alien' radicalism of the French Revolution might infect the [American] polity" led to the passage of the Alien and Sedition Acts.[31] These acts, however, though enacted under the auspices of a looming war with France, were actually devised to quell domestic political opposition during peacetime.[32] The Alien Act made it lawful for the president to order the deportation of "all such *aliens* as he shall judge dangerous to the peace and safety of the United States, or shall have reasonable grounds to suspect are concerned in any treasonable or secret machinations against the government."[33] In a context rife with domestic political tensions, where republicanism in general was considered by many to be dangerous to domestic peace and safety, the Alien Act had the effect of associating republicanism itself with the "foreign," thus also implicitly placing republicans under suspicion of holding treasonous sympathies.[34] The legal repression of political opposition was extended to citizens as well by means of the Sedition Act, which criminalized collective efforts "to oppose any measure or measures of the government of the United States."[35] In the two years during which they were operative, only the Sedition Act was enforced, and was done so only against republican opposition to the federalist administration of John Adams.[36]

One can note a similar pattern throughout the twentieth century. Though opposition to Mexican American studies in TUSD revived Cold War rhetoric with the claim that the program was promoting "the overthrow of the United States government"—a catchphrase that during the Cold War became synonymous with communism—the legal origins of this rhetoric must be traced back to 1903, when, after the assassination of President William McKinley at the hands of avowed anarchist Leon Czolgosz, Congress passed an immigration law that "barred entry to 'anarchists, or persons who believe in or advocate the overthrow by force or violence of the Government of the United States or of all government or of all forms of law.'"[37] Significantly, Czolgosz was himself a US-born citizen. Yet the supposed foreignness of his political ideas—amplified by his "foreign-sounding" name—enabled the government to shift the perception of potential threat onto foreign nationals in order to push through restrictive measures that would have encountered widespread opposition had they been initially applied to citizens. It is thus that despite at first being restricted to foreign nationals, the 1903 law became "the template for all future anti-Communist laws," many of which were directed against citizens as well.[38] "Within two generations," explains legal scholar David Cole, "the prohibition on advocacy of violent overthrow was the central feature of an extensive web of federal and state laws, ultimately penalizing not just speech but association, possession of literature advocating forbidden views, and even belief in disfavored doctrines."[39]

After 1917, as the vector of radical politics shifted to Russia (and later to the Soviet Union), the discourse of the anti-anarchist provisions was extended to target socialists and communists. Because there were people in the United States that "enthusiastically supported this new [Bolshevik] regime," recounts William Wiecek, "the old pattern, fear of an ideologically alien foreign power leagued with a subversive domestic movement, suddenly seemed grounded in reality," much like it had been at the end of the eighteenth century.[40] The passage of a new Sedition Act in 1918 marked an escalation in the suppression of political dissent. Given that the authority of the Sedition Act, along with that of the Enemy Alien Act and the Espionage Act, was limited to wartime, the problem emerged of how to maintain a check on political dissent after the end of World War I. J. Edgar Hoover, who had worked in the Justice Department's Alien Enemy Bureau during the war, found a way to solve this problem after the end of the war as head of the Justice Department's Alien Radical Division.[41]

In 1919, the fear of a domestic subversive movement led to actual panic when several bombs were discovered, and some detonated, around the country. One such bomb exploded in the home of the attorney general, A. Mitchell Palmer. From the remains of the bomber, who had died in the blast, authorities determined that he was an anarchist Italian alien from Philadelphia.[42] While the identities of other suspected bombers were never found, this nevertheless gave Hoover cause to direct a sequence of roundups of foreign nationals deemed politically dangerous—in so doing, Hoover made use of the laws dating back to 1903 governing the political speech and association of noncitizens.[43] The "Palmer Raids," as they came to be known, began in November 1919 with a raid on the offices of the Union of Russian Workers and continued into early 1920 with nationwide raids on the Communist Party and the Communist Labor Party.[44] "The net was so wide and the bureau detectives were so careless," explains William Preston, "that some ten thousand persons were arrested including many citizens and many individuals not members of either party."[45] The roundups' extensive reach was itself made possible by the fact that their targets were noncitizens. "The reason for targeting noncitizens was not that they were the prime suspects," Cole determines, "but that the law made it easier to round them up."[46] Hence the association of radical politics with the alien not only serves the ideological function of externalizing an antagonism that is immanent, but it enables recourse to a set of mechanisms that ease legal restrictions on the suppression of this very antagonism. The lack of legal protections for noncitizens is precisely what facilitated the overreach toward citizens and non–party members.

Repeating another historical pattern a few decades later, the latent threat attributed to noncitizens was imbricated with the question of race—and with the racialization of citizenship and nationality—after the Japanese attack on Pearl Harbor and US entrance into World War II.[47] Most significantly, given the long history through which American citizenship has itself been racialized as white—the legislative origins of which can be found in the Naturalization Act of 1790, which restricted naturalization to "free *white* person[s]"—racial difference was made to function as a marker of foreignness in a way that bridged the gap between citizens of Japanese descent and noncitizen Japanese. Not only was the loyalty of Japanese nationals placed under suspicion, but the loyalty of citizen Japanese Americans was also put in doubt because they were of Japanese descent. Racial difference, as a marker of the "un-American," became a central ideological alibi for Japanese internment.[48] The legal grounds for the internment of Japanese and Japanese Americans can also be traced back to the passage in 1798 of the Alien Enemies Act.

Enacted as part of the Alien and Sedition Acts, the Alien Enemies Act is the only one that remains. It gives the president the power in times of war to apprehend, restrain, secure, and remove as "alien enemies" citizens fourteen years or older of the country with which the United States is at war—though it has been used against foreign nationals after the end of hostilities as well.[49] It holds that such extraordinary powers are needed to preempt potential actions on behalf of the enemy country by citizens of the latter that reside in the United States. The act's logic hinges on the assumption that one's loyalty lies primarily with the country of which one is a citizen, and thus depends on the distinction between US citizens and foreign nationals. This distinction, however, was cast aside with the detention and internment of US citizens of Japanese descent.[50] Significantly, its extension to citizen Japanese Americans contradicted the act's own logic since it supposed that these citizens were in fact *not* loyal to their country of citizenship. Conversely, the very undoing of the supposed correspondence between citizenship and loyalty should itself have placed in doubt the presumption of the disloyalty of foreign nationals from enemy countries in the first place.

In this context, race served a vital function, as it allowed for this contradiction to be dispelled by substituting citizenship with a racial determination of supposed national belonging. If citizenship tends to presuppose national belonging, here it was a racialized conception of foreign national belonging that at once overrode and displaced legal citizenship to the degree that it was one's belonging to the "foreign" Japanese race-cum-nation, rather than one's citizenship, that placed one's loyalty under suspicion. Implicit was the idea that though people of Japanese descent were citizens, they were not really nationals of the United States since their race not only suggested their inassimilability to the latter but compelled their belonging to a racialized Japanese nation—with loyalty assumed to correspond to the "nation" to which they belonged rather than to their country of citizenship. Race thus became a signifier through which the state sought to fix the contingency of political loyalty. This enabled General John L. DeWitt, one of the most vocal proponents of Japanese internment, to notoriously declare in 1943 that "[a] Jap's a Jap. It makes no difference whether he is an American citizen or not."[51] Thus, irrespective of official American citizenship, but because of the concurrent racialization of American and Japanese nationality, Japanese Americans were attributed the mark of foreignness and inassimilability to the American nation.[52]

Inassimilability, however, has also been attributed at times to other ethnic and racial groups, such as Mexicans and people of Mexican descent. On January 29, 1853, for example, in the midst of the panic roused by the forays of legendary rebel Joaquín Murrieta in California, the *San Joaquin Republican* newspaper reported the following with regard to popular anti-Mexican sentiment:

> If an American meets a Mexican he takes his horse, his arms, and bids him leave. . . . We understand that a Mass Meeting was held at Double Springs, on Wednesday morning, and resolutions passed . . . making it the duty of every American citizen at all events to exterminate the Mexican race from the country. The foreigners should first receive notice to leave, and if they refused they were to be shot down and their property confiscated.[53]

This account also evinces the imbrication of race with citizenship and nationality. While the concept of inassimilability is not explicitly mentioned, it is nevertheless implicitly present as the excerpt replicates some of the same assumptions that would structure the logic used to justify Japanese internment nearly a century later.[54] "Mexican," in this excerpt, becomes a racial category incompatible with "American citizenship," a move that racializes as "non-Mexican" American citizenship as well. The "Mexican," which in this passage also functions as the embodiment of social conflict and antagonism arising from the US annexation of California and the encroachment of Anglo settlers after the Mexican-American War—a conflict in which Joaquín Murrieta became a symbol of resistance to Anglo domination—is expelled from, and made "alien" to, the new

juridico-political and racial order. The "Mexican race" is made antithetical to American citizenship to the extent that among the duties of American citizens is the extermination of the former.[55] The extermination of
the Mexican race, in fact, is figured as necessary to the new juridico-
political order—with the act of extermination itself being performative
of racialized American citizenship—in that it promises to eliminate the
source of racial conflict and of social, economic, and political antagonism
hindering the new order's formation. As a precondition for achieving and
securing the new order, the extermination of this "alien" race is also part
of a process of primitive accumulation through dispossession that is constitutive of, and immanent to, this very order. Alienated from land and
citizenship, Mexicans and people of Mexican descent are the proletarian-
ized foundation (though certainly not the only one) of the nascent racial
capitalist politico-economic order.

While the purpose of my analysis here is to draw out the logic
expressed in the preceding newspaper excerpt, which purports to be an
account of popular sentiment at the time, the category of "Mexican" was
historically more heterogeneous from the perspective of Mexican citizenship. The "nuanced, multiracial nature" of Mexican citizenship was lost
and replaced with "the immutable categories of U.S. racism," however,
in the very process by which *some* Mexican citizens in the former Mexican territories crossed the threshold into US citizenship.[56] The Treaty of
Guadalupe Hidalgo provided that Mexicans who chose to remain in the
former Mexican territory and did not explicitly declare their intention to
retain their Mexican citizenship would, "at the proper time," become US
citizens and be able to enjoy full citizenship rights.[57] This stood in tension
with the racial conditions of US citizenship, especially in light of the fact
that Mexico had previously granted citizenship to "civilized" Indians and
blacks.[58] In order to make Mexican citizens assimilable to US citizenship,
explains María Josefina Saldaña-Portillo, "all Indians were deemed unas-
similable to U.S. national character and so retroactively rendered noncitizens of Mexico."[59] The same occurred with Afromestizos and blacks.[60]
In short, Mexican citizenship was retroactively whitened, with the racial
logic of the newspaper fragment (and the violent dispossession it fos-
tered) displaced mainly onto the Indian population.[61] Thus, in the years
that followed, citizenship rights were extended to "white" Mexicans, a
move that denied legal protections to Indians and opened the door to
their utter decimation—and, indeed, their virtual extermination.[62]

The fact that Mexican, Japanese, and Indian inassimilability has been articulated through similar logics at different historical junctures implies an equivalence in these figures' function, and thus an exchangeability between them.[63] Theirs is a "negative" equivalence, however, since it is established via their function as markers of the "inassimilable," as figures of radical heterogeneity in excess of whatever specific characteristics are attributed to them to rationalize their exclusion at different times.[64] The fact that today the Japanese, along with other Asians, are often considered a "model minority" relative to African Americans and Latinas/os precisely suggests both that the particular characteristics identified as causes for their inassimilability are not inextricably tied to these groups and that their designation as inassimilable can tell more about the *function* that such groups are made to serve at different times than about the "real" identity of the groups themselves.[65] Despite changes in differential racial hierarchies that enable a previously disparaged group to become a model for others, the *place* of the inassimilable remains as the nonidentitarian real within any figuration of national identity—modifying General DeWitt's statement, one could say that what the figure of the inassimilable teaches is that "a gap's a gap," regardless of the particular signifier that at different times is made to stand in for it.

Indeed, this is one of the main lessons of Lacanian psychoanalysis, which holds that *"the place logically precedes [the] objects which occupy it,"* and that "what the objects, in their given positivity, are masking is . . . simply the emptiness, the void they are filling out."[66] The positioning of race as determinant of the parameters of political community in the previous examples turned race into an object that allowed for dominant conceptions of US citizenship and nationality to cohere by accounting for their own, and immanent, errant indeterminacy. Yet while racialized nationality seeks "natural" grounds for the nation, the fact that the inassimilability of the real is immanent to political community voids its foundational core. Regardless of the fact that some marginalized groups have been more or less beneficially included into the liberal-democratic order, the inassimilable remains at, and as, the necessary limit of inclusion. If the inassimilable as such could ever be "included"—that is, if it could ever be the site of an agency that forces effects upon the existing structure—it could only do so in excess of the particularities of whatever groups occupy its place.

The anxious desire to safeguard the nation through the determination of political loyalty gave way, especially after World War II, to the near obsessive concern with the ascertainment of political ideas. Due to communism's association with the foreign, communist and other leftist radical political ideas positioned those who held them at the margins of juridico-political community, much like race had done. In the legal discourse of the time, communists were considered almost a species apart. They were regarded by many "as *sui generis*, different from other radical groups like the Klan, and uniquely threatening to America's national security. The Court therefore assigned Communists a special status under the Constitution, with diminished protections for their speech, press, and associational liberties," explains Wiecek: "Communists were different from other fringe or radical groups. . . . Annoying or obnoxious as such groups may have been to their contemporaries, they retained their human nature. But the manufactured image of the domestic Communist . . . made of Communists something less than full humans, full citizens, fully rights-endowed."[67] Thus, while Nazism and fascism also had associations with foreignness, their anti-leftist position, their social conservatism, and their racial politics showed them to be quite compatible with anticommunist reactionary ideologies in the United States.

In 1939, legislation was passed that barred federal employment to any member of an organization that advocated for the "overthrow of [the] constitutional form of government in the United States."[68] The Alien Registration Act of 1940, also known as the Smith Act, required that all aliens fourteen years of age or older register and be fingerprinted at a local post office and notify authorities of any change in residence. It also made immigrants deportable for *past* membership in proscribed organizations, even during a time when membership in these organizations had not been prohibited, thus authorizing the act's ex post facto application.[69] The Nationality Act of the same year both barred from naturalization anyone who belonged to an organization that advocated the overthrow of the government and permitted the denaturalization of citizens who had belonged to the Communist Party.[70] Despite the Alien Registration Act's explicit reference to aliens, it also included provisions that affected citizens directly by making it a federal crime, to be punished with up to ten years in prison, "for anyone to advocate the overthrow of the government by force and violence, to organize a group to so advocate, or to belong to such a group with knowledge of its ends."[71] These provisions made it the first peacetime federal sedition law after the Sedition Act of 1798.[72] While the Alien Registration Act criminalized radical politics, the federal employee loyalty program of 1947 opted for administrative mechanisms to bypass the due process protections of criminal law. Employees whose loyalty was under review were assumed guilty until proven innocent, were subject to guilt by association, could be found disloyal for past membership in groups that had been perfectly legal at the time of their membership, and could find their loyalty determined on the basis of secret evidence.[73] Subsequent laws, such as the Taft-Hartley Act of 1947, the Internal Security Act of 1950, and the McCarran-Walter Act of 1952, furthered the trends established by the laws just mentioned. It was through this constellation of antiradical legislation that many political activists and labor organizers were expelled from the country during this time.[74]

"These People Are Not Aliens," or Are They?
Luisa Moreno and Bertolt Brecht

In 1940, Luisa Moreno delivered a speech during the annual conference of the American Committee for Protection of Foreign Born. In the wake of the mass deportations of Mexicans and Mexican Americans during the 1930s, and underscoring the contradictions between renewed domestic anti-alien sentiment in the United States and the US government's simultaneous efforts to promote hemispheric unity under the Good Neighbor policy, Moreno outlined an alternative vision for unity and labor rights. "Luisa Moreno's address," argues Alicia Schmidt Camacho, "stands as the most expansive vision for migrant and labor rights in any period of Latina/o militancy before or since."[75] Born into a wealthy family in Guatemala in 1907, Moreno left home during her late teens to build a life outside the bounds of her class privilege. Moving first to Mexico City, where she formed part of the vibrant postrevolutionary cultural milieu of the time and befriended the likes of Frida Kahlo and Diego Rivera, she moved to New York in 1928.[76] She worked as a seamstress and a steam press operator in the garment factories around Spanish Harlem and soon became involved in labor organizing.

Moreno's talent as an organizer transformed her into "the most visible Latina labor and civil rights activist in the United States during the Great Depression and World War II."[77] Throughout her astonishing career she organized and advocated for cigar rollers in Florida, cane workers in Louisiana, pecan shellers in San Antonio, Texas, beet workers in Denver, Colorado, and cannery workers in California.[78] She became vice president of the United Cannery, Agricultural, Packing, and Allied Workers of America, making her the first Latina vice president of a major union.[79] Together with other renowned Latina/o organizers, such as Josefina Fierro, Bert Corona, and Eduardo Quevedo, Moreno was central to the creation, in 1939, of El Congreso de Pueblos de Habla Española (The Congress of Spanish-Speaking Peoples).

El Congreso's expansive vision enabled it to establish affiliations with a wide array of leftist organizations, ranging from Mexican unions to the Communist Party. Among its basic tenets was its "refus[al] to draw distinctions between U.S. citizens and foreign-born members of the Latino population."[80] With regard to this, El Congreso differed from other prominent organizations that were its contemporaries, like the League of United Latin American Citizens (LULAC).[81] In many ways, El Congreso was ahead of its time and at the forefront of progressive advocacy. It concerned itself with police repression, education, racial discrimination and segregation, affordable housing, the minimum wage, the extension of the National Labor Relations Act to domestic and agricultural workers, and the defense of immigrants against deportation.[82]

Speaking on behalf of El Congreso, it is this vision that Moreno sets forth in her 1940 speech "Non-Citizen Americans of the South West." "The stage is set. A curtain rises. May we ask you to see behind the scenery and visualize a forgotten character in this great theater of the Americas?" begins Moreno, with a literary flair still present from her early years as a poet.[83] The character to which she brings attention is a people split by citizenship status yet united by language and class: "They are the Spanish-speaking workers of the Southwest, citizens and non-citizens working and living under identical conditions, facing hardships and miseries while producing and building for agriculture and industry."[84] Therefore, "[t]he purpose of this movement," Moreno declares, "is to seek an improvement of social, economic, and cultural conditions, and for the integration of Spanish speaking citizens and non-citizens into the American nation."[85] Stressing that "[t]hese people are not aliens," the speech is a demand for inclusion into the national body.[86]

Important to note is the way in which the logic that bridges the gap between citizens and noncitizens both resembles and differs from the logic used against Japanese nationals and people of Japanese descent in World War II. Instead of race, here it is language that bridges the citizen/non-citizen divide—though surely in a way that feeds into the construction of ethnicity. Unlike in the previous example, where race functioned to impose cohesion upon a group that was made foreign, here language is used to create a group that can make a unified claim on national belonging. That both citizen and noncitizen Spanish speakers demand integration into the American nation again implies a gap between citizenship and national belonging, at the same time that it presupposes a critique of formal equality. To the degree that national belonging undergirds citizenship, integration into the nation is sought both to endow noncitizens with citizenship—one of the speech's main calls is for legislation that would make it easier for noncitizens to naturalize—and to make effective the citizenship rights of those who already enjoy formal citizenship.[87] While in the previous case American national identity was deemed incompatible with Japanese identity, Moreno and El Congreso's stance—and here one can note a challenge to the similar assumption of the incompatibility between the Mexican "race" and American citizenship evinced in the 1853 news article—represents an attempt to diversify the dominant identitarian construction of American nationality, since the integration that is sought hinges on Spanish speakers being recognized as linguistically, culturally, and ethnically *different*—"[w]hile encouraging immigrants to become citizens, delegates [of El Congreso] did not advocate assimilation but rather emphasized the importance of preserving Latino cultures," Vicki Ruiz underscores.[88]

At the heart of Moreno's speech is the construction of a (linguistic-cum-ethnic) national minority identity upon the recognition of which social and political claims can be made.[89] Despite its implicit critique of formal equality and the fact that the very gesture of emphasizing the "Spanish speaking" as a collective endows the group with a kind of distinction that pushes against cultural assimilation, the speech's model of multicultural integration, however, remains rooted within a nationalist framework that compels it to position itself against the figure of the alien—and, by extension, the truly inassimilable. Though constitutive of a demand for national inclusion that promises effective citizenship rights, the rejection of their status as "aliens" is also *the* foundational nationalist gesture. Even as the speech advocates for the belonging of noncitizens, the collective it creates appeals directly to a form of national belonging that places this collective on the "correct" side of the national/foreign divide. The citizen/noncitizen division, which is usually considered to coincide with the national/foreign distinction, is bridged through claims to national belonging, while the distinction between national and foreign is reified. It is thus that when it advocates for legislation that would facilitate the naturalization of "all natural born citizens from the countries of the Western Hemisphere," the speech implicitly sets the extensional limits of those who would benefit from such legislation against the "real" foreigners, those "inassimilable" others.[90]

If Moreno's speech evinces its own assimilationist tendency in dissociating itself from the "alien" in order to seek admission into the American nation, one can find in Moreno's own life a set of actions that push the other way. Luisa Moreno, in fact, was born Blanca Rosa Rodríguez López. It was during her time organizing Latina/o, black, and Italian cigar rollers in Florida that she chose to change her name to Luisa Moreno.[91] "Deliberately distancing herself from her past," Ruiz argues, "she chose the alias 'Moreno' (dark), a name diametrically opposite her given name 'Blanca Rosa' (White Rose)."[92] Ruiz speculates about the reason for this name change:

> Simply put, Moreno made strategic choices regarding her class and ethnic identification in order to facilitate her life's work as a labor and civil rights advocate. With her light skin, education, and unaccented English, she could have "passed"; instead she chose to forego any potential privileges predicated on race, class, or color. Furthermore, she made these changes in the Jim Crow South where segregation and white domination were a way of life.[93]

Consistent with her earlier decision to seek a life outside of the class privilege into which she was born in Guatemala, Moreno's name change can be read as a rejection of the racial privilege to which she could have had access due to her light skin—a privilege symbolically supported by her birth name.[94] Accordingly, Moreno symbolically racialized herself through her name change in a way that positioned her closer to the racialized workers she was trying to organize. Even so, the radical gesture in her renaming, I hold, lay not in taking on a *morena* identity herself (as if a mere change of name would have been enough to do so), but in the way she created a cleavage at the center of her own identity by symbolically negating and distancing herself from the elements of race ("Blanca") and class ("Rosa" and the aristocratic connotations it evokes) that were supposed to ground her identity and the privileges that stemmed from it.

It was an act of self-alienation that would not have necessarily led toward another identity, but would instead have marked a point of immanent separation from "herself." She would repeat this alienating refusal at other moments as well.

At the end of the 1940s, Luisa Moreno had all but retired from her almost twenty-year career as a labor organizer when she was singled out as a "dangerous alien" by the California legislature's Joint Fact-Finding Committee on Un-American Activities.[95] Despite being an advocate for naturalization, as evinced by her speech in 1940, Moreno herself did not file for citizenship until after her marriage to Gray Bemis in 1947, around the time that she became a target of the Immigration and Naturalization Service.[96] Her attempt to officially become part of the American nation would be undone by her association with a form of politics deemed foreign and retroactively prohibited. "We are right back in the pages of that revealing book on the 'Asiatic and the Alien,'" declared Moreno: "No Constitution for us, who are neither citizens nor persons, but a freakish creation called 'aliens.'"[97] Finding herself positioned at the margins of legal personhood, Moreno's statement acknowledges the overlap of race and politics in the statist delimitation of the kind of subject worthy of legal protection. To the extent that a noncitizen may still be regarded as a "person," the claim that she and others like her are "neither citizens nor persons" suggests that Moreno now situates herself beyond the citizen/ noncitizen divide and on the side of the radically foreign in the foreign/ national distinction.[98] She acknowledges her location on the side of the inassimilably "alien." It is thus no coincidence that she finds herself close to the figure of the "Asian," a figure against which her earlier speech was still implicitly positioned.

Moreno was subpoenaed to appear before the committee on September 8–10, 1948. Throughout the ordeal it was suggested to her that her citizenship application could be negatively affected if she refused to cooperate.[99] At one point Moreno was offered citizenship if she would agree to testify against Harry Bridges, the Australian-born leader of the longshoremen's union made legendary not only for his work as an organizer, but for the extraordinary effort that the US government had exerted in trying to deport him.[100] Moreno famously rejected the offer by saying that she refused to be a "free woman with a mortgaged soul."[101]

If one of the models for the performance of "Americanness" during this period was the "friendly witness" eager to cooperate with the various committees charged with rooting out "un-American activities," as Joseph Litvak argues, then the committee had given Moreno the opportunity to prove herself worthy of American citizenship by performing just such a role.[102] In enacting the conventions of the friendly witness by becoming an informant, she would have performed her assimilation into the American nation. If successful, Moreno's iteration of this model of Americanness could have finally turned her into a true national. Hence her refusal to inform was, at bottom, a powerfully anti-assimilationist, and decisively alienating, gesture. It is thus after refusing to either inform on others or to answer if she herself had been a member of the Communist Party— which in fact she had been from 1930 to 1935, during a time when it was not against the law to do so—that Moreno was found to be a "hostile witness." Shortly thereafter, on September 30, 1948, a warrant was issued for Moreno's arrest "as an alien 'affiliated with an organization [that] teaches the overthrow, by force and violence, of the government.'"[103] After several years of fighting to stay in the country, and feeling that she had exhausted any chance of reversing the ruling against her, Moreno left of her own accord in November of 1950, accompanied by her husband.[104]

Three years before Moreno's final departure, another "dangerous alien" took the stand before the House Un-American Activities Committee in Washington, DC. Having arrived in the United States in July 1941, before being officially designated an enemy alien with the US entry into World War II at the end of that year, by 1944 the activities of the German playwright and poet Bertolt Brecht were considered by members of the US government to be a matter of internal security.[105] This was so even though, as James Lyon observes, while living in California,

> the revolutionary dramatist behaved like a law-abiding German burgher. He observed the curfew for enemy aliens while it was in force; he registered annually with the Immigration and Naturalization Service and he always notified them of his current address; he requested and received permission to travel from the local US District Attorney's Office each time he went to New York; he registered for the draft; he took out a California driver's license; and, so far as is known, he paid income taxes.[106]

In short, Brecht adhered to the legal restrictions placed on foreign nationals of the time (especially those from enemy countries), and appeared to have adapted himself to American life. Nevertheless, when the committee began to investigate communist infiltration of the movie industry, Brecht was among the first witnesses called to testify.

He appeared before the committee on October 30, 1947, assisted by attorneys Bartley Crum and Robert W. Kenney—the latter would also go on to represent Luisa Moreno. Held in the Old House Office Building, the hearings attracted unprecedented media attention for a congressional investigation. The abundant media presence, which included television coverage as well as live and delayed broadcasts by all the radio networks, endowed the hearings with the air of spectacle.[107] The committee members present during Brecht's hearing were J. Parnell Thomas (chairman, R-NJ),[108] John McDowell (R-PA), and Richard B. Vail (R-IL). They were aided by chief investigator Robert E. Stripling, who asked most of the questions.

In some ways during the hearing, Brecht clearly played the part of the foreigner, and did so to his advantage. Claiming that he was merely a "guest in this country," he notified the committee that he would avoid entering "into any legal arguments" and promised to answer their questions as fully as possible.[109] This seems both to have surprised the committee, given the refusal to cooperate by the first ten witnesses that had taken the stand prior to Brecht, and to have had the effect of warming its members up to him. Similarly, the fact that his works were in German meant that they would have to be translated into English. This played in his favor since it enabled him to dispute the basis of some of the questions by claiming that his texts had been mistranslated.[110] It allowed Brecht to maneuver his responses to his benefit and to undermine the soundness of the evidence that buttressed the committee's authority in the public's mind.

If, again following Litvak, one remembers that the friendly witness was a model of American loyalty and citizenship, then in agreeing to answer the committee's questions, Brecht also showed himself to be far from un-American.[111] In responding to the committee's questions in a way that at times even exhibited the trace of eagerness, Brecht styled himself as "friendly" (and thus as "American") a witness as those hoping to ascertain his loyalty could have hoped. Regardless of the fact that he had no interest in actually becoming "American"—Brecht always considered himself an exile while in the United States, he never applied for citizenship, and he planned to return to Europe from the beginning of his stay in the country[112]—it was precisely the conventions of "Americanness" that he put on display in his testimony. Yet, unlike Ayn Rand, the naturalized American who ten days earlier had shown herself to be as "American" as one could get in her anticommunism, Brecht, the theorist of alienation, opened up a breach within the performance of Americanness itself.

I thus turn to the testimony. Despite Brecht's promise to cooperate fully, the committee members seem at first unsure about what kind of witness he will actually be. Asked by Mr. Stripling if he is or has ever been a member of the Communist Party, Brecht responds by asking if he can first read a prepared statement before he answers the question. He is asked by Mr. Stripling to submit the statement to the chairman, who, after reading it off record, says that it is not pertinent to the inquiry and denies Brecht permission to read it.[113] Perhaps the real reason that Thomas did not allow Brecht to read his statement, however, is the statement's implicit comparison of the House Un-American Activities Committee with Nazism. Recalling how Nazism began with the suppression of free artistic expression and free speech, Brecht's statement calls attention to the way in which

> [h]umanist, socialist, even Christian ideas were called *"undeutsch"* (un-German), a word which I hardly can think of without Hitler's wolfish intonation. . . . The persecutions in the field of culture increased gradually. Famous painters, publishers and distinguished magazine editors were persecuted. At the universities, political witch hunts were staged, and campaigns were waged against motion pictures such as *All Quiet on the Western Front.*[114]

Had Brecht been allowed to read his statement, especially since the hearing was being aired live across the country, it could have swayed already divided public opinion against the committee.[115] Remembering once again that the previous ten witnesses had refused to answer the question of their membership in the Communist Party, it would not be far-fetched to assume that the committee expected Brecht to respond in similar fashion. With his statement refused, Brecht is again asked if he is or has ever been a member of the Communist Party. Declaring that he will not try to avoid the question, he responds: "I was not a member, or am not a member, of any Communist Party."[116]

Even when Brecht answers the committee's questions directly, there is often a shade of indeterminacy in his answer. This is best evinced in the exchange that ensues halfway through the testimony, after a question with regard to his attendance of Communist Party meetings during his time in the United States:

> Mr. Stripling: Mr. Brecht, since you have been in the United States, have you attended any Communist Party meetings?
> Mr. Brecht: No, I don't think so.
> Mr. Stripling: You don't think so?
> Mr. Brecht: No.
> The Chairman: Well, aren't you certain?
> Mr. Brecht: No—I am certain, I think, yes.
> The Chairman: You're certain that you've never attended.
> Mr. Brecht: Yes, quite, I think so. [*Audience laughter*] You see I'm here six years. I'm here six years. I do not think so. I do not think that I attended political meetings.
> The Chairman: No, never mind the political meetings, but have you attended any Communist meetings in the United States?
> Mr. Brecht: I do not think so, no.
> The Chairman: You are certain?
> Mr. Brecht: I think I'm certain. [*Audience laughter*]
> The Chairman: You think you are certain?
> Mr. Brecht: Yes, I have not attended such meetings . . . in my opinion.[117]

Though Brecht is clearly not refusing to answer, his responses are not unequivocal, given his tendency to undermine the definitiveness of almost every answer by his use of "I think"; the "in my opinion" with which the exchange ends does not help either. The indeterminacy of his answers provokes laughter from the audience several times as Brecht's testimony begins to take on the quality of a comedy routine. With the audience, one is led to wonder if Brecht is serious, or if he is beginning to toy with the committee—especially when one cannot but detect a trace of mischief in his tone when he reiterates, "I think I'm certain," toward the end of the exchange. Is Brecht being sincere, or is he simply putting on an act?

Notably, Lyon lists among the "two significant dramatic performances" that marked Brecht's last months in the United States the staging of *Galileo* under his supervision and "a hearing by the House Un-American Activities Committee, [where] he himself was one of the principal actors."[118]

Indeed, as mentioned before, the committee hearings themselves evoked a sense of spectacle and were (and continue to be) considered by many to be little more than political "theater."[119] Accordingly, Brecht prepared for the hearing as if he were preparing for a performance. In the lead-up to his appearance before the House Un-American Activities Committee, Brecht spent six days in New York, where he met with his collaborator Hanns Eisler (who had himself appeared before the committee the previous month) and the journalist Hermann Budzislawski in order to go over probable questions and practice his answers. With Budzislawski, Brecht "rehearsed for what might happen at the hearing as though they were preparing for a play," writes Lyon: "When Brecht arrived in Washington, he was the best rehearsed of the 'unfriendly' witnesses who would testify."[120] Together they devised certain tactics that would enable Brecht to better maneuver his responses. He would challenge the committee's translations of his works and would use an interpreter, even though he considered his English adequate for the hearing, in order to give himself more time to think before replying.[121] He would do something similar with his cigar, which he would use as a prop to manufacture pauses between their questions and his answers.[122]

In light of the theatrical dimension of the hearings, and Brecht's approach to his participation in them, one is led to focus on the question of theatrical method and on the techniques that Brecht himself developed in his own theory and practice. One must wonder whether the famous theorist of alienation stages moments that produce alienating effects during his own testimony. For Brecht, the A-effect consists of unsettling the ordinary and familiar by turning it into the peculiar and unexpected.[123] The A-effect undermines the self-evidence of what is portrayed and denaturalizes it, yet it "does not in any way demand an unnatural way of acting."[124] Most important, it hinders the audience "from simply identifying itself with the characters in the play," and incites the audience to become conscious of the implications of the characters' utterances and actions.[125] In short, the A-effect is meant to remind the audience that what it is witnessing is a performance, and thereby to create a critical distance between the audience and the world represented onstage.[126] During his testimony, I argue, Brecht does precisely this.

Though one may object that the predominant markers of Brecht's foreignness (his name, his accented speech, the foreign language of his writings, among others) already hamper the audience's identification with him, one must remember that it is with the *conventions* of testimony and citizenship, and not with the personal characteristics of the individual testifying, that the hearings prompt the audience to identify. In relation to the clearly identifiable conventions of the "friendly" and "unfriendly" witness, as staged by the witnesses that testified before him, Brecht adopts those of the friendly witness. As can be seen in the preceding excerpt, however, he integrates into his performance particular words, phrases, and forms of intonation that unsettle his status as a friendly witness, which makes the audience begin to take notice. The audience's laughter precisely registers moments in which the development of identification is hindered and the "friendly" status of Brecht's testimony is consciously put in doubt in the minds of audience members. While one of the functions of the A-effect in theater is to induce the audience to remember that the performance it is witnessing is not reality, Brecht's testimony prompts the audience to ask itself whether the reality it has before it is in fact a performance.[127]

If Brecht's method is to employ the A-effect to open up theater to politics by prompting the audience to think, then here he does something similar. Instead of simply playing the part of the foreigner, Brecht produces an immanent cut that alienates the performance of political loyalty and American citizenship from itself. By playing the part of the friendly witness, yet opening a space of undecidability within this very performance, Brecht creates a breach *within* the enactment of political loyalty and American citizenship through which the audience may think, precisely when it is freedom of thought that is at issue. It is the contingency of thought this freedom implies that threatens the state with indeterminate loyalty, which is why it is this very breach that the state tries to eliminate by driving out the "un-American."

The Assimilating Ego and the Hysteric's Discourse

As demonstrated in the previous sections, the coupling of radical politics with the "foreign" has been a consistent tactic since the early years of the US nation-state. There has been a repeated attempt throughout US history to secure the stability of domestic politics via the repression of the threat of an antagonism deemed "foreign." This move has unsurprisingly fed into the articulation of dominant politics in nationalist terms, with the "national" itself articulated via the discourses of race and ethnicity. One of the consequences of the coupling of radical politics with foreignness is the exertion of pressure upon those who seek full entry into the US nation to "assimilate" politically. Accordingly, adaptation to the "American way of life" is conditioned on a similar depoliticizing adaptation to acceptable "national" politics.

It is these same assimilatory pressures that Lacan credits for the development of ego psychology in the United States, the depoliticizing implications of which Viego underscores when its main tenets are adopted by Latina/o and ethnic studies. Furthermore, given the racialization of the national, Viego notes "a kind of privilege that is thoroughly racialized . . . as white that attaches to the conceit in the imperatives of adaptation and adjustment to and harmony with 'North American reality,'" which endows ego psychology's assimilationism with its own "presumption of whiteness."[128] That is, if the "national" is the construct to which the ego must adapt, then the process of the ego's adaptation entails embracing, or at the very least learning to live with, the presumption of whiteness that is one of this construct's defining features.[129] It is in this sense that the discourse of ego psychology, based on "the unity of the subject," ends up feeding, intentionally or not, into the reproduction of racial domination.[130]

Yet it is also the case that assimilation is not *necessarily* antithetical to the recognition of difference, as was demonstrated previously with El Congreso and Luisa Moreno's speech. Viego himself illustrates this point with reference to Lacan's essay "The Freudian Thing."[131] In the case of the European psychoanalysts who had immigrated to the United States after World War II, Lacan argues in this essay, assimilation was a summons to which this "group of emigrants had to respond; in order to gain recognition, they could only stress their difference. . . . The combination of circumstances was too strong and the opportunity too attractive for them not to give in to the temptation to abandon the core in order to base function on difference"[132] In this way, assimilation also proceeds via the inclusion of a group as different. This is because even if the recognition of difference may modify ideological content, the identitarian logic at work (its form) remains the *same*.[133] In basing one's function on difference, furthermore, one is compelled to *reduce* one's function *to* one's difference in a way that facilitates a form of token inclusion—which carries its own set of privileges, not to mention the pleasure of recognition—that not only leaves the structures of power in place, but legitimizes them by lending them an air of inclusivity.[134] To the extent that Lacan's work sought to counter the effects of these assimilationist tendencies in the field of psychoanalysis, which he did in part by proposing a nonidentitarian conception of the subject, then it stands to reason, as Viego does, that Lacanian psychoanalysis may help Latina/o studies critically reflect on its basic assumptions with regard to its conception of the subject and what it considers to be this subject and the field's basic function.

Viego draws on Lacan to both diagnose what he sees as the current function of Latina/o studies in the university (and, one could add, the public school system) and to propose an alternative that would better serve the field's critical and political impetus. In our contemporary situation, he argues, Latina/o studies in the university operates within what Lacan refers to as the "master's discourse."[135] The master's discourse is one of four discourses—the others being the university discourse, the analyst's discourse, and the hysteric's discourse—the core theorization of which Lacan develops in his seventeenth seminar, *The Other Side of Psychoanalysis*.[136] The four discourses are constituted with regard to four signifiers—S_1 (master signifier), S_2 (knowledge), a (the *objet a*), and $\$$ (the barred subject)—and the particular placement of these signifiers around a four-cornered structure, as shown in figure 2.1. Each of the four corners is attributed the structural function shown in figure 2.2.

The claim that the university speaks the master's discourse with regard to Latina/o studies means that the body of knowledge (S_2) produced by the field is put to work for the benefit of the university as master signifier. The knowledge produced is "not allowed to have transformative potential. The only requirement is that the work keeps getting done and that the worker keep doing it," explains Viego: "Let's think of the requirement as that of the ongoing circulation of difference just for difference's sake or, more specifically, as the packaging of Latino cultural difference in the service of teaching about and codifying so-called Latino cultural difference for the delectation of the masses."[137]

University	Master	Hysteric	Analyst
$S_2 \rightarrow a$	$S_1 \rightarrow S_2$	$\$ \rightarrow S_1$	$a \rightarrow \$$
S_1 $\$$	$\$$ a	a S_2	S_2 S_1

agent	$\rightarrow$	other/work
truth		product/loss

Figure 2.1. Lacan's Four Discourses; adapted from Jacques Lacan, *The Seminar of Jacques Lacan Book XVII*.

Figure 2.2. The Four Positions; adapted from Jacques Lacan, *The Seminar of Jacques Lacan Book XVII*; and Bruce Fink, *The Lacanian Subject*.

My intention in drawing on Viego is not to argue that either Latina/o studies or programs like Mexican American studies in TUSD have no critical/political edge, or that they are all too glad to acquiesce to the demands that they produce innocuous knowledge of cultural difference—though Viego's formulation does suggest that mere demands for the recognition of difference, far from posing a challenge to the current function of the university or school system, in fact provide them with material to bolster their legitimacy in the name of superficial diversity and inclusivity. What Viego is referring to is the institutional pressures put upon Latina/o and ethnic studies programs to precisely reduce their function to their difference. HB 2281, then, can be read as the master's reaction when such a program defies its assigned role and develops a course of study that not only makes plain that it will not be complacent with merely celebrating cultural difference, but sets its sights on critically undermining the historical and social narratives that prop up racially ingrained institutional power. The drastic reaction that culminated in HB 2281 registers the threat perceived when such programs do not fall in line. It is this rebelliousness that Viego suggests could be better served by the hysteric's discourse.[138]

The hysteric's discourse is well positioned to undermine the master's discourse because, with the split subject in the position of agent and the master signifier in the position of other, it "keeps pointing to the breach, to the hole in the discourse that wants to be free of lack and division."[139] The hysteric's questioning introduces the subject, as agent, into history.[140] "[T]he hysteric pushes the master . . . to the point where he or she can find the master's knowledge lacking," explains Bruce Fink, which is why "in the hysteric's discourse, object (a) appears in the position of truth. That means that the truth of the hysteric's discourse, its hidden motor force, is the real [as] that which does not work . . . that which does not fit."[141] It is on the basis of the real that the hysteric's discourse seeks to demonstrate that the master, too, is lacking, which is to say that the master, too, is castrated.

In this way, the hysteric unmasks the master, showing that the illusion of his completeness was based on covering over his own lack.[142] Keeping in mind that "Brecht is a thinker of the theatre conceived as a capacity to unmask the real," one may not be amiss if one detects in Brecht's performance before the House Un-American Activities Committee something of the hysteric's discourse.[143] Similarly, to the extent that one of the critical functions of Latina/o studies is to demonstrate the gaps or holes in dominant national narratives, to show that the ideological coherence of structures of domination and exploitation are effected through a series of blind spots, repressions, and contradictions that betray the fact that they are not-whole, the field already goes a long way in doing the work of the hysteric's discourse. Its reliance on the tenets of ego psychology, however, undermines this critical edge by pulling Latina/o studies back into a form of master's discourse precisely at the moment in which it endeavors to think the status of, and its function in relation to, its own figure of the subject.[144] In trying to produce a whole and unalienated subject, Latina/o studies, not unlike the master, denies the fact that its subject, "like everyone else, is a being of language and has succumbed to symbolic castration," which is to say that it is constitutionally split and that this split is irreparable.[145] The critical potential of the hysteric's discourse thus lies in putting the split subject in the driver's seat and proceeding on the basis of the truth of the real.

Alenka Zupančič, however, raises some points regarding the limitations of the hysteric's discourse. Among them is the hysteric's tendency to completely disjoin truth from the symbolic. "It seems that the hysteric places the whole truth precisely in that Lacanian 'other half' of truth that is never covered by the signifier," she points out.[146] The hysteric thus tends to situate all of truth in the place of the gap, in a way that reduces truth to the void itself. This leads to a kind of fixation and fascination with the void that in turn "becomes a source of surplus enjoyment and satisfaction."[147] "The hysteric is satisfied with nothing, in both possible meanings of this expression," Zupančič explains: "It is not only that nothing can satisfy him or her, but that the nothing itself can be an important source of satisfaction."[148] In this sense, one of the drawbacks of the hysteric's discourse lies in finding satisfaction in the mere exposure to the real of lack. This satisfaction, moreover, precludes engagement in a process of structural change via a torsion back upon the symbolic initiated from the position of the real. There is evidence of such a torsion, and thus of a thinking of the subject that pushes through the deadlock of the hysteric's discourse, in Julia de Burgos's poem "To Julia de Burgos."

Julia de Burgos's Theory of the Subject

In "To Julia de Burgos," the Puerto Rican poet Julia de Burgos deploys a version of the border subject. Hers is a subject constituted around the politics of gender, a subject divided between her social existence and her artistic subjectivity, the latter of which is represented in the form of the poetic voice. As a reflection on her divided self, the poem speaks to many of the themes that are of concern to Latina/o studies. It wrestles with and tries to think through the problematics of identity, oppositional subjectivity, and the politicization of antagonism. In its trajectory, I argue, it offers not one but two formulations of the divided subject and, in the shift from one to the other, reconfigures the conception of the nature of its split. The form in which the division is reconfigured resonates with the Lacanian conception of the subject, though it also exceeds this conception as it opens up to a new subjectivation by linking the place of the split to the potential it holds for a form of politicization that is no longer individual, but rather is constitutively linked to the collective through the figure of the masses in revolt. The poem reads as follows:

TO JULIA DE BURGOS

Already the people murmur that I am your enemy
because they say that in verse I give the world your self.

They lie, Julia de Burgos. They lie, Julia de Burgos.
Who rises in my verses is not your voice; it is my voice
because you are the clothing and the essence is me;
and the most profound abyss spreads between us.

You are the frigid doll of the social lie,
and me, the virile starburst of the human truth.

You, honey of courtesan hypocrisies; not me;
in all my poems I bare my heart.

You are like your world, selfish; not me;
who in everything I wager to be what I am.

You are merely the grave self-important lady of the house;
not me; I am life, strength, woman.

You belong to your husband, your master; not me;
I am no one's, or everyone's, because to all, to all
in my clean feeling and in my thought I give myself.

You curl your hair and put on makeup; not me;
the wind curls my hair; the sun colors me.

You are a housewife, resigned, submissive,
tied to the prejudices of men; not me;
I am Rocinante run away
sniffing horizons of God's justice.

You in yourself have no say; everyone governs you;
in you rule your husband, your parents, your relatives,
the priest, the dressmaker, the theater, the dance hall,
the car, the jewels, the banquet, the champagne,
heaven and hell, and the social "what will they say."

Not in me, in me my lone heart rules,
my lone thought; who rules in me is me.
You, flower of aristocracy; and me, the flower of the people.
You in you have everything and you owe it to everyone,
while I, my nothing I owe to no one.

You, nailed to the static ancestral dividend,
and me, a one in the place of the social divisor,
we are a duel to the death that fatally approaches.

When the multitudes run rioting
leaving behind ashes of burned injustices,
and when with the torch of the seven virtues,
after the seven sins, run the multitudes,
against you, and against everything unjust and inhuman,
I will go in their midst with the torch in my hand.[149]

The threat of the poetic subjectivity relative to the social self (i.e., the self bound by the set of social/symbolic conventions that regulate and produce her identity and behavior) is evoked from the opening verses by means of people's concern that the first may reveal too much of the second. The division between the two is not that between public and private selves, since the poetic voice opposes herself to the other in the latter's public *and* private roles—the other of the poetic voice is as much a facade and determined by the same power dynamics in her private functions as in her public ones. To people's murmurs, the poetic voice responds: "They lie, Julia de Burgos. They lie, Julia de Burgos. / Who rises in my verses is not your voice; it is my voice." The two selves thus stand at odds by means of a split created through the very act of writing, an act through which Julia de Burgos is alienated from herself through a (second layer of) symbolic inscription which is itself constitutive of the poetic voice.[150]

In stanzas two to four, however, the subjective division is articulated via a discourse of authenticity through which the poetic voice presents herself as the true subject—as the essence that rises as it sheds the clothing of appearance, one that sides with truth and sincerity against the other who is defined by society's lies and hypocrisies. With these two selves separated by "the most profound abyss," the poem sets up a dialectic of counteridentification where one identity, the poetic voice as true identity, is affirmed against the artifice of the other. While there is no evidence of an attempt or a desire to overcome alienation through a synthesis of both identities, the poem nevertheless figures the poetic subjectivity as a site of counterconsciousness that makes a "whole" out of the half that she is. She resists assimilation into the other self and adaptation to social demands by marking her difference, even while she continues to define herself in the same language of identity.

And yet the content of the poetic subjectivity as counteridentity is evacuated as the poem develops. This is gauged when the poetic voice declares: "You belong to your husband, your master; not me; / I am no one's, or everyone's, because to all, to all / in my clean feeling and in my thought I give myself." Unlike the other self, the poetic voice belongs to no master. She proclaims her freedom, yet immediately conditions it on giving herself up "to all." While this can be read as suggesting that, to the extent that she belongs to everyone, she belongs to no one in particular, this would imply a resubmission to the social (as an object owned by the collective), which is precisely what she resists. She belongs to no one, rather, because what she gives—which is herself made to consist in feeling and thought—cannot be owned; she has been drained of distinguishing traits, and as such breaks with the commodity logic that feeds on identifiable difference. She is everyone's without submission, however, for the same reason. It is through the inability to be owned by anyone— even by the collective—that she passes over into the common. What she gives is herself reduced to "clean" feeling and thought that touch upon the universal in their subtraction from identitarian particularities. This evacuation of self linked to a break with economic logic and the obligations of custom is reemphasized four stanzas down—"You in you have everything and you owe it to everyone, / while I, my nothing I owe to no one"—where she reduces herself to something like an empty set, or an "evental site."[151]

In the ninth stanza, the poetic subjectivity begins to take flight, as the product of thought run wild (like a runaway Rocinante), toward the horizon as the very figure of division.[152] Coupling the limits where artistic creation ventures with the limits (i.e., "horizons") where justice can be found, the poem prefigures the political subjectivation of the poetic voice that will subsequently occur, one that hinges on the creativity of thought unhinged. It is thus that a few stanzas down, the division between the two is reconfigured in class terms when the poetic voice states: "You, flower of aristocracy; and me, the flower of the people." "You, nailed to the static ancestral dividend," the poetic voice accuses the other self, suggesting that she continues to benefit from privileges passed down to her—the kind of privileges from which Luisa Moreno was also primed to benefit, and against which she also turned. Yet a dividend is also that which in a fraction is divided by another number: "and me, a one in the place of the social divisor, / we are a duel to the death that fatally approaches," the poetic voice declares in the following verses. This number is the poetic subjectivity reduced to a minimal existence, to a one as a minimal difference that immanently divides the social to which the other self belongs. The division between the two selves is now displaced onto the level of society: $\text{self}/1 \rightarrow \text{society}/1$. Remarkably, the poetic subjectivity is no longer the site of a counteridentity, but is rather the site where both society and her own social identity are different from themselves. The one bears the mark of the alienation, of the lack of self-identity, which identitarian and statist logics attempt to repress in their effort to make themselves whole.[153] While the elimination of this minimal difference may not affect the value ($\text{self}/1 = \text{self}$, $\text{society}/1 = \text{society}$), the gap of alienation nevertheless brings with it the threat of an antagonism—"a duel to the death that fatally approaches"—capable of disrupting the reproduction of structural inequality.

In this way, the homology of the division that is the nonidentity of the self with the self and of society with itself implies that the "duel to the death" toward which the two selves are headed also harkens the coming to a head of antagonism at the level of the social. In this homology between the individual and the social, both of which are formally split in similar ways, one can thus find the latent presence of psychoanalysis and Marxism. As Bruno Bosteels stresses, however, "the issue is certainly not to couple the psychic and the social into a neat relation of complementarity, but rather to understand how both Marx and Freud are founders of a discourse, whether political or clinical, that is of the order of an intervening doctrine of the subject."[154] In a move that resonates with Marx and Freud, Burgos uses this poem to put forth her own theory of the intervening subject.

The poem implies that the fact that both society and the self are split is the condition of possibility for revolt and for the subjectivation through which one joins (or commences) such a revolt in a manner that exceeds one's socially determined self-interest. It is thus with the irruption of the rioting "multitudes"—which in Spanish is synonymous with "masses" or "crowds"—that the individual conflict will reach a critical point, with the poetic voice turning against the other self as she joins a collective revolt:

> When the multitudes run rioting
> leaving behind ashes of burned injustices,
> and when with the torch of the seven virtues,
> after the seven sins, run the multitudes,
> against you, and against everything unjust and inhuman,
> I will go in their midst with the torch in my hand.

Emanating from the site of division, which is the place of the Lacanian subject, the "multitudes" or "masses" will occupy and exceed this place as an event that forces its way through the gap and conditions a new subjectivation.

The rioting multitudes will emerge from the "abyss," or nonrelation, that Burgos initially situates between the two selves and then reconfigures onto the social, suggesting that what was previously figured as a weak difference supporting counteridentification (and thus a continuity between identitarian logics) is now figured as the site of strong difference and antagonistic causality. The riot will be an event that the poetic voice—herself a figure of artistic creation and of thought that proceeds via a certain unbinding from the demands of gendered social conventions—will join in order to perform a torsion back upon the other self and upon society simultaneously. To a certain extent, then, the trajectory of the poem runs the trajectory of the different conceptions of the subject that I have touched upon, beginning with an identitarian oppositional conception that is subsequently desubstantialized, only to become the site for a politicization that will occur via an opening up to a collective revolt. While from the beginning people suspect that the poetic voice is the enemy of the other self in her break with the pressures of gendered social expectations and conventions, only when the poetic voice joins a wider egalitarian struggle will the division between the two selves really become antagonistic; it is only then that the poetic subjectivity will truly turn against the other, making way, in turn, for the possibility of a wider transformative torsion at the level of the social. It is with regard to the thought of such a torsion that "To Julia de Burgos" has most to contribute to Latina/o studies and to the theorization of revolutionary politics more generally.

Inhering in the Split beyond the Hysteric's Discourse

By now one can see that it is no coincidence that Tom Horne and others draw upon the figure of the "alien" and the "un-American" to target Mexican American and ethnic studies. By linking ethnic studies with the threat of radical politics, and indeed with the implicit threat of communism, Horne associates the program with the specter of political antagonism. In their attempt to repress this very specter, which alienates the national political community from itself, Horne and others reactivate a nationalist discourse in which national unity is premised on the exclusion of "foreign ideologies" that may upset the reproduction of liberal-capitalist social order, while leaving untouched the assumption of whiteness through which the meaning of the American nation has historically been articulated.

In a move not uncommon among those trying to roll back the hard-won political gains of the movements of the 1960s and 1970s, among which stands the creation of ethnic studies, Horne even appropriates the discourse of Martin Luther King Jr. to justify his attack. "In the summer of 1963 . . . I participated in the civil rights march on Washington, in which Martin Luther King stated that he wanted his children to be judged by the content of their character rather than the color of their skin," Horne states in his open letter: "This has been a fundamental principal [*sic*] for me my entire life, and Ethnic Studies teaches the opposite."[155] Though one may note the problems with using King's statement to promote a color-blind discourse that equates the use of race as an analytical and political category with racism, or that suggests that the best remedy for ending racism is the elimination of race from our critical/ political vocabulary (as if ignoring race will make racism go away), one may also remind Horne that earlier in 1963, in Birmingham, King, too, was billed as an "outside agitator" and incarcerated.[156] In his "Letter from Birmingham Jail," in fact, King himself gives a brief genealogy of the reactionary politics that have sought to ground themselves against the figure of the outside agitator. "Never again can we afford to live with the narrow, provincial 'outside agitator' idea," King declares: "Anyone who lives inside the United States can never be considered an outsider anywhere within its bounds."[157] Unlike Luisa Moreno's call for inclusion, King's statement is a universal, axiomatic prescription of belonging that is completely indifferent to *who* such people are. It declares that anyone in the United States belongs in the United States—which is not to say that it implies ignoring the category of race in the politics that take place therein. Its purpose, moreover, is to stress that the antagonism usually attributed to the "outside agitator" is always already immanent.

Hence Latina/o studies must find its strength, rather than its weakness, in the figure of the alien and in the structural fact of alienation. It too may take inspiration from another of King's speeches, one that rings close to Viego's argument in connecting ego psychology's tenets of psychological adaptation to the reproduction of structures of injustice:

Modern psychology has a word that is probably used more than any other word in modern psychology. It is the word "maladjusted." You've heard that word. This is the ringing cry of modern child psychology. And certainly we all want to live well-adjusted lives in order to avoid neurotic and schizophrenic personalities. But I must say to you this evening, my friends, as I come to a close, that there are some things in my own nation, and there are some things in the world, to which I am proud to be maladjusted and to which I call upon all men of goodwill to be maladjusted until the good society is realized. I must honestly say to you that I never intend to become adjusted to segregation, discrimination, colonialism and these particular forces. I must honestly say to you that I never intend to adjust myself to religious bigotry. I must honestly say to you that I never intend to adjust myself to economic conditions that will take necessities from the many to give luxuries to the few. I must say to you tonight that I never intend to become adjusted to the madness of militarism and the self-defeating effects of physical violence. . . . You see, it may well be that our whole world is in need at this time for a new organization—the International Association for the Advancement of Creative Maladjustment.[158]

It is precisely in the "advancement of creative maladjustment" that Latina/o and ethnic studies—and, indeed, the humanities in general—should find their mission. Refusing to be restricted to the parameters of a single nation-state, however, endeavors to promote the advancement of creative maladjustment should look to other such experiments in maladjustment from different places and times. Against inclusion, assimilation, and adaptation, it is from the place of alienation that we must think. As a mode of thought that proceeds from the truth of the real—from the inassimilable real of national liberal-capitalist political and economic order—Latina/o and ethnic studies can contribute to a form of thought of the inassimilable as such, beyond identity. Yet, like the poetic voice in "To Julia de Burgos," we must also remain open to the egalitarian politics that can emerge from the cut of alienation to exert a transformative torsion back upon the structures that configure our present.

3

Criminalization at the Edge
of the Evental Site

Migrant "Illegality," Universal Citizenship,
and the 2006 Immigration Marches

> Any question of the absorption of this surplus humanity
> has been put to rest. It exists now only to be managed:
> segregated into prisons, marginalised in ghettos and camps,
> disciplined by the police, and annihilated by war.
>
> AARON BENANAV, *Misery and Debt*

———

ADVOCATES OF HARD-LINE stances against undocumented immigration often justify their position by stressing that "[i]llegal immigration is illegal. Period."[1] The tautological structure of this proclamation attempts to ground its justification in the "self-evidence" of illegality, and finds support in the assumption that language here simply reflects a stubborn *fact* of illegality. This assumption has led some to wonder why "[t]o many it is not even considered a crime, even though its name, illegal immigration, makes it clear that it is."[2] Hence, according to this line of thinking, "people who enter or stay in this country illegally are criminals by definition."[3] These subsequent statements thus extend the first's logic by reasoning that since illegal immigration is illegal, and since illegality necessarily implies criminality, those who are here illegally are by definition criminals. Statements such as these are sustained by the assumption that criminality is the natural outcome of the violation of any law. Ironically, these statements are themselves guilty of illegitimately crossing a border of sorts, in their conceptual transgression of separate legal spheres, by ignoring a demarcation internal to US law: the difference between civil and criminal law. Indeed, while it is currently a crime to enter the country without permission, those who stay in this country without authorization (either by overstaying their visa or by staying after unauthorized entry) are *not* criminals, because the violation they commit pertains to civil law, not criminal law. The assumption of criminality as self-evident is thus based upon a misconception of the consequences of legal transgression as homogeneous—that is, the idea that any "illegal" act makes one a "criminal." Against this misconception, it is necessary to demonstrate that the threshold of criminality is not that between a homogeneous law and its violation. This threshold, rather, is internal to the legal system itself and is historically produced.

It is thus with the historical production of migrant "illegality," and "criminality" more generally, that this chapter begins. By tracing historical patterns of criminalization, and linking the criminalization of noncitizen behavior to the legacies of postslavery racial subjugation, I demonstrate the connections between the punitive and disciplinary function of the law and labor control. I emphasize how the criminalization of (un)documented immigration and mass incarceration are products of governmental responses to the crisis of structural unemployment under neoliberalism. They are measures that try to impede the advent of politics by seeking to preempt disturbances of neoliberal order. I follow this with a theoretical discussion in which I demonstrate how the thinking of politics from the perspective of the criminalized, and the undocumented in particular, can enable us to reformulate the concept of universal citizenship.

I argue that universal citizenship can be thought to designate a politics initiated from the perspective and with the participation of those upon whose exclusion legally recognized citizenship is founded. To the extent that the "undocumented" and the "criminal" are today two of the primary figures against which neoliberal governmentality is constituted,

I argue that they are foundational of existing order through their very exclusion. As foundational figures, they thus mark a site, which following Badiou I designate as an "evental site," from where a contemporary radical politics can emerge. Insofar as "citizenship" refers to the active political capacity of a subject, I designate "universal citizenship" the prescriptive actualization of this capacity without regard for statist restrictions and in the absence of legal recognition. In its subtraction from legal recognition, I argue that such a politics remains at the margins of the law and of identitarian capture.

The final section ends by analyzing the 2006 immigrant rights marches in the United States as an example of universal citizenship. I argue against the frequent interpretation of the marches through the optics of identity, and posit that the political novelty of the marches consisted in making the figure of the "laborer" exist once again in its political capacity. Thus the "laborer" evoked by the marches functioned as a figure of generic political subjectivation rather than as a simple reference to sociological reality. The revival of the figure of the laborer, moreover, also signaled the effort to develop an egalitarian political logic against neoliberalism's market-driven economic reason—an effort that can once again put on the table the possibility and necessity of transforming the politico-economic system itself, and in this way also transform the conditions productive of the very figures of the "undocumented" and the "criminal."

"Illegality" and the Criminalization of (Un)Employment

The category of "unauthorized immigrant" is the necessary counterpart to restrictive immigration policy. To the extent that any form of restriction is placed on authorized entry, we can expect the existence of those who circumvent their exclusion by entering the country without authorization. Nevertheless, there have been factors that have contributed to the growth in number of those who fit within such a category and to the consequentiality of such a designation. It is precisely this consequentiality, made such by both the advent and proliferation of restrictive laws and the state's capacity to enforce them, which is constitutive of immigrant "illegality." For the most part, the period before the beginning of the twentieth century was characterized by relatively open borders and by few restrictions on the cross-border movement of people.[4]

The main exception during the late nineteenth century was immigration from China, which began to be heavily regulated with the passage of the Chinese Exclusion Act of 1882. According to historian Elliott Young, the figure of the "illegal alien" first emerged as the product of Chinese exclusion and with the bureaucratic apparatus developed in its aftermath to implement its restrictions.[5] Even so, it was with the Immigration Acts of 1917 and 1924, however, that a new era of more generalized restriction was ushered.[6] The 1917 act extended the previous Chinese exclusion laws to encompass a "barred Asiatic zone" that ran from Afghanistan to the Pacific—with the exception of Japan and the Philippines—and further curtailed entry by widening the categories of excludable individuals and subjecting entrants to added restrictions, like an eight-dollar head tax, a literacy test, and a medical examination before being allowed to enter the country.[7] With the introduction of these restrictions, the number of people who entered through unofficial venues began to grow.

The Immigration Act of 1924 also had a significant impact on the production of an unauthorized immigrant population by enhancing entry requirements and legislating the exclusion of individuals who were ineligible for citizenship (which was a racially motivated measure since "whiteness" was a precondition for the naturalization of everyone except those who could claim to be of African descent). It further reduced the national quotas that had been established in 1921, and, most important, it developed both the mechanisms and enforcement capacity for deportation.[8] Though perhaps hard to imagine from today's vantage point, before the 1924 act, for example, being in the country without authorization was in and of itself *not* a deportable offense.[9] Indeed, deportation before this time was rather limited in terms of its target population, focusing primarily on certain "undesirable classes," and its site of enforcement—the latter of which focused mainly on points of entry and had very few means of enforcement beyond those points. The 1924 act changed this by making *all* individuals without valid authorization eligible for deportation and by enhancing enforcement capability through the creation of the Border Patrol.[10] As Jonathan Inda notes, "it was the making of entry without inspection (or without proper documentation) a deportable offense that actually turned these people into 'illegals.'"[11]

It is thus the condition of deportability, together with the state's capacity to enforce more restrictive legislation through detention and

deportation, that transformed general undocumented status into a consequential and thus socially and legally significant category.[12] While people
who had avoided points of inspection certainly existed within national
space before this legislation, it is with the latter that undocumented status became meaningful as a target of government action and significant to the lived experience of those without authorization. Accordingly,
migrant "illegality" is not the automatic result of unauthorized status,
but rather, together with changes in immigration law that make (more)
people eligible for deportation, it is the product of the state's enforcement
capacity, which makes such a status consequential by transforming unauthorized entrants into targets of policing. This occurred at the same time
that more people began to turn to unauthorized forms of entry, given
higher, and increasingly racial, entry requirements.

The next significant period in the production of migrant illegality
begins in the mid-1960s and extends up to our current time. As Nicholas
De Genova explains, the contemporary configuration of migrant "illegality" "is the product of US immigration law . . . [in the] sense that the history of deliberate interventions beginning in 1965, that have revised and
reformulated the law has entailed an active process of *inclusion through
illegalization*."[13] What De Genova proposes, then, is that the phenomenon
of undocumented immigration, as it has been constituted in the United
States after the mid-1960s, is the purposeful creation of immigration policy, the function of which has been not simply to prevent or dissuade people from entering the country, but rather to structure the very inclusion
of migrants *as "illegal"* by orienting the range of possibilities for entrance
toward unauthorized means. While one may be tempted to respond to
this argument by appealing to a nation-state's sovereign right to control entry into its national territory—claiming that it would be up to
would-be migrants to respect such restrictions no matter their severity—
the fact is that such a response misses the point. By restricting analysis
to the legal issue of sovereign right, one misses the politico-economic
context within which immigration occurs and in which immigration policy intervenes. De Genova thus situates the history of US immigration
policy within the context of the larger historical development of the US
Southwest as a regional economy that has consistently relied on Mexican
labor, both documented and undocumented.[14] In this manner, what De
Genova demonstrates with regard to post-1960s legislation is the collu-
sion between immigration law and sectors of capital in *producing* a labor

force adequate to higher rates of exploitation through the very *inclusion* of workers as undocumented, and thus as *excluded.*

De Genova locates in the end of the Bracero Program in 1964 and the passage of the Hart-Celler Act of 1965 a significant moment in the structural production of Mexican migrant "illegality." Prior to this act, authorized migration from the Western Hemisphere—of which migration from Mexico was the largest part—had remained unrestricted by the kind of numerical quotas established for the rest of the world beginning with the quota law of 1921 and the Immigration Act of 1924.[15] After the 1965 act, quota restrictions were also instituted for the Western Hemisphere and set at 120,000 for the entire region. With new amendments in subsequent years, national quotas were established at 20,000 per country and then lowered to a little over 18,000 by 1980.[16] "At a time when there were (conservatively) well over a million Mexican migrants coming to work in the US each year," stresses De Genova, "the overwhelming majority would have no option but to do so 'illegally.'"[17] Given that the quota restrictions went against established labor migration patterns at the same time that the demand for migrant labor persisted, large numbers of migrant workers became undocumented. In this way, one can see that the "undocumented immigrant" is legally produced *as* excluded. This excludability is constituted by reconfiguring the national juridico-political border upon the body of the undocumented person as a latent barrier whose effectivity is activated upon contact with the state and its avatars. Drawing from Agamben, one can say that after 1965, the production of migrant illegality became the rule rather than the exception.[18] This exceptional figure, constituted as such in its very position at the margins of the law, is not itself a marginal phenomenon, but is rather at the center of immigration policy and the neoliberal political economy.

What happened after 1965, then, was a large surge in the undocumented population coupled with a governmental response that increasingly framed the issue as one of "law and order." It is during this time that the label of "illegal immigrant" also began to enter mainstream parlance through a simultaneous surge in media coverage.[19] Indeed, Joseph Nevins notes that as "illegal" became the label of choice of increasing media coverage during this time, "the actual content of the coverage changed in terms of the representation of unauthorized immigrants [toward] an increasing tendency to associate [them] with criminal activity and a declining standard of living for U.S. citizens."[20] Otto Santa Ana and others have also demonstrated that even with the more recent tendency among news outlets to substitute "immigrant" for the label of "alien," the persistent use of "illegal" since the 1970s has continued to facilitate the conceptual link between undocumented people and criminality.[21] By means of the associations evoked by the signifier "illegal," undocumented people enter the public imaginary as the embodiment of an assumed disregard, if not outright contempt, for the law, and thus as an ominous threat to security and social order. As the living and breathing proof of the law's violation, of the fact that they have violated the law and have not repented or suffered retribution as exhibited by their (continued) existence in a place where they should not be, a notion of unreformed criminality is easily grafted onto them at the level of their very being. It is thus no surprise that by the 1980s policy makers, the mass media, and the public were closely associating criminal activity with rising rates of undocumented immigration.[22]

As a way of addressing this concern, the Immigration Reform and Control Act of 1986, which established a set of provisions that allowed certain undocumented immigrants to "legalize" their status, also identified among its conditions for admissibility that a given individual had "not been convicted of any felony or of three or more misdemeanors committed in the United States."[23] Significantly, then, the issue of criminality gained importance as a determining factor in state calculations over naturalization. The preoccupation with criminality, however, was extended to include noncitizens more generally (that is, not only undocumented people, but also authorized permanent residents, etc.), through additional provisions that made noncitizens deportable if convicted of certain crimes. With this piece of legislation, the figure of the "criminal alien" thus became increasingly central to immigration enforcement.[24]

Legislation after the Immigration Reform and Control Act continued to expand on this precedent by widening the range of offenses that make a noncitizen eligible for deportation. Important among them are a class known as "aggravated felonies," first established with the passage of the Anti–Drug Abuse Act of 1988.[25] Though initially only offenses like murder, drug trafficking, and firearms trafficking were included in this category, new legislation in 1996 significantly expanded the list of offenses that counted as aggravated felonies to include "bribery, car theft, counterfeiting, drug possession, drug addiction, forgery, perjury, petty theft, prostitution, shoplifting, simple battery, tax evasion, and undocumented entry following deportation," among others.[26] These violations could also be applied retroactively.[27]

Since the category of aggravated felony is unique to immigration law, however, an offense can be labeled as such even if it is neither a felony nor an aggravated offense under criminal law.[28] Consequently, there have been cases where authorized permanent residents have been subjected to deportation proceedings for aggravated felonies after being found guilty of stealing a ten-dollar video game or of pulling someone's hair.[29] The "gravity" attributed to such offenses is correlated to the severity of the consequences, which range from mandatory detention and expedited removal (that is, removal without a hearing) to being permanently barred from reentering the United States and facing up to twenty years in prison if caught reentering without permission.[30] In this way, it is evident that it is the *citizenship status* of the individual who carries out a certain infraction that subjects him or her to a different set of penalties. It is not solely the violation itself that triggers these penalties, but rather it is the particular status of the one who carries out the action. In other words, it is not only a question of *what* is done, but of *who* does it. It is thus through the function of the aggravated felony that I would like to make a connection to mass incarceration and to the legacy of postslavery racialized labor control.

After the abolition of slavery, former slave states were faced with the problem of how to manage the newly freed labor force. Fortunately for these states, the Thirteenth Amendment, which abolished slavery, also contains within itself a vital exception according to which "neither slavery nor involuntary servitude . . . shall exist within the United States, or any place subject to their jurisdiction," "except as a punishment for crime whereof the party shall have been duly convicted." Given this exception, former slave states passed a series of "Black Codes" that "proscribed a range of actions—such as vagrancy, absence from work, breach of job contracts, the possession of firearms, and insulting gestures or acts—that were criminalized only when the person charged was black."[31] In this way, similar to the aggravated felony that triggers harsher consequences for a set of actions only when committed by a noncitizen, one can see in the Black Codes the criminalization of certain actions only when performed by African Americans. Once convicted, African Americans could then be subjected to captive working conditions, under the convict lease system, that in some ways were far worse than they had been under slavery.[32] As a consequence, stresses Joy James, "[a] hundred years ago, more African

Americans died in the convict lease system than they did during slavery, worked to death by a business venture coordinated by both state and private industry that replaced plantation labor with prison labor, a commodity that could always be replenished by sweeps arresting blacks because they were black."[33]

Despite their differences, what can be seen with the Black Codes, the convict lease system, the category of aggravated felony, and the production of undocumented immigrant labor, are efforts to produce a racialized labor force that is exposed to higher rates of exploitation and disciplined by the fact that its actions are subject to added restrictions and penalties.[34] Indeed, in the case of undocumented people, "[i]t is *deportability*, and not deportation per se, that has historically rendered [their] labor as a distinctly disposable commodity."[35] The threat of deportation helps ensure that they withdraw from public space and acquiesce to exploitative working conditions. Journalist David Bacon, for example, has documented the ways in which employers have undercut their workers' unionization efforts by prompting immigration raids.[36] Making noncitizens in general more easily deportable, however, also functions to discipline their behavior. After all, much like an insulting gesture could trigger the resubjection of an African American to a kind of social death, a petty violation can lead to the expulsion of a noncitizen from national territory.

While in recent decades the expansion of immigrant detention—along with the privatization of the detention system and the exponential growth of criminal prosecutions for unauthorized entry—has dovetailed with the phenomenon of mass incarceration, it is important to note that unlike with the example of the Black Codes and the convict lease system, which were designed to exploit African American labor power, the function of mass incarceration today is less about exploitation than about warehousing a population deemed redundant to capitalist accumulation.[37] As Fredric Jameson has argued, the Marxist conception of structural unemployment has become vital to a contemporary analysis of neoliberal capitalism.[38] Though Marx is clear that the production of unemployment, or what he terms the "relative surplus population," has always been central to capitalist accumulation, Aaron Benanav makes the point that "[i]f the unemployed tend to be reabsorbed into the circuits of capitalism as an industrial reserve army—still unemployed, but essential to the regulation of the labour market—they then equally tend to outgrow this function, reasserting themselves as *absolutely redundant*."[39] As absolutely redundant, sections of the unemployed become completely superfluous to capital with regard to the utility of their labor power. Thus, while the unemployed have always been inclusively excluded from production, they now appear to be fully excluded to the extent that even the hope for future employment is practically abolished.

Their externality, however, finds its limit in the fact that the unemployed to a large extent still rely on capitalism for their survival (i.e., they still need to acquire money to exchange for commodities), just as capital still relies on their consumption for the realization of value, even while they have been abandoned in terms of their labor power. It is thus no surprise that informal and illicit economies flourish alongside the formal economy. To the extent that their labor power becomes superfluous to capital, so does the social context of the former's reproduction. As Cristina Beltrán reminds us, "[i]t is here, when human beings become 'perfectly superfluous' . . . that the right to live is truly challenged."[40] As the turn toward incarceration and the rampant use of deadly force against black and brown people confirm, the life and death of the surplus population also become redundant. If, according to Foucault, the modern biopolitical imperative is to make live or let die, then one can see that today's surplus population is increasingly abandoned to its own devices.[41]

Ruth Wilson Gilmore identifies the problem of structural unemployment to be one of the primary factors that has given rise to the boom in incarceration and prison construction. In the United States, argues Gilmore, "[t]he correspondence between regions suffering deep economic restructuring, high rates of unemployment and underemployment among men, and intensive surveillance of youth by the state's criminal justice apparatus present the relative surplus population as the problem for which prison became the state's solution."[42] Gilmore demonstrates how, similar to the criminalization of immigration, the state itself produced "criminality" by reclassifying certain offenses, like residential burglary and domestic assault, into felonies requiring prison time.[43] This is also evident in the way in which, after 1988, for example, the California legislature went on a "criminal-law producing frenzy" that increased the number of new pieces of criminal legislation from around twenty to twenty-five per year to around one hundred to two hundred per year.[44] New drug laws requiring mandatory minimum sentences, the use of "sentence enhancements" for additional offenses, and the practice of "wobbling" misdemeanors into felonies in efforts to turn convictions into "strikable" offenses that could result in sentences of twenty-five years to life "enhanced the likelihood of prison time for people not formerly on the prison track," Gilmore stresses.[45] Upon release, the convicted felon, much like the noncitizen and undocumented immigrant, is further subjected to regulations and restrictions that apply to him or her, and can result in a return to prison, by the sole fact of having "felon" status. Subjected to a kind of "civic death," again like undocumented people, convicted felons find themselves the targets of "legalized discrimination" with regard to employment, housing, education, public benefits, and jury service.[46]

What can be seen with mass incarceration and deportation, further-more, is a governmental turn toward incapacitation and expulsion as a way of guaranteeing social order. Signaling the way in which much of this has been achieved through popular consent, Gilmore notes that while "[f]or each jobless individual and household, the crisis centers on daily and intergenerational reproduction[,] [f]or voters, the crisis centers on how to ensure that the surplus population, who rebelled in 1965 and 1992, is contained if not deported."[47] Hence incarceration and deportation also function as mechanisms that attempt to preempt the surplus population's possible disturbance of social order. *Mass* incarceration should thus be read as not only referring to a quantitative phenomenon (i.e., to the expo-nential growth of the prison population), but precisely to the "incarcera-tion," or containment, of the masses in their political capacity—that is, as a force capable of making history through a mode of appearance that pro-duces a break in the quotidian reproduction of social order. To the extent that incarceration and deportation seek to arrest the disruptive potential of the masses, they also attempt to foreclose the possibility for politics that such a disruption can make manifest. It is politics as an active intervention against existing social and economic order that they seek to prevent.

Act, Event, and (Il)Legal Citizenship

It is to the theorization of such an intervention that I now turn. To be clear, after making the case for the structural overlap between the fig-ures of the "noncitizen" (especially the undocumented immigrant) and the "criminal," it is not my objective to suggest a program for a politi-cal project that could bring these groups together in coalition. My aim, rather, is to contribute to work that has set out to theorize politics from the perspective of those legally excluded from participation in the field of official politics. As entities at the edges of legal personhood, noncitizens and convicted felons are excluded from the kind of participation reserved for full citizens. Thinking politics from their perspective thus compels us to critically reconsider the very categories of "citizen" and "citizenship" themselves, and to theorize the nature of "unlicensed" political intervention. With that said, the analysis that follows focuses primarily on the issue of undocumented immigration, while also advancing a notion of citizenship that challenges the logic of criminalization.

Julie Dowling and Jonathan Inda have turned to Foucault's concept of "counterconducts" to theorize the "political becoming of undocumented migrants."[48] If neoliberal governmentality seeks to shape the conduct of the undocumented through techniques like checkpoints, workplace raids, and requirements of proof of authorized residency for state services, for example, migrant counterconducts refer to a range of tactics through which the undocumented actively circumvent such efforts to shape their behavior—from protests, sanctuary politics, legal challenges, labor organizing, and sit-ins in public places and government offices, to driving at times during which roadblocks are less likely and creating protection networks to alert others of checkpoints and detentions. In specifying the nature of counterconducts, Foucault situates them between the concepts of "revolt" and "disobedience," given that the former "is both too precise and too strong to designate much more diffuse and subdued forms of resistance," while the latter is "too weak."[49] Thus counterconducts are neither passive forms of resistance, a simple disregard for the rules (as "disobedience" may suggest), nor do they acquire the status of open revolt. Indeed, for Foucault, the concept of counterconduct has the "advantage of allowing reference to the active sense of the word 'conduct'—counter-conduct in the sense of struggle against the process implemented for conducting others," while at the same time distinguishing itself from the notion of "'misconduct,' which only refers to the passive sense of the word, of behavior: not conducting oneself properly."[50]

It is on the active character of counterconducts that Dowling and Inda focus. Thus for these authors, in a situation where migrants are expected to remain politically reticent given their unauthorized status, migrant counterconducts can constitute practices of "unauthorized citizenship" whereby the undocumented actively demand "to be recognized as legitimate political subjects with social, civil, and political rights."[51] Unauthorized citizenship thereby functions as a form of action that, while not anchored on the prior recognition of the agent's legal right to act, nevertheless maintains recognition as a main objective. Given that else-where Inda himself demonstrates the way in which the very recognition of one as a "legitimate" political subject is determined by the degree to which one exhibits the characteristics of the neoliberal "prudential cit-izen," however, this search for recognition proves to be a double-edged sword.[52] Recognition of legitimacy implies an assimilationist logic that, despite resulting from the affirmative demands of the undocumented and providing much needed reprieve from persecution, is in danger of leaving intact (and indeed, of reifying) the governmental reasoning that struc-tures and justifies the exclusion of undocumented immigrants from full rights in the first place. By insisting that they are "legitimate members of U.S. society [who] *deserve* the right to work, to raise families, and to be free from the fear of persecution," the recognition of their claims remains conditioned upon the distinction between deserving and undeserving members of society, of which "illegals" and "criminals" are almost always grouped with the latter.[53] Short of challenging the normative parameters of dominant articulations of citizenship, Dowling and Inda's conception of unauthorized citizenship comes too close to promoting a politics of inclusion through accommodation.

Nevertheless, there remains in the active connotations of countercon-ducts an element of prescriptive politics that deserves further theoretical elaboration. From within the field of citizenship studies, Engin Isin the-orizes as "acts of citizenship" particular moments in which noncitizens, or subjects excluded from the rights and privileges that come with full political belonging, constitute themselves as "claim-making subjects."[54] Countering the frequent tendency to think citizenship in terms of status or routinized modes of behavior, Isin insists that the theorization of polit-ical change requires a focus on rupture and on the interventions through which new political subjects come to be.[55] In other words, given that much contemporary scholarship thinks citizenship in terms of legal status and habitus, it is also necessary that we strive to think the way in which peo-ple without "legitimate" standing intervene politically in a manner that breaks with established patterns of thinking and acting. Designating such interventions as "acts of citizenship," Isin draws attention to the exceptional and creative function of the "act" versus that of "actions." "An act," for Isin, "is neither a practice nor a conduct nor an action, and yet it implies or perhaps makes all those possible."[56] The temporality of an act is momentary, in contradistinction to the temporal extension of actions and (counter)conducts. As a "rupture in the given," an act breaks with the "objective" determination of possibilities.[57] Acts are attributed an onto-logical status, whereas actions occur within the realm of the ontic.[58] The ontological status of the act thus provides the condition of possibility for the ontic status of the action.

The act, then, makes possible the constitution of both the agent of the subsequent action as subject and the scene where such action takes place. "With the creative act," Isin explains, "the actor also creates herself/him-self as the agent responsible for the scene created."[59] Indicating the mutual constitution between actor and scene, however, Isin maintains that "[t]he actor is produced through the scene and is constituted by the act itself."[60] Therefore, neither the subject of the action nor the scene within which the action unfolds preexist the act. While the act may be done by someone, that someone is transformed in and through the act and its effects. The act itself produces a change in the conditions of possibility of the agent's action by opening up a new space through which the actor creates and is created by the reconfiguration of a given scene into a new one. In this way, neither the act nor the actions that follow depend upon an inclusionary imperative, but rather transform the parameters of the context itself.

Given the ontological and creative status that Isin attributes to the act, I turn to Badiou's philosophy in order to delve deeper into the nature of the act (which I rethink in terms of an "event"), and to trace some of its implications both for thinking universal citizenship through the con-temporary figures of the "criminal" and the "undocumented immigrant," and for rearticulating the relationship between the political subject and the law—especially in light of the reactionary legalism that characterizes our current context. I propose that the location of these figures within the juridico-political and economic order of the US nation-state, as con-stitutive exclusions to this order, may be thought of as situated at the edge of an "evental site." Badiou defines an evental site as an element that belongs to a situation but that is not included in it.[61] It is an element that exists within a situation, since to belong to a situation is to exist within it, but that is not recognized as a legitimate element by the state—state recognition being the mechanism of inclusion.[62]

I argue that the figure of the undocumented immigrant can be thought to inhabit such a site. This is so despite Inda's contention that the undoc-umented obtain a certain degree of recognition, for example, by means of

the state's methods of enumerating both the stock and flow of the undocumented population.[63] Given that, for both Inda and Badiou, state recognition is bestowed by means of the counting mechanisms through which
a certain group is endowed with intelligibility and transformed into an
object of knowledge, it would seem that the fact of the state's production
of knowledge about the undocumented would run counter to my claim
that they belong without inclusion—that is, that they elude the state's
count. If one looks at the Department of Homeland Security's population
estimates, however, one can see that it attains its estimate of the undocumented population by subtracting the "legally resident population"
from "the total foreign-born population living in the United States."[64]
The total foreign-born population and the legally resident population are
established through a combination of census figures and data maintained
by other government institutions.[65] Evident in this example is that the
size of the undocumented population is determined negatively. As a subset that is in the country without authorization, and thus has eluded the
count of the state in this regard, it is precisely counted by the state as that
part of the population that is "uncounted." The minimal degree of state
recognition that this subset obtains through the state's estimate of its size
does not so much entail its positive representation, but rather signals the
state's estimation of its own miscount. Despite the statistical soundness
of this estimation, what this example demonstrates is indeed the existence of an eventual site in relation to which the state can only trace its
possible outlines.[66]

What the consideration of the history of undocumented immigration
in the United States can contribute to Badiou's own framework, however, is a more nuanced conception of the miscount under contemporary
neoliberalism by precisely bringing capitalism into the picture, especially
in its relationship to the state. For Badiou, the very function of the state
is to try to achieve an exhaustive count. What De Genova has demonstrated with regard to legislation after 1965, however, is the extent to
which the state itself has produced a miscount in directing migration
toward unauthorized means. Thus, while Badiou holds the impossibility of a full count to be an inherent ontological condition that persists
despite the state's best efforts, undocumented immigration in the United
States also shows the miscount to be the result of specific historical conditions. It demonstrates the way in which the interpenetrations of sectors
of capital and the state can lead to the state aiding a miscount for capital's

benefit. This is at bottom a neoliberal logic through which the state itself adopts a certain antistatism (i.e., it limits its own power of the count) in order to create room through which capital can operate more profitably by more ruthlessly exploiting workers situated at the margins of legality. But this same miscount that benefits capital also presents a latent danger for the state precisely because it delimits its power. Accordingly, the state combines the production of a miscount, on the one hand, with expanded policing and security apparatuses, on the other. It is in this way that undocumented immigration, as a phenomenon where the limiting of state power is simultaneously coupled with other excessive forms of this power (e.g., the legal and material machinery of immigration enforcement) instituted in the name of security, is revealed as a paradigmatic instance of the contradictions of our neoliberal era. The apparatuses of immigration enforcement thus operate within a contradictory situation that both purposefully produces a miscount and tries to contain it by persecuting and capturing *some of* this errant remainder. Their function, given their futile attempts to square up the count, is ultimately only to regulate the miscount, to keep it in check through a range of punitive and disciplinary mechanisms used to shape the behavior of the miscounted.

Along these lines one can also observe that the identification of individuals without immigration authorization is carried out by means of two primary strategies: (1) a strategy that also relies on a negative form of identification by finding those who are unable to prove their documented status—those who are unable to prove that they have already been counted by the state—and (2) an often disavowed strategy that by and large relies on the identification of undocumented immigrants with existing subgroups with socioeconomic, cultural, ethnic, and linguistically definable characteristics (in other words, subgroups that are already intelligible to the state): working-class ethnic minorities, of which Spanish speakers are the group most placed under suspicion, hence the issue of racial profiling. Though any given undocumented person can become an object of knowledge with regard to the usual criteria of knowledge production (age, sex, occupation, income, health, etc.), it is with regard to the recognition of their "legitimate" belonging that they remain on the margins. To the extent that the official political rights of citizenship depend upon the recognition of legitimate belonging, the "illegitimate" belonging of the undocumented implies their exclusion from official politics, and thus their belonging without inclusion.[67]

If from the set of adults that exist in the United States we separate the set of people who have the legal right to participate in official politics within this territory, however, we not only find the undocumented immigrant at the border of inclusion, but we also find near it the figures of the "criminal" (the felon whose rights are curtailed) and the authorized "alien" (the noncitizen visa holder or permanent resident). While these last two are also situated at the edges of the juridico-political community, at least temporarily,[68] they are nevertheless still thought to have *something* in common with this community—as a fellow national, for example, the citizen-felon (in most cases) cannot be deported, while the authorized alien has documentation that attests to the state's recognition of his/her compatibility.[69] With the undocumented immigrant, on the other hand, in a way that condenses the heterogeneity also implied by the other two in relation to the juridico-political community, one sees that this figure is attributed the notion of both criminality *and* foreignness as *illegal alien*. With the category of *criminal alien*, moreover, one can see the way in which criminality functions to exacerbate the element of "foreignness" to the degree that someone who had previously obtained the right to belong based on a prior determination of compatibility (a noncitizen) has that right rescinded and is made deportable because of "criminal" activity. The reason that I articulate this in terms of "foreignness" is that criminality is here taken as a sign of the incompatibility of a person in relation to the juridico-political community as such. Criminality is taken as evidence of a person's "outsider" status with regard to the social, legal, and political realm.

What is most striking about the concept of the evental site is that it is also considered to be "foundational" of the situation to which it belongs. Given that a set is defined by the elements that belong to it, the evental site is significant because with it, belonging itself reaches its limit. Paradoxically, the evental site is the element that belongs as the very figure of nonbelonging, while also being that against which belonging as such commences.[70] Since, from the perspective of the situation, the evental site has *nothing* in common with it, the site emerges as the intrasituational figure of constitutive radical *alienage* and nonidentity.[71]

As a figure indexing an evental site, it is evident that the undocumented immigrant is indeed that against which legally recognized citizenship is negatively grounded; it is the heterogeneity that founds the latter. Demonstrating an overlap with the issue of criminalization in general, Lisa Marie Cacho insists that "people who occupy legally vulnerable and criminalized statuses are not just excluded from justice; criminalized populations and the places where they live *form the foundation* of the U.S. legal system, imagined to be the reason why a punitive (in)justice system exists."[72] This reveals both the "criminal" and the "undocumented immigrant" to serve a structural function as the embodiment of the very limits constitutive of the structure as such. Yet these figures at the edge of the eventual site also mark the location of structural incompleteness and nonidentity, of the fact that the structure is "not-all," and thus point to the real as a stumbling block to the structure's consistency. This is why Badiou links the eventual site to the historicity of a situation as well.[73] As a foundational element situated at the limits of structure, the eventual site marks the location from which a disruptive event can happen that makes actual the possibility of transforming the organizational coordinates of the structure itself.

An "event," then, is the irruption into a situation of the threat of inconsistency contained by the site as structural limit. As the very expression of inconsistency, it occurs as a violation of the law of the state, whose reason for existing is precisely to prevent such a disruption. Given that the state tries to secure the situation's order via its "encyclopedia"— that is, the various epistemological resources through which elements and subsets are endowed with intelligibility, and thus with representational stability—an event, to the extent that it occurs in violation of the law of representation, also proves to be in excess of the encyclopedia's resources.[74] An event is the intrasituational expression of unintelligibility as such. As a result, even the seemingly simple act of determining if an event took place is undecidable from the perspective of the situation.[75] The decision to affirm the event's occurrence can also not rely on the means of evaluation that exist within the situation, since, if it could, that would mean that the event would not have been undecidable after all.[76] This choice is thus made on the basis of a purely subjective wager.[77]

Hence, founded on an undecidable and "illegal" event, the choice to affirm the event and the procedure that investigates its consequences can only occur at the margins of the law, in their subtraction from it, and therefore can also be considered "illegal."[78] Since this very procedure *is* politics (to the extent that the consequences it deduces transform the organizational coordinates of the situation), then one can affirm that to a certain extent, politics is an illegal procedure. The point is not that any violation of the law is a political act, but rather that politics, to the degree that it aims to transform the law through a procedure radically heterogeneous to it, operates on the border of the state's demarcation of legality and illegality. Most significantly, politics understood in this way by definition cannot remain purely within the limits of the state's legal designation of citizenship.

In line with the fact that the "faithful" or "productive" subject for Badiou is the figure that registers such a politics, I posit that it is actually *this* subject that the "citizen" names at its most radical, and has done so at least since the first modern revolutions as the outcome of the prescriptive affirmation of the universal "right to politics." I thus argue that the faithful subject in politics *is* the citizen, and that the very production of a new political present *is* citizenship—both of which remain subtracted from the law. Rather than understanding the exercise of citizenship to be a right that belongs only to a preexisting, legally recognized citizen, the citizen-subject is brought into being through the exercise of citizenship itself; the citizen is nothing but the name, or the formal designation, of the productivity of citizenship as revolutionary praxis.[79] This, in turn, allows one to reaffirm once again the very idea of universal citizenship. Citizenship begins with the forceful actualization of the "right to politics" and is universal in that it stems from the perspective of the structure's limit, from the location that marks the site of the structure's paradoxical foundation, and whose effects, as a consequence, implicate the situation in its entirety.

Despite the evident resonance between Isin and the Badiou-inspired conception of citizenship that I have outlined, it is with the question of universality that a difference emerges between the two. Echoing the rejection of universality in much contemporary theory, Isin counterposes to universal citizenship the notion of "traversal citizenship."[80] With this, Isin proposes a framework that allows one not only to theorize "the right to act across or against frontiers," but to "investigate actors who exercise this capacity not because it is universal or it is a right that belongs to every human . . . [but] because they exercise a right that does not exist."[81] Isin's rejection of universality is thus based on a conception of the latter as a category that supposes all-inclusiveness or evokes some form of substantive foundation upon which to ground the legitimacy of political action. The problem with this form of universality, as I argue throughout, is that such all-inclusiveness is a logical impossibility and such substantive foundations do not exist. In a slightly different formulation of his conception of traversal citizenship, however, Isin further asserts, "citizenship is about conduct and action *traversing* all of the social groups that constitute a body politic."[82] Far from differing with him on these points, I argue that it is exactly *because* of them that such a form of citizenship is universal.

Indeed, universal citizenship is universal precisely because it is a form of prescriptive action initiated from the location of the foundational exclusions that constitute the demarcation of legal citizenship and full political rights. It is an intervention into the political from the perspective of those without the right to do so and, in this way, makes actual the possibility of anyone to do so, regardless of identity and legal status. Since an event surges forth from a site that is foundational of the situation to which it belongs, the event is universally addressed; its consequences are not confined to any particular individual or group, making the procedure that investigates these consequences radically open to participation by *anyone*. This process—which Badiou terms the "generic procedure," and I term "citizenship" itself—thus implicates all of a situation's elements in the double sense that anyone can wager to affirm the event and participate in the production of its consequences, and that the outcome of such a procedure is consequential to everyone present in a given situation.

Badiou refers to both the procedure and the subset it creates (i.e., the collective it gathers together) as "generic" because they cut through existing social groups and identitarian categories. It is precisely this traversality that enables them to elude any identitarian predicate that can fix them within the state's encyclopedia, thus enabling them to remain indiscernible to the latter.[83] "The generic subset . . . contains a little bit of everything, so that no predicate ever collects together all its terms," Badiou explains: "The generic subset is subtracted from predication *by excess*. That kaleidoscopic character and predicative superabundance of the generic subset are such that nothing dependent upon the power of a statement and the identity of its evaluation is capable of circumscribing it."[84] Hence the reason that this mode of politics and the collective that it constitutes are generic is because they cut across all social categories, and they are capable of cutting across all social categories because of the universality of the event's address. Thus, against the opposition that Isin establishes between the traversal and the universal, I would argue, rather, that universality is both the condition and outcome of the traversality he proposes.

This means that despite the intricate link between the history of immigration legislation and the production of particular and exclusionary racial, ethnic, gendered, and classed conceptions of citizenship, the process of universal citizenship does not rely upon a figuration of its subject in identitarian terms. It proceeds neither by seeking inclusion into an identitarian conception of citizenship, nor by affirming an alternative identity in opposition. At the same time, however, the egalitarian politics that motivate universal citizenship cannot ignore the function of such categories in the constitution and transformation of existing social order. To the extent that universal citizenship as generic procedure is in excess of the classificatory resources of a situation, it displaces them in a manner that allows for their egalitarian reconfiguration—which in the case of class could imply its possible dissolution.

The 2006 Immigration Marches: Universal Citizenship, Indistinction, and Labor

In the early months of 2006 the United States experienced a sudden outburst of marches against the criminalization of undocumented immigration and for immigrant rights. From February to the beginning of May, major cities and rural towns alike throughout the country witnessed some of the largest popular mobilizations around these issues in this country's history, as 3.7 to 5 million people in more than 160 cities took to the streets.[85] The March 25 demonstration in Los Angeles, dubbed La Gran Marcha, was the largest protest in the history of the city, while, as a whole, the demonstrations have been billed by some scholars as "likely the largest protests over immigrant rights seen in the world."[86] The marches were an overwhelming repudiation of the US House of Representatives' passage, in December 2005, of HR 4437 (also known as the Border Protection, Antiterrorism, and Illegal Immigration Control Act), a bill that among its provisions would have turned into felons anyone caught residing in the United States without proper authorization, as well as those caught lending nonemergency assistance to them.[87] Far from being a "drastic shift in federal immigration policy,"[88] HR 4437 was an intensification of the trend toward criminalization that has defined immigration policy since the final decades of the last century.

Though many have rightly stressed the ways in which the marches drew on the organizational and communication networks already at work in the advocacy organizations, churches, unions, hometown associations, and ethnic media outlets that participated in the demonstrations,[89] the sheer magnitude, the extension, and the speed with which the protests spread nevertheless registered an element of contingency at the heart of contemporary social order that was in excess of existing organizational structures.[90] From Washington, DC, Chicago, and Los Angeles, the number of participants exceeded the expectations of the marches' own organizers by the tens and even hundreds of thousands, as many of the protesters turned out for the first time.[91] Indeed, in some instances it was the participants themselves who forced organizations into action.[92] Therefore, if one holds that the undocumented immigrant is a constitutive element of the current neoliberal politico-economic and governmental order, and can be regarded as inhabiting an evental site, I argue that the protests index the irruption into the situation of the void at the edge of which this figure is situated. The protests can be said to register an event that opened up the possibility for a politics that evaded the distinction between citizen and noncitizen in its determination of who could or could not participate, and in this way made possible the advent of universal citizenship by being open to anyone.

Cristina Beltrán, out of all the scholars who have written on the marches, has most coherently articulated in theoretical terms their function as a moment of creative rupture and initiation. The 2006 marches are for Beltrán something close to what Isin refers to as an "act of citizenship." Echoing Isin's insistence on the critical importance of "those moments when, regardless of status and substance, subjects constitute themselves as citizens . . . as those to whom the right to have rights is due," Beltrán notes the way in which during the 2006 marches, noncitizens across the country "were actualizing a power they did not yet have."[93] With the participation and from the perspective of noncitizens, the prescriptive affirmation of the marchers' right to intervene in national politics was an act that in and through itself made actual the universal "right to politics"—that is, the right of *anyone* to become a subject of politics. In prescribing their right to politics, they exercised a right that, by definition, many of them did not have, but in the name of which they acted. The marches can thus be read as an act that through its very intervention, "created self-organized sites of transformation that came to exist by virtue of [participants' collective] address"—that "elaborated new citizenships [and] challenged familiar scripts regarding the undocumented, unsettling traditional notions of sovereignty and blurring the boundaries between legal and illegal, assimilation and resistance, civic joy and public outrage."[94] Beltrán likens this intervention to Hannah Arendt's definition of political freedom, as "the freedom to call something into being, which did not exist before, which was not given, not even as an object of cognition or imagination, and which therefore, strictly speaking, could not be known."[95] The act of calling into being the previously inexistent right to politics is, moreover, an act exercised without statist or legal authorization.[96] Given the status of the undocumented as the embodiment of nonstatus, their participation suggested the formation of a collective the inclusion into which was determined by active participation rather than by ascriptive criteria.[97]

Beltrán's Arendtian framing, however, also leads her to evaluate the productivity of the marches in terms of distinction and recognition. Distinction, for Arendt, stems from the fact of human plurality, from the fact that "nobody is ever the same as anyone else who ever lived, lives, or will live."[98] Beyond simple difference, or what Arendt terms "otherness" as "the curious quality of *alteritas* possessed by everything that is," the human capacity for distinction obtains from humans' ability to initiate new beginnings in the exercise of freedom.[99] It is in the political realm, constituted as a collective of individuals that are at once unique *and* equal, that one can distinguish oneself through action coupled with speech.[100] "The action he begins is humanly disclosed by the word, and though his deed can be perceived in its brute physical appearance without verbal accompaniment," explains Arendt, "it becomes relevant only through the spoken word in which he identifies himself as the actor, announcing what he does, has done, and intends to do."[101] "In acting and speaking," she continues, "men show who they are, reveal actively their unique personal identities and thus make their appearance in the human world."[102] The outcome of political action and speech is hence the identification of the actor as distinct individual agent.

It is in the creation of such a space of appearance that Beltrán situates both the political importance and shortfalls of the marches. She holds that at the heart of the marches was the search for dignity and recognition—this is so despite her acknowledgment that "[b]y appearing again and again, participants of this emerging counterpublic engaged in forms of display that emphasized social transformation rather than merely liberal inclusion."[103] For her, the marches were at bottom the manifestation of the human "passion for distinction" that "challenged the dehumanizing effects of anonymity and illegality" to which the undocumented are subject by virtue of their immigration and laboring status.[104] The problem with framing the marches in terms of recognition, however, is that even while she emphasizes the marchers' creativity in actualizing a right they did not have, Beltrán reintroduces identitarian inclusion as the ultimate aim. This stems precisely from Beltrán's Arendtian framing, I argue. Thus it becomes evident that on the one hand, while in the exercise of freedom humans call into being an object in excess of knowledge, on the other hand, the subject constituted through this very act seems to fall squarely within the realm of knowledge (i.e., the encyclopedia), given that the latter is able to recognize the subject's distinction in meaningful terms. The act's creation thus becomes secondary, to the extent that the main objective (the subject's distinction) is attained from within the bounds of existing knowledge and its identitarian predicates. The transformative potential of the act's creation is curtailed, as the latter becomes merely a mechanism for the subject's inclusion into the existing order.

It is thus no coincidence that, in Beltrán's account, the marchers' search for recognition depended on their ability to be identified as "subjects who contribute to (rather than harm) the larger society."[105] Identitarian distinction is in this way articulated through the capacity to make the marchers intelligible in the security-laden terms central to neoliberal governmentality. Their very distinctiveness thus paradoxically relies on their recognition as the same—that is, as "normal" neoliberal subjects. Beltrán's conceptual framework thereby imposes an identitarian logic upon her analysis that tends to reconstitute the distinction between subjects "deserving" and "undeserving" of citizenship, despite her explicit warnings against this very distinction.[106] Against this line of argument, I hold that the radical novelty of the marchers' political intervention, in taking a right without authorization—and thus in taking something that was not "theirs" to take—was registered precisely in making illegible the distinction between contribution and harm, legality and illegality. Contra Beltrán/Arendt, moreover, I propose that the subject constituted through the act/event of the marches remained subtracted from state recognition by evading the identitarian predicates of the encyclopedia.

The question of visibility, however, was certainly at stake in the marches. Given the undocumented's function as a constitutive exclusion to legally recognized citizenship, their function as a marker of the state's miscount, and the role of legislation in forcing their withdrawal from public space, it can be said that the undocumented politically "inexist" in

US society.[107] "Inexistent" are such people who "are present in the world but absent from its meaning and decisions about its future."[108] They are those around an eventual site whose minimal existence, like the undocumented or the incarcerated, "is tantamount to having no existence at all."[109] While inexistence places one at the margins of identity, this should lead one neither to posit a lack of identity itself as the problem, nor to posit identity as the solution, either as the ground for the subject's recognition or as the supposed source of the subject's consistency.

With the marches, the inexistent became highly visible. Despite this high degree of visibility—as can be gauged from the unprecedented levels of participation, the extension of the marches, and the amount of attention they elicited—the marchers nevertheless evaded distinction. This is evident in the anxious yet futile attempts by many observers to pin down who the marchers were and what they wanted. According to some, the marchers embodied the "foreignness, criminality, and threat to the nation" that the very legislation against which they protested tried to contain.[110] For others, the marchers were either an unruly mob or tools of the Mexican government in its supposed attempt to reconquer the US Southwest.[111] Many in support of the marches, on the other hand, sought to counter their perception as a threat by positively identifying the marchers as either Latinas/os mobilizing in defense of their "own," as advocates of the traditional values of family and religion, or as idealists yearning to gain access to electoral politics.[112] Indeed, in their effort to find out who the marchers were in the Chicago area, Pallares and Flores-González demonstrate that despite the high rates of Latinas/os, citizens (including naturalized citizens), and Mexican nationals, the marchers constituted a cross section of society in terms of citizenship status, ethnicity, nationality, gender, and age.[113] As a consequence, attempts at a definitive classification prove difficult, if not impossible.

Beltrán's appraisal of the productivity of the marches is thus in tension with the marchers' lack of distinction. Accordingly, while she points out that the marchers' use of white shirts and the collective chanting of slogans gave the undocumented a level of protection by "mak[ing] it difficult for onlookers to distinguish citizens from noncitizens," she also suggests that "the very practices that promoted inclusive participation and collective visibility risked subjecting the marchers to a dehumanizing discourse of massification—as a seemingly inexhaustible flood of foreigners, dangerous lawbreakers, or an ignorant and easily manipulated group of political pawns."[114] I would argue, rather, that it is precisely in their "massification," in the constitution of the marchers as an indistinct collective, that we find the consequence of the universal egalitarian principle that animated them.

The state, it must be remembered, secures order by assimilating elements into its encyclopedia. The latter works by hierarchically grouping elements according to their various recognizable properties and characteristics. The classificatory categories through which distinct social subgroups are organized serve the function of "separating names."[115] Of these, "[a] state always generates the existence of an imaginary object that is supposed to embody an identitarian 'average,'" such as the "national," or, in today's neoliberal context, the "prudential" citizen.[116] Inexistence befalls the figure that embodies radical deviation from this norm.[117] One can in this way see that the problem with the logic of inclusion is that in its attempt to identify with the norm (as subjects that "contribute" to society and thus "deserve" to be included, despite superficial differences), it overlooks the fact that this norm is constituted through the very production of the undocumented as divergent. The attempt to make the undocumented match the norm does not eliminate the divergent/inexistent as necessary counterfigure, but merely displaces it onto other abject categories, and most often that of the "true" criminal.[118] Further, the distinct individuality posited by Arendt cannot but rely on such separating names, and actually makes their reification the telos of political action.

The egalitarian impulse evident in the prescriptive affirmation of the right of anyone to intervene politically begets "massification" in its very deposition of the state's classificatory categories. The equality it prescribes is not a condition for distinction, as in Arendt, but is instead a subjective principle heterogeneous to the encyclopedia. Political appearance thereby occurs as an obstacle to knowledge rather than through assimilation into it. And remembering once again that one of the basic functions of today's security state is to preclude the appearance of the masses in their political capacity—an injunction of which one finds echoes in Beltrán's rejection of "massification"—it is precisely in the appearance of the marchers *as* the masses that the marches signaled the possibility of a new politics, despite their internally polyphonic and contradictory demands.

As a form of unauthorized and universal citizenship, however, there was also a strong political tendency that sought to challenge reigning economic reason, and that was articulated around the issue of labor. This should come as no surprise given the paradigmatic exploitation of undocumented people under neoliberalism, a phenomenon that marks the political absence, or inexistence, of the figure of the worker.[119] Accordingly, some framed the marches as "actually a sea-size demonstration of workers, for workers and—most importantly—by workers."[120] Carlos Mares, a day laborer who took part in one of the first acts of protest against HR 4437 by running cross-country, insisted, "We demand fair legislation, not just for Latin American workers but also for workers from Africa, Asia and all over the world."[121] Also significant is that the articulation of demands around the issue of labor was able in some cases to go beyond the kind of moralistic appeals for inclusion that rely on adopting the status of the "good" and "obedient" workers sought by neoliberal capitalism.

The efforts to carry out a nationwide strike by undocumented workers on May 1, International Workers' Day, gestured to the international context of undocumented immigration and labor struggle, at the same time that it stressed the right of workers to politically intervene in an economic system that thrives on their exploitation. While the portrayal of the marchers as workers can obfuscate the problem of structural unemployment, and thus once again make invisible those who are systematically excluded from work, it must be remembered that many of the undocumented are also the surplus population of the countries from which they come.[122] Correspondingly, they embody the link between worker and surplus population in a manner that situates them in the context of transnational capitalist accumulation. Likewise, while the logic of refusing to work can be said to presuppose their status as people who contribute to society—as could be seen in slogans such as "We don't run the country, but we make the country run," or "The USA is MADE by IMMIGRANTS"[123]—the very refusal to work constitutes them as a "danger" capable of disrupting the smooth process of accumulation in a way that unsettles the distinction between contribution and harm. With that said, however, I would argue that rather than simply being based on economic notions of what it means to contribute, what these slogans assert is actually the function of the undocumented as excluded foundation of US juridico-political and economic order. In fact, the radical implications of such an avowal were registered within the movement itself in the form of a split between the more moderate middle-class politicians, the church, and many of the unions on one side, and the more radical elements on the other.[124]

Returning to Beltrán, one sees that it is with the political use of the category of labor that she is most critical. Her reservations revolve mainly around three points: (1) the problematic relationship between racialized labor and civic standing throughout US history, (2) the depoliticization of labor given its relationship to necessity, and (3) the failure of labor to provide the conditions within which laborers can gain distinction given the ephemeralness of labor's product and the mundane and repetitive nature of its activity. Hence, while conceptions of American citizenship have historically relied on the connection between wage labor and political standing, this connection has not held true for racialized laborers.[125] As a consequence, Beltrán argues,

> in trying to claim one "central foundation" of American political thought (the civic standing conferred by work), immigrant-rights advocates have failed to comprehend the second "core dilemma": the history of race in America and the question of how the civic status conferred by work is complicated by racialization. . . . [T]he capacity to work hard and earn confers little or no civic standing on raced subjects. Instead, the undocumented occupy a subject position defined by their willingness to engage in undesirable labor.[126]

Part of the problem, according to Beltrán, is thus that the labor of people of color does not confer upon the laborer the same civic status as does the labor of Anglos, due to the devaluation of racialized labor itself. This is only compounded by the fact that the racialized labor of the undocumented is also articulated as the kind of low-wage labor that is not "fit" for American citizens. Beltrán's criticism here, however, is still premised on the assumption that the marches were wholly centered on the goal of recognition and inclusion. It holds that the undocumented, as racialized laborers, could not hope to be fully recognized and included as laborers deserving civic standing since the racialization to which they are subject has historically functioned to block this very recognition.

Yet the framing of the marchers' demands from the perspective of undervalued labor was also problematic, Beltrán argues, in that such labor situates the laborer within the realm of necessity rather than serving as a basis for the independence required for political action. Hence she declares:

I argue that emphasizing labor as the way to gain political standing is, simply put, a bad idea, for in identifying immigrants in terms of the jobs they do, the discourse of labor frames undocumented subjectivity in terms of economics and survival rather than of democratic action. Because the undocumented already struggle with a public identity still powerfully enmeshed in their capacity to labor, emphasizing labor promotes the tendency to see the undocumented as subjects of *necessity* rather than *natality*.[127]

Framing such laborers as "subjects of necessity" constructs them as prepolitical and thus disqualifies them from being capable of having political agency.

The repetitive and ephemeral tasks often performed by the undocumented, moreover, fail to provide the conditions through which such laborers can gain distinction as individuals—remembering again that for Arendt and Beltrán, individual distinction is constitutive of political subjectivity. "Instead of revealing each individual's uniqueness, labor highlights the interchangeability of activities done in the private realm," Beltrán points out, before insisting, "If undocumented subjectivity is indeed excessively defined by labor, then the marchers of 2006 were fighting an uphill battle against a logic that treated them as subjects of little worth or individuation."[128] The problem with the undocumented's emphasis on labor, in other words, is that it channels the articulation of their demands through a category that, given its already denigrated status as prepolitical, forms the very conceptual basis that constructs the undocumented as subjects worthy of excessive exploitation in the first place. By anchoring their political claims on labor, they inadvertently do so on a category that precisely cancels the status of their claims as political.

Considering that Beltrán is sympathetic to the plight of the undocumented (and, indeed, regards the marches as a political act par excellence), following her own logic, one is led to ask whether there is a similar problem with turning to a theorist of politics for whom the political is fundamentally constituted through the depoliticization and exclusion of the disenfranchised.[129] As Judith Butler points out, such a tension is evident in the work of Arendt herself. "In 1951, [Arendt] opposed the nation-state for the ways in which it was bound to expel and disenfranchise national minorities. The 'public sphere' and the notion of 'polity' emerge precisely as alternatives to the 'nation-state' and its structural link with nationalism," Butler explains, before wondering, "[B]ut if the public sphere, ten years later, is elaborated through the example of classical Athens, has Arendt simply substituted the class and race politics of classical Athens for the nationalism of the nation?"[130] Despite her preoccupation with the stateless, Arendt's conception of the political is founded on the production of an analogous figure, also rendered politically illegible, as the political's very condition. Hence, Butler states, "Arendt's description in *The Human Condition* leaves uncriticized this particular economy in which the public (and the proper sphere of politics) depends essentially upon the non-political or, rather, the explicitly depoliticized."[131] Seen in this way, Beltrán's argument that the use of labor as a rallying point is politically counterproductive, since undocumented labor for many is an activity that does not measure up to the status of the political, is itself a conceptual move that threatens to reinforce the devaluation and exclusion of labor from politics.

Contra this line of argument, I maintain that we need to think from the perspective of those upon whose disenfranchisement and denigration the political is founded, not in order to recognize their status as such, but to transform the very structure through which such a status is made to exist and function as it does. In the specific terms of labor, this would imply not simply the recognition of the undocumented as exploited and an attempt to value their labor as such, but would rather imply an attempt to transform the politico-economic system that breeds exploitation itself. The marchers' mobilization around the category of labor, as part of an "act of citizenship," itself entailed an enactment of civic standing despite and against the historically troublesome relationship between racialized labor and civic standing that Beltrán points out. After all, does Beltrán's own emphasis on the marches as a moment of initiation not demonstrate that such power to begin can and does occur from the perspective of labor, and thus precisely demonstrates labor's civic political capacity?

At play in this problematic, I argue, is a distinction between labor as a sociological category, on the one hand, and as a figure of political subjectivation, on the other—a figure that may very well signal the return of the name "proletariat." Rancière, in fact, links the depoliticization of the figure of the (undocumented) immigrant worker to "the end of the visibility of the gap between politics and sociology, between subjectification and identity."[132] When this gap is eliminated, politics is itself foreclosed by reducing the thought of antagonism to the logic of the police and by containing political subjectivity within the parameters of social reality. Badiou also registers this distinction when he stresses that the "subject is a product of a break, and not of the idea that it represents a reality, not even that of the working class."[133] The signifier "proletariat," as "the name of the power of the generic,"[134] is thus the name of a subjective figure irreducible to the sociological parameters of the "working class," much like the "citizen" names a subjectivation that breaks with the state's demarcation of the political.

Hence, while the 2006 marches put labor back on the agenda, the figure of the laborer that marked their subjectivation was irreducible to "laborer" as sociological category. As the name for a subjectivation with regard to the inexistent proper to neoliberal capitalism (since the undocumented *immigrant* is at bottom the undocumented *worker*), the consequences deduced by a politics thought from its perspective would implicate the situation in its entirety, including the surplus population in its various forms. The indistinction that Beltrán finds inherently depoliticizing—which she attributes to the marchers' tendency toward massification and their insistence on labor—is rather the indistinction proper to a subjectivation that does not take the parameters of social clas-sification as its political frame—one that, rather than attempt to gain political recognition of the undocumented as good laborers worthy of reprieve, registers a mode of universal citizenship that makes possible the transformation of not just the meaning but the conditions of existence of labor, and thus makes possible the abolition of exploitation itself.

Conclusion

The 2006 marches can thus be taken as an example of an event that enabled the emergence of universal citizenship. From the initial outburst to the attempts to sustain its consequences, the marches demonstrated a politics subtracted from state recognition. Situated at the margins of the law, they sought to challenge the law itself in its exclusionary, crim-inalizing, and exploitation-enhancing functions—a challenge that also entailed the revival of "labor" in its subjective political capacity. What this analysis of the figures of the "undocumented immigrant" and "crim-inal" has demonstrated is that "criminality" is not self-evident. The anal-ysis of criminalization demonstrates that it is precisely on the contingent demarcation between the criminal and the noncriminal that one must focus. Given the function of "crime" as a framework for governmental action in its attempt to resolve the contradictions of neoliberal capitalism, it is necessary to denaturalize and reformulate conceptions of legality and illegality—especially as they pertain to politics—and to take aim at the structure of the politico-economic system itself. Insofar as criminalization and incapacitation (be it through incarceration, detention, or deportation) function as mechanisms that aim to prevent the possibility of the advent of radical politics that social unrest occasions, one must stress that true egalitarian politics always occurs at the margins of the law and of existing "legality." By demonstrating the marginal status of politics with regard to the law, this chapter has attempted to challenge wholly legalistic conceptions of citizenship, while arguing that it is precisely from the perspective of a politics initiated from a situation's constitutive exclusions that a nonidentitarian universal mode of citizenship can and should be thought.

Oscar "Zeta" Acosta and Generic Politics

At the Margins of Identity and Law

AN ENIGMATIC AND CONTROVERSIAL figure during his lifetime, Oscar "Zeta" Acosta has continued to intrigue generations of literary critics, artists, and activists after his mysterious disappearance in Mexico in 1974. Though often remembered primarily for his two semiautobiographical novels, *The Autobiography of a Brown Buffalo* (1972) and *The Revolt of the Cockroach People* (1973), Acosta was also active as a militant lawyer during a pivotal moment in the development of the Chicano Movement in Los Angeles during the late 1960s and early 1970s. It is on the basis of his contentious experience with the law that the present chapter offers a rereading of *Revolt*. While his multifaceted engagement with the Chicano Movement complicates any attempt at a conclusive assessment of his political thought, it is nevertheless possible to identify in *Revolt* several thematic threads that give insight into his thinking of revolutionary politics. This later work, I contend, presents an implicit theory of politics conceived as a "postevental" process initiated with the 1968 East Los Angeles high school walkouts—one that displaces identity as a basis for the unity of a political collective and reassesses the relationship between law, politics, and representation.

The Chicano Movement, as is often noted, was in large part charac-terized by a "quest for identity."[1] Beyond the social implications of val-orizing Mexican American cultural heritage against its denigration by Anglo society, ethnic pride was frequently seen as the necessary "com-mon denominator for uniting all Mexican Americans and making possi-ble effective political mobilization."[2] The development of a strong ethnic identity was thus considered politically imperative as a way to provide the movement with the common ground required for unified action. The problem, however, is that in taking a specific identity as the basis for political action, such a politics produced a set of internal exclusions in the very process of identitarian definition on which it depended. These exclusions, often based on gendered and heteronormative conceptions of difference integral to the existing organization of the social, reproduced some of the same discriminatory logics that sustained (and continue to sustain) the status quo.[3] Given this, one can see that "a set of exclusions confronts identity politics and prevents it from doing justice to the con-cerns of the excluded and marginalized" from the very outset.[4] Insofar as politics as a collective endeavor cannot rid itself of a notion of the common, and yet the representation of commonality relies on the iden-tification of constitutive limits as a condition for its intelligibility, the question thus turns on how one can think commonality in a manner not determined by identitarian definition. Such a notion, I argue, requires that commonality be thought with regard to a form of negativity; that it be thought beyond the realm of positive representation. I propose that Acosta points the way to such a conception in *Revolt.*

Without denying the evident existence of heteronormative and sex-ist discourse in *Revolt,* and despite a frequent tendency among critics to analyze Acosta's work in line with the identity politics of Chicano nation-alism, I nevertheless propose that one can also find in Acosta's writing a thinking of politics unsutured from both identitarian and legalistic lim-itations. More specifically, I argue that *Revolt* can be read as a reflection on politics as a postevental and generic procedure founded on the incur-sion of the void. Yet I am not the first to bring Badiou's framework into dialogue with Acosta's work. Carlos Gallego has also drawn on Badiou to read *Revolt* as figuring a nonidentitarian and universalist politics of the void. With Gallego, I see as an advantage of Badiou's philosophy its enabling a critique of identity politics that neither jettisons the category of the subject nor reduces it to an effect of structure—be it as a remainder that resists structural capture or as a product of interpellation.[5] Gallego's reading, however, does not take sufficient account of the way in which a politics of the void consists as postevental *process* in the novel, or of its implications for an alternative conception of what a political collective holds in common.

An "event" is an intrasituational dysfunction "on the basis of which the void of a situation is retroactively discernible."[6] Inasmuch as a situation's order is constituted by means of an injunction against the void (since the void is inconsistency as such), an event, which occurs as a contingent yet fundamental violation of a situation's law of presentation, evinces the void's incursion. The event makes evident a breach in the structure of existing order, yet does so in a way that brings into being the possibility of its transformation. The function of a postevental "generic procedure" is to bring to bear upon a situation the transformative consequences made possible by an event. It is precisely because the void is subtracted from any substantive predicate that a politics drawn from it is universal. "The void, the multiple-of-nothing, neither excludes nor constrains anyone," explains Badiou: "It is the absolute neutrality of being—such that the fidelity [i.e., the generic procedure] that originates in an event, although it is an immanent break within a singular situation, is none the less universally addressed."[7] Since the void is *no-thing*—it is inconsistent being, or dissemination without limits[8]—and therefore is subtracted from any positive predicate, there is nothing particular in it that can restrict the extension of its address. Yet despite the universality of its address and the fact that the consequences implied by an event are not confined to a particular individual or group, the collective formed around the process that traces the event's consequences does not include *everyone* within a given situation. This collective, rather, is formed by *anyone* that endeavors to actively transform the situation on its basis, which is to say on the basis of a possibility brought into being by the fact that the situation is not-all. Such a politics, held together by a subjective wager on an event, thus allows us to move away from considering any form of identity or positive characteristic as a supposed basis for what the collective has in common. The only thing members share is that they *are* in a place where an event (might have) occurred—though they share this with those that do not partake in such a politics as well—and they hold in common a wager on a possibility without guarantees.

In *The Revolt of the Cockroach People*, I argue, Acosta thematizes a generic politics of the void via the very category of Cockroach. More than simply a synonym for Chicanas/os in the novel, at an initial level this signifier designates all marginalized and oppressed people as being similarly situated.[9] By standing in as a name for all those upon whose marginalization rests existing social order, it designates a structural site, an evental site at the edge of the void. At several moments in the narrative, however, Acosta gestures toward a politics initiated from this site. With regard to such a politics, Cockroach also comes to designate the generic political collective constituted through it, a collective whose common "ground" is the groundlessness of the social as such. Exceeding the bounds of identity, the novel evinces the thinking of a mode of politics that touches upon the void.

A creative work written after the bulk of his time as a lawyer, *Revolt* provided Acosta with a medium through which to critically reflect on his previous legal work and activism, on the nature of politics and political participation, and on the (non)relationship between politics, law, and representation. Accordingly, after providing a brief overview of the 1968 East LA walkouts (the historical event that conditioned Acosta's own participation in the Chicano Movement), I analyze the trial work in which Acosta engaged in their aftermath. With regard to the group distinction requirement he had to meet as part of his grand jury discrimination challenge in defense of Chicano activists, I propose that the law's own logic undermined the potential universality implied by the walkouts by containing subsequent politics within the sphere of identity. This occurred in a way that ultimately fed into the development of Chicano nationalism outside of the courtroom. I follow by reading *Revolt* as comprising a critical reflection on both the shortcomings of the identity politics of Chicano nationalism and the limitations of trying to effect political change from within the law, at the same time that it develops a conception of a nonidentitarian and universal mode of politics via the category of Cockroach. It is this confrontation between a universal generic politics (subtracted from the law and representation) and the cultural and historical context it transforms that appears in the novel by means of the author's distortion of historical information and the diegetic motifs of the lie and the secret—thus signaling the presence of an unrepresentable politics as an absent cause of the inconsistencies that plague the symbolic coherence of the narrative.

The Walkouts

The conditions of East LA public schools at the beginning of 1968 were dismal, with dilapidated, overcrowded, and underfunded schools producing a graduation rate that hovered around a mere 50 percent among its Mexican American students.[10] Compounding the issue was an administration and school board whose often bigoted views made them unresponsive to complaints by these students and their parents, while simultaneously producing a culturally biased curriculum that conditioned Mexican American students for low-skilled jobs. Mounting frustrations erupted during the first weeks of March of that year when nearly ten thousand high school students from Wilson, Garfield, Lincoln, Roosevelt, and Belmont left their respective schools in protest.[11] With the walkouts, or "blowouts" as they also came to be known, it was evident that a new phase of political activity had begun. "Overnight, student activism reached levels of intensity never before witnessed" explains Chicano scholar and participant Carlos Muñoz: "[It] was the first time students of Mexican descent had marched en masse in their own demonstration against racism and for educational change."[12] In their repudiation of the school system, the walkouts of that spring were an unprecedented event that "drew the largest Mexican [American] community in the United States onto the turbulent field of popular protest."[13]

It is clear that the walkouts and the students' demands were guided by a perception of Mexican Americans as an underrepresented and disparaged community. The students' calls for the inclusion of Mexican American history and culture in the curriculum, the creation of a Mexican-oriented cafeteria menu, and the appointment of Mexican Americans to administrative positions demonstrate being motivated by particular cultural and identitarian concerns.[14] Yet there is also evidence that the walkouts cannot be fully circumscribed into purely identitarian considerations, and that at the same time that one acknowledges the emphasis on identity, one can nevertheless see in the *fact* of the walkouts and the demands themselves, in the very act that constituted the latter *as* demands (transforming them from mere noise that could be ignored), an affirmation of equality with universal implications. The fact of the walkouts as a collective act was itself a declaration that actualized the right of those who lived in and around East LA to participate in a decision-making process that shaped their lives. Indeed, one can gauge in the walkouts the affirmation of the right of all residents of a given area to participate politically.

The element of universality of the walkouts is further evidenced by the degree to which in their wake, student acts of this kind were neither confined to East LA nor restricted to Mexican American students. Garnering national attention, the walkouts inspired similar acts throughout California, Arizona, Colorado, Texas, and into the Midwest.[15] Without denying the predominance of Mexican American involvement, it is also clear that other schools with lower numbers of Mexican Americans participated as well. This was the case with Jefferson High School and Edison Junior High School, predominately African American schools that also joined the walkouts and expressed their own demands. Likewise, over a thousand students from the predominantly Anglo Venice High School joined the protests by also walking out during the week of March 11.[16] Hence one can see in the walkouts and their demands an affirmation of equality the consequences of which extended beyond their particular context.

One of my aims is therefore to analyze the ways in which this universality runs up against the issue of identity, especially in thinking the nature of the political collective. I thus move to examine the way intuitive notions of Mexican American identity were rearticulated and given sharper definition through the legal strategy adopted in defense of two groups of activists associated with the walkouts and with subsequent actions emanating from the protests, as well as the way in which this redefinition fed into larger processes through which Chicano nationalism came to predominate. The first group of defendants, known as the "East LA Thirteen," faced potential sentences of up to forty-five years for conspiracy charges stemming from the walkouts.[17] The second group, known as the "Biltmore Six," faced possible life sentences for several alleged felonies (burglary, arson, conspiracy) committed in an attempt to disrupt Governor Ronald Reagan's speech during a conference on education held at the Biltmore Hotel in the spring of 1969.[18] Acosta served as defense attorney in both cases.

The Court Cases

In both, Acosta sought to challenge the legitimacy of the grand jury indictments by arguing that the equal protection clause of the Fourteenth Amendment had been violated by the relative absence of people

of Mexican descent from the indicting body.[19] Vital to the success of
the equal protection argument, however, was Acosta's ability to prove
the existence of Mexican Americans as a distinct social group. "To
prevail on the discrimination claim," explains legal scholar Ian Haney
López, "not only did Acosta have to demonstrate bias but, first and
foremost, he had to prove that Mexican [Americans] constituted an
identifiable and distinct minority group in Los Angeles."[20] This was due
to the precedent previously set by the Supreme Court in *Hernández v.
Texas* (1954), in which it ruled that the Fourteenth Amendment prohibited the exclusion of Mexican Americans from grand juries in Texas.
Significant for Acosta's challenge was that even though the court in
Hernández held that Mexican Americans did not deserve constitutional
protection as a *racial* minority, it held that they nevertheless could still
merit protection in instances demonstrating their existence as a distinct social group shown to be the target of prejudice, thus making the
issue of group identity a central concern.[21] Indeed, with the grand jury
challenge, Louis Gerard Mendoza points out, "[i]dentity [became] a
basis for action."[22]

Acosta was thus compelled to employ the support of both expert
witnesses and "documentary and statistical evidence in order to legally
establish their identity as a people separate and distinct from the majority,
thereby meeting the constitutional requirement of 'classification' which
is a pre-condition to a demand for consideration and representation for
their group on the Grand Jury."[23] He used the testimony of sociologist
Joan Moore, of demographers from the Los Angeles County Regional
Planning Commission, and of staff from the Los Angeles Commission on
Human Relations to prove that "Mexican Americans [met] all accepted
criteria for ethnic classification, including both internal and external
identification."[24] Such criteria pertained to "group distinctiveness as recognized by society as a whole; concentrated socioeconomic patterns;
shared cultural traditions; and intergroup relations."[25] Acosta argued that
these criteria were met by the existence of common values and behavior
patterns, the collection of statistics on "Mexicans" by state institutions,
socioeconomic patterns in education and employment, poverty levels,
housing issues, and spatial segregation. The predominant adherence to
Catholicism and the use of Spanish proved continuity of cultural traditions, and low rates of intermarriage with other groups established cultural, economic, and residential distinction.[26]

Despite his success in convincing the court that Mexican Americans constituted a distinct social group, Acosta was nevertheless unable to persuade the court in either case that this group had been the object of discrimination. The reason for this was that even after subpoenaing and questioning on the stand dozens of the Los Angeles County Superior Court judges responsible for nominating individuals to the grand jury, he was unable to prove that the absence of Mexican Americans was a result of an *intentional* desire on the part of the judges to exclude this group—something the presiding judges in both cases regarded as necessary.[27] Yet, notwithstanding the ultimate failure of the grand jury challenge, what I would like to focus on is the way in which the challenge's group distinction requirement itself entangled the defense strategy within an identitarian matrix that, in making the defense empirically identify the factors constitutive of Mexican American commonality, exerted an influence over the ideological disposition of the movement outside the courtroom.

Inasmuch as Acosta saw in the grand jury challenge a way to politicize the courtroom, the legal requirement to prove group distinction forced him to adopt a course of action that made Mexican American identity the centerpiece of his political work. Indeed, keeping in mind that the cases stemmed from a larger movement that Acosta sought to represent in the courtroom, I suggest that his legal strategy had significant repercussions *outside* of the courtroom by exerting an influence on the development of the self-conception of the Chicano Movement during this time in ways that fed directly into the consolidation of Chicano nationalism as its ideological anchor. Thus, as Haney López insists, "in the end, whether they convinced the judges who sat over them mattered less than whether they convinced the Mexican [American] community as a whole, and themselves in particular."[28] In this way, Acosta's legal work in relation to his activism provides a privileged view into an important moment in the development of Mexican American identity politics.[29] In particular, it gives insight into a way in which a certain Mexican American proto-nationalism, in the form of "feelings of collective belonging which already existed," was rearticulated into Chicano nationalism by lifting to the status of legally recognized empirical truth the roots of such common feeling.[30] Whereas Ernesto Chávez has pointed to the anti–Vietnam War protests as influencing the transformation of proto-nationalism into nationalism, here we also see the importance of legal battles in giving impetus to this transition.[31] Alongside the mythic dimensions of Chicano identity construction,[32] we also find such sources as social-scientific knowledge and litigation.

Turning to the work of Jacques Rancière, I suggest that what one sees here is a particular historical moment where "politics" runs up against the "police." For Rancière, the "police" refers to

> an order of bodies that defines the allocation of ways of doing, ways of being, and ways of saying, and sees that those bodies are assigned by name to a particular place and task. . . . Policing is not so much the "disciplining" of bodies as a rule governing their appearing, a configuration of *occupations* and the properties of the spaces where these occupations are distributed.[33]

In other words, the police, much like Badiou's encyclopedia, is an operator that classifies by identifying differences and allocating roles.[34] It organizes society into its constitutive parts by making them *intelligible* as such and ensures the stability of this order by assigning each to its proper place. In a newspaper article about the East LA Thirteen, Acosta describes the effects of the defense strategy in similar terms. In a statement strongly resonating with the classificatory function of the police, Acosta recounts:

> The staccatoed, computerized, analytical statistics "justified" their very existence; what had been but an inchoate propaganda of their own now became a rational truth to serve them not only in their confrontations with the Anglo establishment, but more importantly with their painful attempts at the proselytizing of a Mexican community which condemned the walkouts along with their patent nationalism and which winced at the racial rancor in their verbosity.[35]

Here a previously intuited yet equivocal identity becomes an object of knowledge via the work of the defense's strategy. The social-scientific framework that sanctions what is counted as admissible knowledge by the court raises the degree of group intelligibility from "inchoate propaganda" to that of "rational truth." Objectively proving their social existence as separate and distinct, their legal challenge and the political sequence from which it originates are also endowed with the legitimacy of facts needed not only to convince the judges and stand up to the "Anglo establishment," but, "more importantly," to win over the skeptical members of their own community to the nationalist cause—thus evincing the effect of the defense strategy on the self-conception of Mexican Americans outside the courtroom.

This being so, I argue that the legal requirement to prove group distinction forced the defense to adopt a police logic that is constitutive of existing social order. Expert testimony and statistical and demographic evidence defined the sources of commonality of a social group considered isomorphic to a political collective whose capacity for concerted action was thought to depend on the same foundations—thereby aiding the transformation of an existing proto-nationalism into a "self-evident" nationalism. To the extent that the latter established the ideological parameters for conceptualizing the political subject, the police framework that the defense adopted contributed to undermining the potential universality expressed by the student walkouts in the spring of 1968.

If, as Rancière suggests, politics is "a mode of expression that undoes the perceptible divisions of the police order by implementing a basically heterogeneous assumption, that of a part of those who have no part, . . . [and] demonstrates the sheer contingency of the order,"[36] which I believe to be a fitting description of the walkouts, then the logic that the defense had to adopt to meet the legal requirement for establishing group distinction fed into a form of nationalism that undermined the universalist politics first implied by the walkouts. Far from demonstrating the "sheer contingency of the order," the defense strategy reified it, even while it aimed to challenge it, by adopting the very terms of social classification. The defense was thus caught fighting at the level of inclusion into the police order on the latter's own terms in that its strategy was still dependent on the logic of identifiable groups and places. It challenged the count of the police, but not the logic that structured it. Rather than prescribing a logic heterogeneous to the police order, Chicano political reason was instead determined by the latter's "perceptible divisions" in taking as its basis for action the existence of Mexican Americans as a distinctly classifiable group—a group that then sought to promote its self-interest in relation to other established social groups, even in its attempts at coalition politics.[37] To the degree that such classification defines the group's priorities and course of struggle, it should also come as no surprise that the taking of existing forms of sociality as basis for action often led to a lack of willingness within the movement to subject intragroup gender and sexual roles to critical reevaluation, since the latter would precisely strike at the ideological heart of group identity.[38]

Revolt and the Critique of Identity Politics

To associate Acosta with identity politics, however, is to stay within the range of usual interpretations of his work. As a prevalent theme across the spectrum of his writings, many critics have channeled their analyses through the prism of identity.[39] Along these interpretive lines, it would be tempting to read *The Autobiography of a Brown Buffalo* and *The Revolt of the Cockroach People* as simply being a continuation of what Acosta did in the courtroom. Much as the court cases established their own conventions for demonstrating group distinction, here Acosta would symbolically enact a process of identity formation by adhering to the conventions of the autobiographical genre. Acosta's narratives would be a means through which to define himself and the ethnic group to which he belongs; to establish the "reality" of their experience and enable both to obtain the recognition necessary for their inclusion into a wider historical narrative.[40]

Yet Frederick Aldama and Kimberly Kowalczyk have demonstrated that Acosta actually violates some of the distinguishing features of the autobiographical genre, and that these violations occur precisely to call attention to the gap between mimesis and reality. A glaring example of this is the fact that as Buffalo Z. Brown, the main protagonist in *Revolt* does not even share the same name as the author, thereby introducing a lack of congruence between the author and the character.[41] Furthermore, in *Autobiography*, the narrating "I" gives information—such as his age at a particular moment in time—that is contradicted at another point in the narrative. Since this contradiction is revealed within the text itself, it signals a distancing between Acosta as author and Acosta as narrator, at the same time that it constructs the latter as not being fully reliable.[42] At other times Acosta also creates a breach between narrator and character when the narrator begins to describe the character in the third person.[43] At the beginning of *Revolt*, for example, as a group of activists try to find a way into St. Basil's church to disrupt its Christmas Eve service, the narrator describes: "There are fifty pigs waiting for us to make the wrong move. . . . 'Come on,' our lawyer exhorts. I, strange fate, am this lawyer."[44] In this way, a space of incongruity is introduced that moves these works beyond the confines of autobiography. I argue that it is precisely in these gaps between autobiography and fiction where Acosta develops a critical reflection on Chicano nationalism, identity politics, and the unrepresentability of a politics subtracted from the legality of the police order.

Indeed, critics such as Marcial González and Carlos Gallego have made important contributions to this line of analysis with regard to Acosta's critical stance toward Chicano nationalism in *Revolt*.[45] Both critics focus on a particular moment in the narrative where Acosta as author reprimands the Chicano Movement via a dialogue in Acapulco between Acosta as character (i.e., Buffalo "Zeta" Brown) and his fictive twin brother, Jesus. By means of this blatant manipulation of historical fact (he did not have a twin brother named Jesus), Acosta signals a self-critical posture by literally setting up a double of himself.[46] After spending several days listening to Brown go on about the "*movida* in East LA," Jesus finally questions him regarding just how serious he and his fellow militants are about their struggle.[47] He challenges Brown's self-designation as a revolutionary by arguing that until the movement develops a level of commitment that embraces death as a real possibility, it will remain "just an exercise in ego-tripping."[48] "Jesus's question," explains Gallego, "is meant to both criticize facile identification with a revolutionary ethics and foreground the sacrifice of death that such an ethics requires."[49] Through this decisive move, González argues, "*Revolt* pits Chicano cultural nationalism against a kind of political consciousness characterized by the political rebel's acceptance of death as a possible outcome of struggle."[50] Both critics thus see in the motif of death a central category through which Acosta critiques Chicano nationalism. For González, however, the target of Acosta's critique is not so much the identity politics that Chicano nationalism espouses, but rather the lack of revolutionary commitment to real social transformation that it exhibits. Real revolutionary commitment here hinges on the subjective acceptance of death as a possible consequence. Gallego, on the other hand, suggests that the motif of death does offer "insight into Acosta's conceptualization of a non-identity-based politics" to the extent that death constitutes a "negation of self" that signals toward a revolution-ary universality based on anonymity.[51]

While I agree that Acosta links political subjectivation with a "nega-tion of self," I would like to point to a different moment in the narra-tive where he can be read as proposing another model of subjectivation untied from the motif of death. Here, subjectivation occurs via a break with liberal individualism and hinges on a decision to affirm one's sub-jective capacity, a decision beyond strictly rational calculation. This moment of subjectivation occurs early in the narrative after a conversa-tion Brown has with his cousin, Manuel, upon arriving in Los Angeles. Manuel, a former star high jumper for the University of Southern Cal-ifornia, still blames his failure to qualify for the 1952 Olympics on the negligence of his coach who "had deliberately not taught him to jump higher" because he disliked Chicanos.[52] When Brown changes the sub-ject to the Chicano militants,

> [Manuel] laughs and tells me that they are just a bunch of young punk communists who don't know their ass from a hole in the ground. "They blame all their troubles on everybody but themselves."
>
> I laugh at the irony. I ask if he isn't doing the same thing with his failure to qualify for the Olympics.
>
> So he screams at me: "That's different! I worked my ass off! I made it on my own. No one gave me a thing. You don't see me going around crying, asking the government for a handout."
>
> We get into heavy arguments. He refuses to acknowledge that his sports scholarship to USC was a handout just like any other handout. I find myself defending a group I don't even know.[53]

As a small business owner—he owns his own restaurant, "Manny's Fish Bowl"—Manuel echoes the petit bourgeois claim that one's success is wholly a consequence of one's individual work ethic, and disavows the role of structural factors like racism or poverty in affecting one's life chances. He acknowledges that racism played a role in *his* inability to qualify for the Olympics but refuses to acknowledge that racism could be a structural problem, choosing instead to restrict it to the individual pathology of his coach. When it comes to his success, however, he ignores the role of assistance, like his scholarship, in order to represent himself as a hardworking individual who has attained all he has purely on self-merit.

It is after this conversation that Brown begins to reflect on his own principles: "As I trot up the ten flights to my room, my mind begins to whirl. My own arguments to Manuel have impressed me. If I didn't give a shit, why was I bothering to argue? . . . In a way I agree with Manuel. The best way to accomplish what you want is simply to work for it, on an individual level."[54] Here the tensions that structured Brown's conversation with his cousin are reproduced within his own mind. While he ultimately agrees with Manuel that the most effective kind of action is as an individual working for one's own best interest, there is a glimpse of another logic that challenges this mode of thought, to his own surprise. He is confused by the appearance of a mode of reasoning that contradicts what he believes himself to believe. That this confusion comes in the form of a question points to the fact that the arguments he levied at Manuel evince the trace of a commitment that he did not know he was able to make (thus his surprise at his own arguments), and to the fact that the object of his commitment remains unclear. With the very next sentence he continues: "I open my room and an army of cockroaches disperses into the cracks and darkness. My evening set of calisthenics is full of 'and yets . . .' Didn't I argue!"[55] Again evoking a sense of contingency, of something unknown swirling around him, Acosta directly links this uncertainty to the political collective to come through the image of "an army of cockroaches" that immediately "disperses into the cracks and darkness"—that is, while located at the edge of the situation's void, the cockroaches still dissipate into it, for the moment remaining as the mere *potential* for a future politics. As he tries to get on with his workout, however, he is repeatedly confronted by a series of "and yets . . ." that interrupt and disconcert him.

These "and yets . . ." interrupt the logic of liberal individualism precisely at the moment when Brown is inclined to resign himself to it. They mark the site where an exception to this logic can and has occurred. It is an exception that confronts Brown with a breach in the given order of things and marks a place from where another logic can emerge. The "and yets . . ." evince the trace of the agency of a lack, the void, surging forth from this site, and like an event they force a choice. Thus Brown declares:

That night I get no sleep. My brain goes off like explosives and by dawn I have made innumerable resolutions. I will change my name. I will learn Spanish. I will write the greatest books ever written. I will become the best criminal lawyer in the history of the world. I will save the world. I will show the world what is what and who the fuck is who. Me in particular.[56]

While the predominance of the "I" here can be read as signaling an intensification of an individual sense of self, I would argue that this "I" is merely the point of departure for the subject. Pushing through the hole made manifest by the "and yets . . . ," these "innumerable resolutions" force Brown's opening toward his own subjective capacity; a capacity that in the context of collective politics will be in excess of either individual or collective identity. Though still falling short of an initiation into collective politics, this episode both conditions his subsequent involvement in the Chicano Movement and is accompanied by the return of a previously repressed memory of his first fraught attempt at collective politics.[57] Thus, while this account of subjectivation is not, strictly speaking, an example of *political* subjectivation, given the absence of an active incorporation into a political sequence, the specter of collective politics nevertheless haunts the entire episode. Beginning with the change of name, and proceeding with the list of extraordinary things he will do, what one sees here is the way in which Brown, by having the courage to affirm the consequences of the "and yets . . . ," forces himself to overcome his limitations; he forces himself to become something more than "himself." Though at first sight Acosta seems to conform in many ways to the developmentalist paradigm that María Josefina Saldaña-Portillo identifies as pervasive to revolutionary thought—a paradigm wherein "[t]he underdeveloped subject must make the ethical choice to enter development and thereby history, to leave behind a prodigal life in favor of a productive one"[58]—what Acosta's account of subjectivation demonstrates, rather, is the gap between a subject marked by an event (in this particular case, the "and yets . . ." as exceptions to the logic of liberal individualism) and the continued existence of the individual as human animal with particular desires. The process of subjectivation here does not imply the death of a prior subjectivity or the elimination of one as an individual.[59] Indeed, what Acosta signals here, and will continue to thematize throughout the narrative in the form of Brown's productive *and* prodigal behavior, is the enduring tension between individual and subject. What is certainly maintained, however, is the affirmation of a certain subjective voluntarism bent toward the future.[60] Hence the repeated "will" has double significance in both employing the future tense to mark the distance between the individual "I" and the process by which the "I" will exceed itself as subject, and in suggesting that the decision indeed lies within the proper purview of an affirmative will.

COCKROACH: EVENTAL SITE AND GENERIC COLLECTIVE

Acosta's most poignant challenge to the identity politics of Chicano nationalism, however, is developed through the category of Cockroach. Gallego notes the shift toward a thinking of nonidentitarian politics by Acosta in the manner in which he favors the signifier "cockroach" over that of "Chicano."[61] According to Gallego, Acosta "chooses the 'cockroach' as a means of representing all 'the people' who are similarly situated, or excluded in a similar manner from the public sphere."[62] As the "little beasts that everyone steps on,"[63] "cockroach" comes to designate the abject status shared by all those whose exclusion is constitutive of existing social order, thereby becoming "a generic symbol of oppression . . . reminiscent of Badiou's definition of the void."[64] In its particular situatedness, however, I would argue that Cockroach, especially when Acosta writes the first letter in uppercase, becomes a proper name for a situation's evental site—that is, for the site from which an event can occur—rather than for the void itself. Additionally, I argue that one can also see in Acosta's use of this signifier in the narrative a further function tied specifically to the question of the foundation of a political collective and of the requirement for participation in this collective once an event has occurred. Rather than simply indexing an immanent site of exclusion that holds the *potential* for disruption, Acosta begins to think the nature of politics once this potential has been actualized—that is, after the cockroaches have revolted (hence the title), and thus after the void's evental incursion into the situation.

I thus maintain that in the novel, Cockroach is also the name of the collective constituted *after* the moment of revolt. Given the evental site's positioning at the edge of the void and its function as the limit condition of existing order, by giving the collective the proper name of the site as its own name, Acosta signals a process that attempts to transform a situation from the perspective of its negative foundation. It is their wager on a universal possibility without guarantees, one brought into being by the evental act of revolt, that founds what this collective's members have in common and holds them together, thus disenabling any substantive particularity as condition for participation or cause for action. Hence it becomes evident that into the category of Cockroach are included not just Chicanos, students, women, the poor, Vietnamese peasants, beatniks, or Jews—those who in different instances can be said to be systematically excluded—but also lawyers, Anglos from wealthy areas, wealthy celebrities, politicians, and members of the church—people belonging to groups that at different times in the narrative are identified as sources of oppression, but who become Cockroaches after joining the movement. The narrator thus speaks of Duana Doherty, "the street nun who once worshipped wearing black robes while her head was bald. Then she joined with the Chicanos and became a Cockroach herself."[65] As a member of the church, even in her condition as a "street nun," Doherty formed part of an institution against which the Chicano militants organize precisely for "its refusal to involve itself in the cause of social justice for Mexican Americans."[66] It is only after she became an active participant of the movement that she also became a Cockroach.[67]

Acosta dramatizes the universality of the political address early in the novel when Brown, standing on a stage during the protests after the arrests of the East LA Thirteen, declares to everyone present: "I am the chief counsel for these men. I will be needing a lot of help in the days to come. We will need lawyers, law students, leg men, secretaries, and the support of anyone who is in agreement with our position."[68] Similarly, during Brown's campaign for sheriff of Los Angeles County, he states:

> The publicity from the trials and my numerous contempt of court charges have brought hordes into my camp. Cockroaches from Hollywood and Venice, *vatos* from car clubs, elderly churchgoers. Cockroaches from the barrios and beaches have begun to pass out bumper stickers. Posters drawn by nuns and hippies. . . . Lawyers from the National Lawyers guild, from the ACLU and from the Legal Aid Societies have joined up to elect the radical Chicano lawyer.[69]

Acosta here signals the existence of a political sequence open to anyone who chooses to actively support the call for equality and justice, regardless of their particular identity, occupation, or social status. I thus suggest that the category of Cockroach affords a glimpse into Acosta's thinking of the political subject as such, to the extent that Cockroach begins to function as something close to a "generic" collective, and the political subject's existence is gauged by means of the transformative effects that this collective brings about within a situation. The distance from the state that this politics takes is figured in the narrative by means of Brown's increasing antagonism toward the law and his ultimate rejection of it as a tool for politics.[70]

OF SECRETS, LIES, AND FORMAL DISTORTIONS

Consistent with a conception of politics as a generic procedure that remains illegible to the state, revolutionary politics in the novel remains at the margins of representation, with the reader's approximation to it mediated through the lies and formal distortions exhibited by the narrative. Revolutionary politics in the novel is situated in the interplay between form and content; or rather, as the absent or unrepresentable cause that formally distorts the story's content. Perhaps the most conspicuous distortion of historical fact presented thus far is Acosta's invention of a twin brother as a means to develop a critical stance toward Chicano nationalism. Adding an interesting twist to this episode, González briefly suggests that the entire account of Brown's trip to Acapulco, where the encounter with his brother takes place, could be a lie.[71] While informing Black Eagle that he is coming back to LA after finding out about reporter Roland Zanzibar's death during the Chicano Moratorium, Brown is forced to justify his time in Acapulco and tells his friend:

> I've been trying to set up . . . sanctuary . . . I've been talking to some . . . real heavy people . . . I've got a deal going where if . . . you know, like if you need a place to hide? OK, I can't say nothing more . . . I've been tailed down here by . . . I know it sounds paranoid . . . . [. . .] I'm telling you, the State of Guerrero is still in revolt [. . .] but you tell the dudes that I've been working . . . I just haven't been fucking up . . . All right?[72]

The information he gives Black Eagle is a lie, since the reader knows that Brown has really spent his time in Acapulco indulging in drugs and prostitutes. Yet the very obviousness of the lie brings attention to the fictive status of the narrative. This, according to González, can make "one . . . wonder: has the entire chapter been constructed as a lie? . . . Can one sense a bit of authorial transparency here—a plea to his audience to grasp the truth behind the lie?"[73] After all, it is within this very chapter that another lie (that of having a twin brother) is also used to expose a truth (his critique of Chicano nationalism). In this way, the possibility is opened up that what Brown tells Black Eagle is closer to the truth, and that what the reader has been told throughout the chapter is the lie. This possibility is given further credence by the fact that in reality, Acosta had actually been present in Los Angeles during the Chicano Moratorium, rather than having been in Acapulco.[74]

In addition to Brown's conversation with Jesus, moreover, this chapter also marks the further political radicalization of Brown following a series of incidents that make more acute his disillusionment with the possibility of working for change within the law. Although Acosta had experienced previous disillusionments with the law since his time as a legal aid attorney in Oakland, his early work in Los Angeles was characterized by his belief that as a radical lawyer, he could use the law against itself. Mirroring the intensification of his disillusionment and his ultimate renunciation of legal practice in real life, this belief in the ability to effect change from within the law is tested and finally abandoned in the course of *Revolt* as well.

A significant turning point comes after a coroner's inquest into the death of a young Chicano while in police custody. The young man, Robert Fernandez, is alleged to have committed suicide in his cell, but his family suspects that he has been murdered.[75] Though the inquest works under different rules from those of a criminal case, it still works under the authority of the judicial branch.[76] After Brown is able to arrange for the coroner's inquest into the cause of death, however, he realizes that its proceedings are structured to the advantage of the police and their account of the incident. He becomes aware that its rules actually function as an impediment to the inquiry's ability to really find out what happened. Its failure to adhere to the basic rules of evidence by making hearsay admissible, as well as its disallowing of direct questioning and cross-examination of witnesses by Brown, tilts the advantage toward the police, whose own account of the events is able to stand without being significantly challenged. Rather than trying to get to the bottom of what actually occurred in an unbiased manner, furthermore, the district attorney's representative does all he can to lend credibility to the police's story. "It is an impossible procedure. . . . Even if it is a suicide situation, we are not getting at the truth," exclaims a frustrated Brown.[77] It is thus despite the police's inability to "explain how Robert could have tied the noose more than seven feet off the floor without something to stand on,"[78] or to adequately explain why the piece of cloth with which he hung himself does not match the dimensions of the hole in the blanket from which the piece of fabric was allegedly cut, that the plausibility of the police's account remains strong enough for the jury to unanimously determine suicide as Fernandez's cause of death. Convinced of the existence of a structural bias in the legal system meant to maintain an oppressive social order, it is after this episode that Brown and some of his friends first turn toward illegal and violent forms of action by firebombing a Safeway store.[79] That this episode signals Brown's further politicization is also evinced by the way in which "Zeta," as a kind of nom de guerre adopted by Brown earlier in the narrative, begins to take precedence over his other names.[80]

Even though in the story Brown takes part in the bombing of the Safeway before his trip to Acapulco, it is after his return from this trip that a more militant stance really develops among him and his associates. The beginning of this more militant phase is signaled by references to a string of bombings that occur throughout Los Angeles (mostly targeting government buildings), and by increasing references to guns. It is with regard to these references, I claim, that one can approximate Acosta's reflection on revolutionary politics—though it is important to point out that the bombings themselves are not "revolutionary" in the novel. Indeed, the reader is never given information as to any revolutionary consequences stemming from them. Thus I don't believe that Acosta uses the bombings to suggest their necessity as a tactic, but uses them rather to point to a turn toward a form of action antagonistic to the law—which can, after all, take either peaceful or violent forms. The bombings can in this way be read as a metaphor for the unrepresentable force that is revolutionary politics subtracted from the law.[81] With the exception of one of the final scenes in the novel where the militants bomb the Hall of Justice, the bombings and the references to guns merely function as a technique through which the narrative points to something else, something outside the law and representation that the reader can never fully know, and that is occurring behind the scenes of the action to which the reader is given access.

After his return from Acapulco, Brown again accepts the role of lead defense for a group of militants, this time arrested while leaving the area of Laguna Park in the aftermath of the Chicano Moratorium. In this case, known in the novel as the case of the "Tooner Flats Seven," seven militants, including Rodolfo "Corky" Gonzales, are "charged with Arson, Riot, Conspiracy and a host of other travesties."[82] Significantly, it is during this case, and not in that of the East LA Thirteen, that Brown puts forth the grand jury discrimination challenge in the novel. This particular manipulation of historical fact allows Acosta to directly juxtapose the demonstration of structural racism in the legal system with the adoption of "illegal" tactics after the events around the Chicano Moratorium. That the militants' political focus has shifted elsewhere—beyond the courtroom, and thus beyond the confines of the law—is initially hinted at when, during a noon recess in the trial, Brown remarks, "I grab my briefcase, which is empty except for a gun, and push off."[83] Remembering once again that at one point the courtroom was regarded as a place where politics could happen, here one sees that the very tools with which Brown could effect such a politicization—that is, all the materials required to make a case—are absent, having been replaced instead by a gun.

A few pages later, the reader is made aware that the existence of the gun is consistent with a set of resolutions made by Brown upon his return from Acapulco. After a quick meeting with the Tooner Flats Seven defendants, Brown is riding in a car on his way home when he describes:

I am spinning around in emptiness, thinking of what my brother Jesus told me. Who have we killed? Just how heavy *are* we? I am confused, but by the time we reach the house I have made two decisions. When I have finished this trial, I will write my book. Without fail. And win or lose, I will destroy the courthouse where the *gabachos* have made me dance these last years with lead in my belly and tears in my heart.[84]

Obviously still hounded by his brother's questions, Brown anxiously ponders just how far he and his fellow militants are willing to go in their militancy. The way in which this account closely mirrors the earlier moment of subjectivation in the narrative—with the figure of the void this time evoked as the "emptiness" around which he is spinning—points to its similar function as a subjectivizing turning point, this time with regard to the adoption of extralegal tactics. The extralegality of these tactics is highlighted by the fact that it is precisely the courthouse that he vows to destroy. Given the courthouse's status as representative of the law and the legal system, its destruction also entails the symbolic destruction of the law by force rather than by legal arguments. Accordingly, the fact that bombings and guns, as metaphors for force, have come to replace legal arguments also points to a breakdown in the efficacy of communication; it points to a zero point in the confrontation between two competing logics—the police on the one hand and politics on the other—where communication is impossible. Recalling Rancière's notion of disagreement, what is at stake here is the very ground upon which these two competing logics confront one another.[85] The fact that Brown will destroy the courthouse regardless of whether he wins or loses the case further emphasizes that what happens in court is politically inconsequential.

It is in this context that the basement in Brown's house enters the narrative and begins to function as a source of extralegal action that resists representation. Though the basement is referenced several times in the narrative after Brown's return from Acapulco, it remains a signifier without clearly definable content. The first time the basement is mentioned occurs before the Tooner Flats Seven trial begins, when Brown organizes a meeting at his house between Corky Gonzales and the rest of the defendants. The purpose of the meeting is to assuage the other defendants' worries about whether or not they can trust Corky as an outsider from Denver. During the meeting the issue of tactics comes up immediately. The defendants want to know if Corky and his associates want to continue to march and protest, or whether they support armed struggle. "No. We don't. It doesn't serve our purposes now," answers Corky: "If you guys are throwing bombs, it must be because you feel that it's necessary to do so in order to accomplish your objectives. . . . We don't. . . . Not at this time."[86] Though Corky disagrees with the rest of the militants, he nevertheless expresses his tacit support and thus "passes his colors."[87] Still, Brown and the militants refuse to divulge their plans to him. "I don't tell him a word about our plans. I simply tell him that if I get caught I will not involve anyone from any of the organizations," asserts Brown.[88] Immediately after the meeting ends, "Gilbert and Pelon get down to work in the basement, a little room with dirt walls. The trap-door is in my bedroom. Only we three know about it. It is our secret."[89]

Before the end of the meeting, however, the issue of writing briefly comes up. Brown, knowing that Corky is also a writer, tells him that he has just received a letter from "some broad up in Frisco . . . about doing some article or book."[90] When asked about what he is going to write, Brown suggests that he will write about what has been happening in Tooner Flats. "You going to tell them *everything?*" asks Corky with concern. "Heh, heh . . . just enough to get you in trouble," responds Brown facetiously.[91] Though brief, this exchange once again calls the reader's attention to the uncertain status of the narrative in terms of its degree of historical accuracy, because Brown's comment expresses ambiguity with regard to what he will or will not reveal. His answer evinces his acknowledgement of the implications—legal or otherwise—of disclosing too much. Especially in light of the fact that Brown is a *lawyer*, one can assume such concerns to be at the forefront of his calculations—and those of Acosta as author as well. Thus, implicit in his response is that he will not tell everything. When we add to this self-reflexive gesture the fact that Brown refuses to tell Corky all of their plans, and refers to the basement and what is going on in it as "our secret," this scene can be read as a multilayered thematization of the withholding and manipulation of information. Consequently, and given that what one is reading is precisely Acosta's written account of what (might have) occurred, the question of what is (partially) true and what is (partially) false in the narrative is again brought up. Adding to this the fact that the reader is never brought into the basement itself, one can surmise that the reader, too, is excluded from the secret(s).

In another important instance, the function of Brown's house (and the basement, by extension) as a source of extralegal activity is actually brought up within the context of the trial, yet it proves to exceed the capacity of the law, once again, to determine what is going on. It is through the testimony of an undercover policeman, Fernando Sumaya, that Brown's house first comes up in court. Sumaya has succeeded in infiltrating the Chicano militants, and the night before the Chicano Moratorium he had attended a meeting at Brown's house. "The place was loaded," testifies Sumaya: "There were all kinds of guns and rifles. Dynamite . . . flares . . . Gasoline, everything."[92] He also tells the court that some of the defendants had obtained their firebombs from Brown's house, "the house on Sixth Street."[93] A similar account is given by the chief of police, Judd Davis, during his testimony:

"Well . . . we had information that your house was being used to store weapons and dynamite. [. . .] We knew that you were the reputed mastermind. . . . Our information had led us to believe that you were the person primarily responsible for all the bombings, the burnings . . . That is, that you were the brains behind the operation. [. . .] [O]ur information is that you directed the bombings during the riots."

"From Acapulco?" [asks Brown].

"No, not the riot of the twenty-ninth."

"Which one?"

"Well . . . they say that you've been the leader ever since you got kicked out of the inquest."

"You mean the inquest into the death of Zanzibar?"[94]

"They say that ever since then, you have been directing the activities of the Chicano Liberation Front."

I laugh. [. . .] I can hear the dudes who presently live in my own pad on Sixth Street. . . . Right now the bastards are probably brewing up some molotov for tonight's action and here I'm being called the *mastermind*. [. . .]

"Now, Chief . . . Tell me . . . Do you believe those stories your undercover spies tell you? I mean, do you really believe that I am the leader of those persons who are throwing firebombs every other day at banks and schools and government offices? [. . .] Do you think I'm telling the people to pick up the gun? Come on, Davis!"

"No . . . I told them that you probably just let them use your house. . . . I can't say that I have any hard information that you actually *direct* people to commit acts of violence."[95]

The first thing to notice in this exchange is the pervasiveness of ambiguity and inconsistency. In fact, even before this exchange, the reliability and accuracy of the testimony of Sumaya—who, unlike Chief Davis, had supposedly been inside Brown's house—is put in doubt when at one moment he seems to conveniently forget important information, like whether he was the one who had called in the report alleging the presence of a gunman in the Silver Dollar Bar, and at another moment claims that he failed to notice the body of Zanzibar a yard away after the latter was shot in the head with a tear gas projectile.[96] In light of the unreliability of Sumaya's testimony and the fact that the rest of Chief Davis's sources are not named, the "they say" that grounds the validity of Davis's testimony is reduced to *hearsay.* There is even inconsistency regarding the incidents that are the object of inquiry. Chief Davis claims that Brown "directed the bombings during the riots" but then adds that he does not refer to the riot of August 29, the one that provides the context within which the seven defendants were arrested. When Brown presses him to clarify to which other riot he refers, Chief Davis changes the subject by making reference to an inquest as a turning point in Brown's activities toward the adoption of violent tactics. While the reader knows from the narrative that it is after the inquest into Fernandez's death that Brown and his associates first turn toward violence, this is not actually the inquest to which Chief Davis refers. He refers to the inquest into the death of Roland Zanzibar, a character based on famed reporter Rubén Salazar, who was killed by a sheriff's deputy the day of the Chicano Moratorium under similar circumstances.

Though the inquest into Zanzibar's death is not included in the narrative, there really was an inquest into the death of Salazar, and there are several similarities between this inquest and the Fernandez inquest as it is portrayed in the novel. In both instances, Norman Pittluck[97] served as the inquest officer in charge of the hearings.[98] Similarly, Acosta was also present at the Salazar inquest, though not as the attorney representing the Salazar family. He was there as a member of a "blue-ribbon" committee, a group of twenty-one inquest observers who had been organized by the Congress of Mexican American Unity to monitor the proceedings. Even in this capacity, however, Acosta was nevertheless able to get involved in verbal confrontations with Pittluck much like they occur in the novel.[99] Most significant still is that a person by the name of Robert Fernandez was also present at the Salazar inquest. According to several sources, this Robert Fernandez was a Loyola University law student who interrupted the hearing in protest and then provoked a walkout by other spectators after he was ejected by deputies.[100] Consequently, here one might wonder if, via the name of Fernandez, the inquest that appears in the novel also points one in the direction of the militants' actions after the inquest into the death of Zanzibar/Salazar.[101] This claim can find support in the narrative since at one point Brown himself states, "Ever since the death of Zanzibar, government offices have become the favorite targets for the bombers of the underground."[102] While he distances himself from the bombings here, elsewhere he declares, "I have no desire to make a martyr out of Zanzibar. I know he has been murdered. Only Gilbert and Pelon know how we intend to avenge him."[103] Since Gilbert and Pelon are the ones who are involved in what is happening in the basement, and were also involved in firebombing the Safeway, one can perhaps link their activities to the other string of bombings.

While an explicit reference to the basement is absent in Brown's exchange with Chief Davis, I would argue that its absence here precisely points once again to its positioning at the margins of representation. The reader knows that whatever the militants are up to is being shaped by their activities in the basement. Thus, both Chief Davis's testimony and Brown's own thoughts regarding what is probably going on in his house are articulated in relation to this referent that eludes representation in the courtroom. The basement, as the source of the actions that motivate the exchange, is present in the exchange through its very absence. Though one may be tempted to say that in this exchange Brown actually lets the reader know exactly what is going on in his house/basement, it is important to keep in mind that the reader's knowledge is still mediated here by Brown's imagination. It is through what he imagines to "probably" be happening there during the hearing that the reader is told that molotovs are being prepared, yet the reader is still kept away. Thus it is only through hearsay or the imagination that one is allowed glimpses into what could possibly be occurring in the basement. In this way, much like Chief Davis, the reader is also left without "any hard information."

In a final move, Brown redoubles his efforts to get Chief Davis to confess to a conspiracy on behalf of the police to assassinate Zanzibar:

> "Do you know who the man was that called in reporting that there was a man with a gun inside the Silver Dollar?"
>
> "No, sir."
>
> "*Isn't it a fact that Wilson killed Zanzibar because you felt he knew too much?*" The jury is leaning forward.
>
> Judd Davis looks me straight in the eye. "That's no more true than the allegation that you're personally ordering the bombing of our government buildings. . . . You're getting paranoid, Brown."
>
> "I have good reason for it, Chief."[104]

Instead of clearing things up, Chief Davis's testimony merely adds to the confusion and uncertainty as to the causes shaping events. While he seems to admit that the allegations regarding Brown's involvement in violent actions are untrue, what he actually does is simply make the truth or falsehood of Brown's allegations against him rely on the truth or falsehood of his own allegations against Brown. The reader is thus given the option of interpreting Chief Davis's statement as *either* a claim of innocence *or* an admission of guilt. If the reader believes that Brown is involved in the bombings, then the reader must conclude that the police really did assassinate Zanzibar.[105] In the latter case, then, one would also be made to notice a certain correlation and confrontation between the extralegality inherent in a politics subtracted from the law and the extralegality inherent in the law's excess over itself as it tries to safeguard social order.

In sum, everything that can be gathered with regard to the bombings, to what is going on in the basement, and to the timeline of events does not coincide with definite knowledge. Insofar as the reader never knows what is really taking place, he or she is forced to try to put the pieces together around a missing core that impedes them from neatly adding up. One can thus link the figure of the basement precisely to an *underground* and hence unrepresentable form of politics once Brown returns from Acapulco—a politics whose unrepresentability is correlated to its subtraction from the law. Likewise, the basement can be read as signaling the withholding and distortion of information evident in the semiautobiographical novelistic form itself, a form that is adopted by Acosta in order to retell the story of a historical political sequence. What the reader becomes aware of, however, is that Acosta cannot actually tell that story, or at least, not all of it, leaving much of it to be gauged through the distortions and inconsistencies that serve as its narrative traces—that is, as traces of the fact that the story he points to is precisely a story of the not-all.

In the novel's final pages, though, the pattern of hiding knowledge of the bombings is broken as Brown and his associates make good on his promise to blow up the Hall of Justice after the Tooner Flats Seven trial concludes. With the intention of killing Judge Alacran, they place a bomb in the bathroom one floor below his chambers.[106] After the bomb goes off, however, the radio identifies as the only victim "[a] young man of presumably Latin descent."[107] Adding the death of an innocent Latino bystander to their failure to kill Alacran, the reader cannot but expect a remorseful reaction from Brown approximating his earlier behavior during Fernandez's second autopsy.[108] Brown violates these expectations by declaring:

> No, I don't feel guilty about the kid that got killed. I feel terrible.
> But not guilty. Lots more will die before this fight is over. The truce

we've signed for the moment doesn't mean anything. Just because the
Viet Cong or the Chicanos temporarily lay down their arms doesn't
prove shit. For me, personally, this is a kind of end. And a beginning. . . . Somebody still has to answer for Robert Fernandez and
Roland Zanzibar. Somebody still has to answer for all the smothered
lives of all the fighters who have been forced to carry on, chained to
a war for Freedom just like a slave is chained to his master.[109]

For González, this incident can be read as a final symbolic negation of Chicano nationalism, "a negation that necessarily implies transformation to a
broader level of political commitment."[110] Adding to González's analysis,
though, I think that one must also read in Brown's gesture not just the
negation of Chicano nationalism, but the subjective exhaustion of the Chicano Movement itself and of Brown's participation in it in particular. Just
as the firebombing of the Safeway—the only other bombing that the reader
is permitted to witness—marks the symbolic beginning of their truly militant phase, the bombing of the courthouse marks its end. Far from (symbolically) destroying the law (the courthouse is only slightly damaged), the
law continues to live unfettered in the figure of Alacran. This political end,
however, is simultaneously accompanied by the specter of a recommencement in the form of a new beginning. Via imagery that recalls Hegel's
master/slave dialectic, but perhaps through a nonhumanist lens this time,
Brown alludes to future subjectivations as others (and perhaps even himself, once again) subject themselves to the process necessary for the struggle for freedom to be won.[111] In this way, he leaves open the possibility,
and indeed the urgency, for the recommencement of a new sequence in the
future—one that can continue the struggle for universal emancipation.

Conclusion

The Revolt of the Cockroach People can thus be read as a sophisticated work
in political thought in critical tension with the politics that both inspired
it and constituted its subject matter. Especially when read against the
consequences of Acosta's legal work, *Revolt* demonstrates a discerning
consideration of political subjectivation, the nonidentitarian foundations
of the political collective, and the (non)relationship between politics,
law, and representation. Its insights, moreover, are expressed by means
of techniques that belie its seemingly impetuous style. It is precisely at

the limits of the semiautobiographical novel's narrative universe, in the interplay between form, content, and history, that radical politics can be found at work in its subtraction from representation.

Through his experiences as a radical lawyer and a political militant, Acosta became disillusioned with the possibility of using the courtroom to further revolutionary objectives. Forced to submit to the law's police logic, the consequences of his grand jury discrimination challenge outside the courtroom had the effect of assisting the development of a nationalist Chicano political identity that sought to make intelligible the sources of its political unity. In *Revolt*, however, Acosta provides a critical response to the limitations of his legal work and to the restrictive nature of Chicano nationalism. By paying attention to how group formation is figured in the novel, one can reconsider Acosta's relationship to the identity politics of Chicano nationalism in more nuanced ways.

Though he reconfigures this relationship in a variety of manners, perhaps the one with the most implications for thinking politics unsutured from identity is his use of the category of Cockroach. Functioning in a first instance to designate an evental site where, in their social marginalization, Chicanos find themselves similarly situated alongside other excluded groups, it is when Cockroach begins to function as the name for a political collective that Acosta's vision of a universal politics is gauged. Cockroach serves in the novel as a signifier for a collective made up of anyone who chooses to participate in the production of postevental consequences. To the extent that this process cuts across established social categories, rather than bringing existing groups together in alliance or combination as in the case of coalition politics, Cockroach is constituted as a "generic" collective held together by a subjective wager in excess of identitarian constraints.

In this way, Acosta posits an alternative to the supposed necessity of substantive identification as a condition for collective action. Beginning from the incursion of the void in its interruption of the logic of liberal individualism, the process that traces the consequences of this event can only be gauged at the borders of representation, in excess of the identitarian self that is also the subject/object of autobiography. This process can thus only be approached in the novel through the inconsistencies it creates with regard to the relationship between the story and historical fact, through the themes of the lie and the secret, and through the figure of the basement that indexes an underground politics.

5

Between Crowd and Group

Fantasy, Revolutionary Nation, and the Politics of the Not-All

IN THE WAKE OF THE Black Lives Matter movement, the philosopher of race George Yancy conducted a series of interviews with prominent intellectuals for the *New York Times* philosophy series The Stone. Among those interviewed was Judith Butler, who was asked to respond to a tendency among (mostly white) people outside the movement to counter the slogan "Black Lives Matter" with the universalizing retort: "All Lives Matter." "When some people rejoin with 'All Lives Matter,'" Butler explains in the interview,

> they misunderstand the problem, but not because their message is untrue. It is true that all lives matter, but it is equally true that not all lives are understood to matter which is precisely why it is most important to name the lives that have not mattered, and are struggling to matter in the way they deserve. . . . If we jump too quickly to the universal formulation, "all lives matter," then we miss the fact that black people have not yet been included in the idea of "all lives." . . . But to make that universal formulation concrete, to make

that into a living formulation, one that truly extends to all people, we have to foreground those lives that are not mattering now, to mark that exclusion, and militate against it.[1]

The problem with the slogan "All Lives Matter" is that it ignores the extent to which the intelligibility of the collective grouped under the universal quantifier "all" continues to be constituted through an exception in the form of an immanent exclusion: black lives as the very exclusion that founds the intelligibility of the "all." The "all," far from being neutral, appears racialized as nonblack. Viewed from this perspective, the universality affirmed by the "all" merely works to reestablish the hegemony by which a social part founded on the benefits of racial privilege is able to simultaneously project itself onto, and disappear into, the social whole. To the extent that the "all" is constituted through the exclusion of "blackness," the slogan "All Lives Matter" reproduces the root of the problem against which the Black Lives Matter movement is organized: the fact that in a context where race-blind discourse has increasingly become the norm, the seemingly neutral universal still turns out to not be neutral after all, but rather continues to be propped up by ingrained racial exclusion. The social and literal death to which black bodies are exposed does not designate a purely external position made such by a preexisting political field, but rather designates an immanent site that has been externalized, one whose very externalization is central to the creation of that from which it has been expelled. Given its status "as that which stands in a relation of internal exclusion to the hegemonic," one might very well conceive of "blackness" as inhabiting the place of sub-alternity.[2] Its position with regard to a racially charged substantive universality, however, also implies a certain universality for this subaltern position. As a constitutive exclusion, "blackness" marks a paradoxical site that is both foundational to and the weak point of the structure from which it is excluded.

As Butler points out, the slogan "Black Lives Matter" forms part of an attempt to effect a transformation from the perspective of "black lives," one that would create a new context in which "all lives matter."[3] Yet one should be wary of the suggestion that this can be brought about by including the "black" into the "all," by widening the latter's extension. Insofar as any meaningful totality relies on a negative counterfig-ure for its intelligibility, this hope immediately runs up against its own limits—the same limits against which it struggles: the still exclusive status of the "all." In all probability, the creation of an "all" inclusive of black lives would still constitute itself through the exclusion of such figures as the "truly" dangerous criminal, or the undocumented person whose lack of permission to be in the country has made his/her exposure to death official policy, just to name a few possible examples.[4] This is why, as Bosteels reminds us, "[a]ny project to bring this remainder into the political arena . . . runs the risk of always already being nothing more than a reaction formation that as such remains inscribed within the bounds of the existing state of affairs."[5]

The "black" in "Black Lives Matter," then, should perhaps instead be taken to mark a site that resists incorporation, one that "represents an antagonism or demand that cannot be satisfied through a transfer of ownership/organization of existing rubrics"[6]—a site, I would add, that points beyond "blackness" as substantive specificity. Thus, far from being one identity among others, "blackness" can be understood as situated at the limits of identity itself, as the nonidentitarian foundation *and* remainder in the constitution of any identity formation. As the name for the immanent negation of the "all," "blackness" marks the site, and with "Black Lives Matter" calls forth a politics, of the not-all.

Though the focus of this chapter is not directly about the Black Lives Matter movement, the visibility and force it has gained makes it a relevant point of departure through which to introduce some of the basic themes that guide the chapter, namely the possibility of thinking a political collective the consistency of which does not depend on identitarian constructions that formally reproduce the logics against which they struggle. Thus, beyond a coalition between brown, black, and other people of color, what the Black Lives Matter movement prompts us to think, I argue, is the possibility of a singular politics initiated from the nonidentitarian perspective of the not-all—a politics sustained by a collective subject capable of maintaining its nonidentitarian character, its genericity, in the process of its unfolding. Evidence of such a conception can also be found in the Haitian Constitution of 1805, where it is declared that "Haytians shall hence forward be known only by the *generic* appellation of Blacks."[7] More than a racial category, "black" was a political category into which were included white Europeans, such as the German and Polish soldiers, who had fought for the Haitian cause against Napoleon.[8] Accordingly, "black" functioned as a generic political category the inclusion into which was established by participation in anticolonial struggle rather than by ascriptive criteria. Far from simply serving as an example of another racialization of the "all," it named a collective constituted from the perspective of the "not-all"; that is, from the perspective of those upon whose denigration, murder, exploitation, and null political existence the old order had been founded, and thus from the limits of the substantive hegemony of the "all."

Beginning with Freud's work on group psychology and Laclau's theory of populism, I analyze their theorization of how groups are constituted. I focus on the role they attribute to identity and the identification of commonality as necessary for the development of a social bond that allows an aggregate of people (i.e., a crowd) to coalesce into a group. At a basic level, while one of Laclau's main concerns is with "the nature and logics of the formation of collective identities," my concern is with the nature and logic of the formation of nonidentitarian collectives.[9] As an alternative to Laclau's theory of populism, I draw on Badiou's concept of the generic collective, a nonidentitarian collective constituted through the material process that transforms a situation on the basis of an event. The generic collective, moreover, decenters the necessity of an intracollective social bond for its consistency in favor of a process of unbinding the consistency of which is determined by political deduction. The tension between an identitarian conception—which, as I will demonstrate, closely adheres to Lacan's formula for fantasy ($\$ \lozenge a$)— and a generic one is also evinced in Frantz Fanon's writings, particularly around his theorization of nation. In moving between these logics, Fanon's thought inheres in the parallax shift from one to the other. In the concluding section, I return to psychoanalysis and attempt to reformulate the ontological consistency of the generic collective by means of Lacan's formulas of sexuation. While beginning from the female side of the not-all, a political sequence, in its confrontation with the material and symbolic context it seeks to change, runs up against and must appropriate and void a masculine logic of cultural intelligibility in a way that enables it to remain open to the real that functions as both its own cause and the source of its (in)consistency. This hinges on a "hollowed out" discourse or ideology, I argue, that, in giving limited intelligible expression to the political logic that drives it, is still able to void (and thus avoid) the structure of fantasy.

Crowd or Group: Commonality, Identity, and the Generic

With the publication of *Group Psychology and the Analysis of the Ego* in 1921, Freud sought to intervene in the field of mass psychology. Among this field's concerns was the study of the formation and behavior of human collectives, including the psychological dynamics (both individual and collective) at play in these processes. The interest in mass psychology during the late nineteenth and early twentieth centuries, however, was also in many ways a reaction to historical social upheavals like the Paris Commune of 1871 and the French Revolution before it. Intellectuals unsympathetic to revolutionary politics, and weary of the threat of violence and disorder implied by the revolting masses, sought to characterize such collective action in negative, pathological terms.[10]

Writers such as Gustave Le Bon were concerned with the effects of the "crowd" upon individual behavior. Under the influence of the crowd, the individual, in Le Bon's view, often "descends several rungs in the ladder of civilization. Isolated, he may be a cultivated individual; in a crowd, he is a barbarian—that is, a creature acting by instinct."[11] This supposed regression in behavior was also thought to occur at the level of the collective itself. Thus, summarizing Le Bon, Freud reports the characterization of such collectives as impulsive, irritable, led by the unconscious, overriding personal interest, incapable of perseverance, impatient, immune to reason, extremist, unswayed by the constraints of reality, averse to innovation, possessing a desire to be ruled and oppressed by strong leadership, and having an unlimited respect for tradition.[12] At the same time, however, Freud also notes that "under the influence of suggestion groups are also capable of high achievements in the shape of abnegation, unselfishness and devotion to an ideal. While with isolated individuals personal interest is almost the only motive force, with groups it is very rarely prominent. It is possible to speak of an individual having his moral standards raised by a group."[13] Indeed, Freud points to language itself as one example of the collective's creative genius.[14]

In light of such contradictory accounts of collective behavior, Freud suggests that what is actually at stake is the existence of different kinds of collectives. Those that are usually attributed negative characteristics, he posits, are "groups of a short-lived character, which some passing interest has hastily agglomerated out of various sorts of individuals.

The characteristics of revolutionary groups, and especially those of the great French Revolution, have unmistakably influenced their descriptions."[15] On the other end of the spectrum are the stable groups, "which are embodied in the institutions of society."[16] The distinction that Freud proposes makes evident the implicit political judgment of the theorists of mass psychology. As the name "mass psychology" suggests, it is the *masses* as collective phenomenon that figure as one of the field's primary concerns.[17] The negative characteristics attributed to the first kind of collective are in line with a general preoccupation and disdain for the intrusion of the masses into the political field.

Yet what interests Freud is also the question of what holds these collectives together, which leads him to investigate the nature of the constitution of their social bond.[18] He turns to William McDougall, who further contributes to resolving the contradictory character of different collectives by distinguishing between a "crowd" and a "group" proper. A "crowd" is a type of collective with the most minimal and rudimentary level of organization, while a "group" possesses an organizational structure that enables it to achieve a higher degree of stability and temporal continuity.[19] "Before the members of a random crowd of people can constitute something in the nature of a group in the psychological sense of the word, a condition has to be fulfilled," notes Freud:

> [T]hese individuals must have something in common with one another, a common interest in an object, a similar emotional bias in some situation or other, and ("consequently," I should like to interpolate) "some degree of reciprocal influence." . . . The higher the degree of "this mental homogeneity," the more readily do the individuals form a psychological group, and the more striking are the manifestations of a group mind.[20]

Hence, a condition for the transition from crowd to group is the existence of commonality, of something that the members share in common (a common interest, disposition, purpose, or way of thinking) and that brings them together. Yet the existence of commonality is not enough. An additional requirement is that the members themselves raise the perception of their commonality to an idea of the group as a whole. Thus McDougall, who attributes the existence of a "general will" to the organized group, posits that "a collective or general will only exists where some idea of the whole group and some sentiment for it as such exists in the minds of the persons composing it."[21] "The diffusion of this idea among the members of the group, which constitutes the self-consciousness of the group mind, would be of little effect or importance," McDougall argues, "if it were not that, as with the idea of the individual self, a sentiment of some kind almost inevitably becomes organised about this idea and is the main condition of its growth in richness of meaning."[22] Therefore, the idea of the group, as the self-conception of the group qua group, does not simply serve a conceptual function, but rather forms the basis of an *affective* attachment tied to the experience of the group as meaningful. One can begin to note that one is not very far from that ideological identitarian investment that structures our desire, which Lacan will later articulate as fantasy, and which, in bringing a certain degree of consistency to experience as meaningful, is also implicated with the production of affect.[23]

Indeed, Freud finds in the economy of the libido the key to understanding the development of the social bond.[24] As just mentioned, the bond between members of a group begins with the identification of a commonality that anchors their self-conception as a group. This self-conception, moreover, is embodied in an object, which most often takes the form of the leader.[25] In groups that have achieved a level of stability beyond that of the crowd, Freud argues, "*a number of individuals . . . have substituted one and the same object for their ego ideal and have consequently identified themselves with one another in their ego.*"[26] Similar to the way the ego ideal of an individual orients that individual's actions, the substitution by a number of individuals of a common object for their ego ideal provides orientation for the group and is constitutive of group ties by enabling its members to identify with each other.[27] The vertical raising of commonality to the status of an object is the means through which the horizontal identification and social bond between members takes place. What can be referred to as an initially "weak" sense of commonality present in the coming together of individuals into a crowd is made "strong" (i.e., it is transformed into an affective bond) through its embodiment in an object upon which the members bestow their "love" and in relation to which they are able to develop a feeling of the group as such.

The logic of group formation outlined by Freud thus hinges on the mutual reinforcement of commonality, identity, and affect and has continued to have an impact over subsequent theories of human collectives. My interest, however, is not with human collectives in general but with political collectives in particular—with those radical collectives that endeavor to change the organization of human collectives as such. Inasmuch as identity and affect bring coherence to human collectives and help ensure their continuation, it follows that at least part of the work of radical collectives is to intervene at the level of the reproduction of existing structures of identity and affect. But if such a collective undoes identity and affect, the question remains of what holds it together if it is going to exist beyond the temporality of the outburst.

I thus turn to Laclau, who draws on Freud's work on group psychology to theorize hegemony and the constitution of oppositional collectivities.[28] Laclau begins with the "demand" as a basic unit in the constitution of political subjectivities. "[S]ince it is in the nature of all demands to present claims to a certain established order, [the demand] is in a peculiar relation with that order, being both inside and outside it," explains Laclau: "As this order cannot fully absorb the demand, it cannot constitute itself as a coherent totality."[29] The very existence of demands thus attests to the advent of conflict and contradiction within the existing order. This order's inability to satisfy a given demand, in turn, betrays the fact that it is lacking. The demand cannot be accommodated; it cannot be situated in a meaningful way vis-à-vis the existing order's symbolic coordinates. Accordingly, "[a] first form of heterogeneity emerges when . . . a particular social demand cannot be met within that system: the demand is in *excess* of what is differentially representable within it. The heterogeneous is what lacks any differential location within the symbolic order (it is equivalent to the Lacanian real)."[30] The existence of unfulfilled demands, insofar as they bring into play something heterogeneous to established order—akin to the order's own real—is for Laclau the very condition of possibility for politics.[31] A demand's excess over the field of representation also implies its excess beyond its particular content and beyond its relation to a particular social group. The heterogeneity it introduces, in other words, touches upon the nonidentitarian limits of both the demand and the system to which the demand is made.

A demand's nonidentitarian excess over its particularity thus implies a degree of universality that allows for the development of an initial "vague feeling of solidarity" between the various social groups making demands.[32] "What gives them an initial and weak equivalential tie is the mere fact that they all reflect the failure of the institutional system," Laclau states.[33] Yet, as previously seen with the example of the group, something else is required for this initial solidarity to transform into a bond: "[T]he *unity of the equivalential ensemble, of the irreducibly new collective will in which particular equivalences crystallize, depends entirely on the social productivity of a name.* That productivity derives exclusively from the operation of the name *as pure signifier.*"[34] This "pure" or "empty" signifier—a signifier whose particular signified has been reduced to a minimum but which has not been altogether eliminated[35]—is, through the very evacuation of its particularity, able to attain a level of universality that allows it to stand in for unfulfilled demands in general, at the same time that it retroactively crystalizes those demands into a unity of equivalences.

The empty signifier, in its function as the representative of the dislocation of the system as such, produces the unity of the collective (that is, a collective made of unfulfilled demands unified as equivalent) by standing in for its commonality. "[I]f an equivalential link is going to be established between them, some kind of common denominator has to be found which embodies the totality of the series," Laclau points out: "Since this common denominator has to come from the series itself, it can only be an individual demand which, for a set of circumstantial reasons, acquires a certain centrality. . . . This is the hegemonic operation."[36] Like the leader, which for Freud embodied the idea of the group's commonality, the empty signifier is a member of the series that, in the process by which it comes to stand apart from the collective as representative of its commonality, totalizes the equivalential chain into a whole.

Laclau's innovative break with earlier theorists rests on his negative figuring of commonality, because commonality is determined in relation to structural lack. It is a nonsubstantive commonality. What the elements have in common is that each touches upon the order's structural limits, with one of the elements in the chain becoming the representative of this negative commonality by coming to occupy the place of this very lack. Thus, it is crucial "not to conceive of the common denominator expressed by the popular symbol as an ultimate positive feature shared by all the links in the chain," stresses Laclau.[37] Nevertheless, the empty signifier endows this negativity with some degree of consistency since it indexes an emptiness from within the realm of signification.[38]

But even if it is itself positioned at the limits of identity, the very function of the empty signifier raised to the hegemonic position is to transform the equivalential chain into a stable collective by making it coalesce around a discursive identity. Thus, even if the equivalence of the elements is established via a negative commonality, the collective as such acquires a positive identity, which Laclau situates under the signifier of "the people." This discursive identity not only makes the collective intelligible qua collective, but also endows it with internal consistency in the form of a social bond that is stronger than any initial vague feelings of solidarity.[39] In this, Laclau thus remains in line with the theorists of mass psychology, for whom the meaningful representation of the group qua group is necessary for the crowd to transition into a bounded collective.[40]

Insofar as this collective first begins to form through the equivalence of unfulfilled demands, it is evident that its initial coming together presupposes a coalition between marginalized elements,[41] even if Laclau does say that once constituted, popular identity is "something qualitatively more than the simple summation of the equivalential links."[42] Despite being united by a discursive identity into something more than the sum of the collective's parts, each component of the collective remains attached to its particularity. Indeed, if the hegemonic element is the one that has been *most* emptied of its particularity, then this must imply that the demands of the other elements in the equivalential chain continue to maintain a stronger connection to the particularity of their own interests. Consequently, with this self-interest as a persistent point of reference, one can expect identitarian factionalism to reemerge within the collective. This factionalism, moreover, would be based on identities that are themselves a product of, and integral to, the social order they seek to change. One can expect that with each subgroup vying to promote its own interests, the "general will" that collective identity strives to create is bound to disintegrate into the summation of particular wills—what Rousseau designates as the "will of all."[43]

Notwithstanding the vital role of emptiness and negativity in producing the chain of equivalence and quilting it into a group, however, hegemony for Laclau still proceeds upon the desire and promise of social fullness, even if ultimately unachievable. On the one hand, "the popular identity expresses/constitutes . . . the fullness of the community as that which is denied and, as such, remains unachieved."[44] It functions as the embodiment of the failure of society to be sutured into a totality, and does so in a way that gives positive expression to this failure. On the other hand:

> No social fullness is achievable except through hegemony, and hegemony is nothing more than the investment, in a partial object, of a fullness which will always evade us because it is purely mythical. . . .

> The logic of the *objet petit a* and the hegemonic logic are not just sim-
> ilar: they are simply identical. . . . The only possible totalizing hori-
> zon is given by a partiality (the hegemonic force) which assumes the
> representation of a mythical totality.[45]

The identical status of the hegemonic logic with that of the *objet petit a*
points to the fact that Laclau's theory of hegemony reproduces the Lacanian formula for fantasy ($\$ \Diamond a$)—fantasy and hegemony are homologous.

The In Lacanian terms one can say that the equivalential chain is established by the convergence of demands "emptied" of their particular object.
The hegemonic element comes to occupy the place of the missing object,
thereby giving a common orientation to the desire of the elements in the
chain and providing them with a certain unity. Like in Freud's account,
the hegemonic element occupies the place of the object and enables the
identification between members, giving way to the emergence of an affective bond between them. The hegemonic element "completes" the group.
This is what Laclau also terms "radical investment": "making an object
the embodiment of a mythical fullness."[46] Thus, though the equivalential
chain is first brought together by a nonsubstantive universality, the function of the hegemonic articulation is to posit this universality as a mythical fullness.[47] Hegemony, like fantasy, "functions as a construction, as an
imaginary scenario filling out the void."[48]

Accordingly, while the new collective results from the fact that existing order cannot be totalized, it nevertheless finds its own unity by structuring its desire in the direction of just such a totalization. This imaginary
hegemonic scenario, which Laclau refers to as "mythical," can then just
as accurately be called "ideological." The advent of collective identitarian fantasy (i.e., hegemony) is for Laclau that which enables the transformation of a weak equivalence (a crowd) into a strong one (a group).
Given that existing social order, as the product of existing hegemony,
itself functions on fantasy, politics in Laclau's conception is articulated
around the substitution of one fantasy for another. Without dismissing
the possibility that the new hegemony may be significantly different in
content from the old one, such politics nevertheless reproduces a logical form constitutive of the social order against which it struggles (one
built on the suppression of its own real) in a way that also reproduces
some of the same problems that gave cause to this politics in the first
place.[49] While a new hegemony's inability to ever deliver on the fullness

it promises is surely also the condition for future politics, its stoking of the very desire for a total and unalienated experience also makes future politics particularly susceptible to the lure of essentialist nationalist and xenophobic ideologies that may vie to take the new hegemony's place following the disillusionment that will inevitably result when the jouissance it promises remains unfulfilled.[50] In the meantime, its attempt to sustain the fantasy of fullness and cover over its own real will most likely result in the repression of some among its own base—those who do not understand that the time for disorder has passed.

As I have argued, however, Badiou's work allows us to posit the existence of a different form of politics, one that in going through the fantasy does not rely on an identitarian affective bond for its cohesion. In *Metapolitics*, Badiou touches on this question when he remarks:

> [I]f party discipline is genuinely political . . . does it, strictly speaking, constitute a bond? I seriously doubt it. . . . For the real substance of political discipline is quite simply the discipline of process. . . . A genuinely political organisation, or a collective system of conditions for bringing politics into being is the least bound place of all. Everyone on the ground is essentially alone in the immediate solution of problems, and their meetings, or proceedings, have as their natural content protocols of delegation and inquest whose discussion is no more convivial or superegotistical than that of two scientists involved in debating a very complex question. . . . Ultimately, what true politics undermines is the illusion of the bond.[51]

Politics is a process that advances upon a loosening, and even breaking, of existing affective attachments.[52] It proceeds on the basis of an unbinding.[53] Insofar as existing bonds are constituted through fantasy, a political process undermines these bonds to the degree that it pierces fantasy. Indeed, politics here supposes the ability of anyone to think and act beyond the ideologically determined self-interests that define one's social position and identity, whether as an individual or as a member of a social group. "We can therefore say that politics is of the masses, not because it takes into account the 'interests of the greatest number,'" Badiou argues, "but because it is founded on the verifiable supposition that no one is enslaved, whether in thought or in deed, by the bond that results from those interests that are a mere function of one's place."[54] Far from being passive material there to be organized into a group, the masses in revolt give cause to politics as the material force of an initial subjective unbinding (from already constituted groups into a crowd). While Badiou should not be read as arguing for a politics *completely* devoid of affect (a type of "cold" politics reduced to scientific calculation—albeit he does refer to a "faint coldness that involves precision"[55]), his remark also posits the political collective itself as *minimally* bound.[56] This allows the role of the bond in politics to be decentered. The affective bonds that may exist between members are thus central neither to the constitution, cohesion, nor the continuation of the collective. The bond is neither the collective's point of departure nor the glue that holds it together.[57]

In fact, Mladen Dolar draws our attention to several instances in which Freud himself ponders the possibility of a similar kind of collective.[58] In his exchange with Einstein over the causes of war and its possible elimination, for example, after repeating his views on emotional ties and identification, Freud proposes that "[t]he ideal condition of things would of course be a community of men who had subordinated their instinctual life to the dictatorship of reason. Nothing else could unite men so completely and so tenaciously, even if there were no emotional ties between them"; yet immediately he adds, "But in all probability that is a Utopian expectation."[59] If one grants that there are instances when the improbable happens, then perhaps one can liken such a conception to those rare occasions when events occur in the field of politics and a collective is constituted around the logical deduction of its consequences. Badiou refers to such a process as a "truth" or "generic" procedure; I call it "universal citizenship."[60]

The collective constituted around this procedure is indistinct and nonidentitarian. While it can function as a vague subset associated with the trace of an event, what it *is* is beyond the capacity of the situation to define. All that can be said from within the situation is that the elements that belong to this collective *are* in the situation, which is why Badiou identifies the generic set with the truth of a situation's being.[61] The evental trace, as a statement or new possibility, is what remains of the event as absent (because vanished) cause of the procedure. Though the trace provides the collective with its orientation, it functions neither as an image of the group itself nor as a particular part that comes to stand in for the whole. Similarly, while the members of the group hold the trace of an event in common, and the trace may be said to give some positive expression to their "negative" commonality (i.e., inconsistent being), it does not function to totalize a discursive identity around the collective; it says nothing with regard to *who* its members are.

Inasmuch as the collective cuts across all social groups, it also departs from the logic of coalition politics. While it will include elements from every social group, these elements do not function as representatives promoting the interests of their respective group. Like the persistence of particularity in Laclau's equivalential chain, however, self-interest is not fully eliminated in Badiou's conception either.[62] Yet unlike in Laclau's framework, what Badiou terms "disinterested interest" does not need to reconnect back to the interests of the members that comprise the collective, since the event enables a logic not inherently connected to any particular interest—and in this way, I would add, conditions the possibility of a "general interest."[63] What brings the collective together is the *subjective wager* of its members to affirm an event and deduce its consequences.[64] A close reading of Frantz Fanon's writings on the Algerian fight for independence will enable us to see the tensions between the competing logics I have outlined in this section with regard to identitarian fantasy, on the one hand, and a generic politics, on the other.

Fanon and Nation

As a thinker deeply immersed in the struggle for Algerian independence, Fanon was a theorist of politics in action. Like the engaged theorization of the politics of their time by revolutionaries before and after him, Fanon's "Algerian" texts were written in the heat of the political moment, often in spurts of intense creative energy. While the richness of Fanon's texts allows for multiple and sometimes contradictory readings, as has been evinced by the varied commentary on his work, my approach, rather than seeking to fully reconcile the contradictory aspects of Fanon's thought, seeks instead to trace the varied logics at play, with a specific focus on the question of nation.[65]

Regarding the nature of colonial/anticolonial antagonism, for example, there is a frequently observed tension in Fanon between a Manichaean conception and a more nuanced one that undermines the categorical and monolithic opposition between colonizer and colonized. Thus, while on the one hand Fanon affirms that "the Manichaeanism that first governed colonial society is maintained intact during the period of decolonization.

In fact the colonist never ceases to be the enemy, the antagonist, in plain words public enemy number 1," on the other hand he also states:

> It was once all so simple with the bad on one side and the good on the other. . . . On their arduous path to rationality the people must also learn to give up their simplistic perception of the oppressor. . . . They realize that certain colonists do not succumb to the ambient climate of criminal hysteria and remain apart from the rest of their species. Such men, who were automatically relegated to the monolithic bloc of the foreign presence, condemn the colonial war. The scandal really erupts when pioneers of the species change sides, go "native," and volunteer to undergo suffering, torture, and death.[66]

Despite the contradiction between these statements, however, one is tempted to argue that the tension here is only illusory, since, if these statements are inscribed within a temporal and dialectical frame, as the second statement suggests, it is evident that the Manichaean view merely pertains to an initial moment, after which it is undone through the process of struggle. Situating these accounts "within the *moving body* of verbal and representational acts that [constitute] Fanon's dialectical narrative," Ato Sekyi-Otu stresses how "the finality of propositions made in various scenes is rendered suspect."[67] This view, though, more than requiring that the finality of the first statement be rendered suspect, essentially requires that one disregard the first statement altogether. In its attempt to resolve the contradiction by making the second conception develop from the first, what this interpretive move really obliges is a choice of the second over the first, since only the second allows for the dialectical movement that undoes the initial Manichaeanism. Therefore, the contradiction remains.

What I would like to argue is that not only can this contradiction not be reconciled in this way, but such conflicting statements, rather than simply resulting from conceptual inconsistencies in Fanon's work, issue from the existence of different logics simultaneously operating across his writing. In the preceding quotations, then, Fanon describes an identitarian logic that formulates the anticolonial struggle around the Manichaean opposition between colonizer and colonized *and* one that displaces strict identitarian opposition in favor of a splitting of the social and political field based upon individuals' subjective decision on which side to take.

These logics differ from each other with regard to the criteria (preexisting identity for the first, or subjective political decision for the second) by which belonging to either camp in the struggle is established. Yet, as I hope to show, Fanon's thought consists in the very back-and-forth shift between these two logics. Along these lines, the productivity of Fanon's thought can be situated in the nonrelation between them, within a space akin to that of parallax.

According to Kojin Karatani, parallax obtains from the change in perspective between one's point of view and the point of view of others.[68] Rather than trying to form a complete picture of a phenomenon out of both points of view, parallax inheres in the in-between space produced through the very shift in perspective. In the words of Slavoj Žižek, whose own book *The Parallax View* is indebted to Karatani's elaboration of this concept, a parallax view entails the renunciation, when faced with an antinomy, of "all attempts to reduce one aspect to the other (or, even more so, to enact a kind of 'dialectical synthesis' of opposites); on the contrary, we should assert antinomy as irreducible, and conceive the point of radical critique not as a certain determinate position as opposed to another position, but as the irreducible gap between the positions itself."[69] In his Algerian writings, I hold, Fanon's thought inheres in the oscillation between identitarian and nonidentitarian conceptions of nation, between socially predetermined and voluntaristic criteria for belonging, between the old and the new, and between organization and spontaneity.

Accordingly, Fanon's writings evince an identitarian conception of nation, one that I will call "nationalist" and that adheres closely to the logic of fantasy, and another that I will call a "generic nation," whose contours are indeterminate and to which belonging is determined by political choice. This second form of nation, however, is not simply a crowd or the opposite of a group. It is a collective formed through the torsion by which the crowd, which is also to say the masses, brings consistency to its forceful intrusion into history. Generic nation is not just another position. It is the indeterminate collective that sustains the apositionality of the masses in their unbinding.

My approach is thus to read Fanon as himself engaging with and thinking through the different logics at work in the political sequence of which he was a participant. The Manichaean logic of the first conception of nation is gauged when Fanon explains: "Equally victims of the same tyranny, simultaneously identifying a single enemy, the physically

dispersed people is realizing its unity and founding in suffering a spiritual community which constitutes the most solid bastion of the Algerian
Revolution."[70] The Freudian/Laclauian resonance is unmistakable. The
equivalence among members of the colonized population is established in
relation to a common object: "the same tyranny," "a single enemy." Maintaining this object in common allows for mutual identification among
the colonized—identification based on the acknowledgment of equal vic-
timhood and common suffering—and gives way to the affective bond of
a "spiritual community" that functions here as the core for revolutionary politics.[71] Even if the common object here is not one of love but one
of hate or rejection, it is still consistent with Laclau's formulation. In
Laclau's words:

> If I refer to a set of social grievances, to widespread injustice, and
> attribute its source to the "oligarchy," for instance, I am performing
> two interlinked operations: on the one hand, I am constituting the
> "people" by finding the common identity of a set of social claims in
> their opposition to the oligarchy; on the other, the enemy ceases to be
> purely circumstantial and acquires more global dimensions.[72]

Having identified the enemy as the source of conflict, nationalist fantasy
is formed upon the promise of totalization via the enemy's elimination:
"Decolonization unifies this world by a radical decision to remove its
heterogeneity, by unifying it on the grounds of nation and sometimes
race. . . . The minimum demand is that the last become the first," states
Fanon.[73] Though this formulation refers to the initial moments of the
anticolonial movement, one also sees its logic reemerge *after* independence with the coming to power of the national bourgeoisie.[74] Therefore,
even if one grants Fanon's account according to which Manichaeanism is
overcome through the process of anticolonial struggle, one nevertheless
sees a reversion back to it after independence. In this sense, the possible
finality attributed to the account of the displacement of Manichaeanism is
itself rendered suspect. Indeed, Manichaeanism and the identitarian fantasy that supports it, far from being confined to an initial moment that is
dialectically overcome, reappears as a persistent parallel logic.

The national bourgeoisie attains a position of leadership after independence. It is the part of the previously colonized that now stands apart
from the others and orients the postindependence national project. It is

the part that becomes "hegemonic," in Laclau's sense. Its status as a sub-group that has supposedly reduced the particularity of its self-interest to a minimum, however, is immediately put in question. From the moment it comes to power it calls for nationalization, but in name only, since far from "placing the entire economy at the service of the nation or satisfying all its requirements," it merely wants to take over the privileges previously held by the colonists.[75] The national bourgeoisie, in pushing for its self-interested appropriation of wealth and resources, revives a discourse of nationalization and Africanization "tinged with racism."[76] Fanon explains:

> [W]henever this national bourgeoisie has proven to be incapable of expanding its vision of the world, there is a return to tribalism, and we watch with a raging heart as ethnic tensions triumph. Since the only slogan of the bourgeoisie is "Replace the foreigners," and they rush into every sector to take the law into their own hands and fill the vacancies, the petty traders such as taxi drivers, cake sellers, and shoe shiners follow suit and call for the expulsion of the Dahomeans or, taking tribalism to a new level, demand that the Fulani go back to their bush or back up their mountains.[77]

Guided by its own self-interest and narcissism, and unable or unwilling to satisfy the demands of other sectors of the population, the only way the national bourgeoisie is able to attain a modicum of hegemony is by redirecting the frustration felt by the other sectors toward the "foreigners" that remain. "We have switched from nationalism, to ultranationalism, chauvinism, and racism," Fanon describes: "There is a general call for these foreigners to leave, their shops are burned, their market booths torn down and some are lynched."[78] After the national bourgeoisie reveals its inability to bring forth the fullness of a wholly reconciled society, xenophobia reemerges as the blame is shifted onto the foreigner. And here one must note that the slogan "Foreigners must leave" also once served as the zero point of national struggle.[79] Fanon's critique of the national bourgeoisie makes evident that when the hegemonic element disregards the demands of other groups, prior social divisions reemerge, which demonstrates that this "nation" was only ever a coalition of interests that breaks down after independence.

If for Laclau the emptiness of the empty signifier expands with the extension of the equivalential chain, one can nevertheless see that regardless of the scope of this extension, the particular self-interest that remains in the demands of the member turned empty signifier still functions as the ultimate point of reference for its actions. Even if the relative evacuation of its particularity is the condition for other social groups to channel their demands through it, this particularity still serves as the basis for its decisions, and hence implies that any given hegemony will most likely end in the betrayal of the project of which it is hegemonic. This may be especially true of any "bourgeois" hegemony. After all, the historical task of the national bourgeoisie, according to Fanon, can only be "to repudiate its status as bourgeois and an instrument of capital and become entirely subservient to the revolutionary capital which the people represent"; its duty is to "betray the vocation to which it is destined."[80] In other words, the only way in which the national bourgeoisie could play a progressive role would be to reject its very function *as* the national bourgeoisie; it would have to betray itself and its own interests in order to not betray the nation. Yet, given its status as the representative of capital, and thus as the embodiment of capitalist market logic, it cannot but act in its own interest, which is the self-interest that sustains capitalist reason. Indeed, for this very reason Fanon suggests that the national bourgeoisie has never been able to attain sufficient hegemony: "Because it is obsessed with its immediate interests . . . the national bourgeoisie proves incapable of achieving simple national unity and incapable of building the nation on a solid, constructive foundation."[81] This is why from the moment it rises to power its deficient hegemony is compensated for by a turn toward outright domination.[82]

Fanon also signals the existence of a different conception of nation, however. "We want an Algeria open to all, in which every kind of genius may grow," he declares.[83] Contrary to the restrictive nationalist conception, this one remains open. *"For the F.L.N., in the new society that is being built, there are only Algerians,"* Fanon stresses: *"From the outset, therefore, every individual living in Algeria is an Algerian."*[84] In this conception, to say that in the society under construction there are only Algerians is not to say that, as opposed to "foreigners," only Algerians matter. According to this political logic, *everyone* who lives in Algeria is Algerian, which is to say that everyone living there legitimately belongs.

This is a striking departure from the nationalist identitarian formulation that constitutes itself through the exclusion of whatever "foreigners" may live there. To say that everyone in Algeria is Algerian is not to propose a substantive identity but rather to reduce identity to a minimum. "Algerian" is not defined by a substantive property (language, culture, religion, history, etc.) or a combination of such that those who fall within this category are thought to have in common. "Algeria" is here nothing but the proper name of an extension—that is, of a place or territory. It does not define what an "Algerian" is. It only says that to belong to the set "Algeria" makes one an "Algerian," and belonging is determined by location: to live in Algeria is to belong.[85] And the definition of "Algeria" is simply that which belongs to it.[86] Like in mathematical set theory, where its most basic element, the set, is beyond explicit definition, so is the nation in the FLN's conception, as described by Fanon.[87] If with Badiou one takes set theory as ontology, one can say that to the extent that the FLN's formulation coincides with the logic of set theory, implicit in it is an ontological conception of nation.[88] Like a set, nation is extensional in this conception—the nation/set is defined solely by the elements that belong to it. It is defined as "the result of a simple collecting together of previously existent elements, which may or may not share any unifying properties."[89] Consequently, there is nothing keeping the Algerian nation from being multiracial and multireligious.[90]

This extensional determination, however, does not legislate the end of contradiction or antagonism within the nation, as is obvious by the fact that this pronouncement is made in the midst of the Algerian Revolution. The set/nation continues to be subject to a politics aiming to transform social order. Indeed, in Fanon's depiction, the fight against colonialism entails not simply the achievement of national sovereignty, but the transformation of social relations through the very process by which "Algeria" comes to be and sustains itself as an independent nation. And here one arrives at yet another component of this conception of nation: the generic revolutionary collective.

With regard to the Egyptian uprising that overthrew Hosni Mubarak at the beginning of 2011, Badiou writes: "[I]n Egypt the people who had rallied to the square believed they were Egypt; Egypt was the people who were there to proclaim that if, under Mubarak, Egypt did not exist, now it existed, and them with it. . . . Throughout the world it [was] accepted that the people who [were] there . . . [were] the Egyptian people in person."[91] The mass uprising, more than a metonymy of the nation, connects the part to the whole much as in a hologram, where a given part *reproduces* the whole. As a kind of short circuit between the part and the whole, it reproduces the whole without becoming intelligible as a distinct group, much less by functioning as a distinct social group that takes the role of leader. The crowd or masses are the nation *because* of their very amorphousness, because they are an indistinct part of it. This nonidentitarian aspect of the mass uprising is carried over into the collective that comes together to produce and sustain the mass uprising's consequences.

If the nation is conceptualized as a set, then the revolutionary collective is the "generic" subset of this nation in that it gathers together some of everything of the set, thus assembling together some of everything that makes up the nation. Returning to the Algerian context of Fanon's writing, beginning from the position of those who do not count in the colonial order, the fight against colonialism creates a collective that works at the level of universality. Taking the title of perhaps the most well-known of his Algerian texts, *Les damnés de la terre*, from the anthem "L'Internationale" ("Arise, the damned of the earth"), Fanon in his writings traces this logic by following the trajectory laid out in the last verse of the same stanza from which the title originates: "We are nothing, now let's be all." Yet, as I will demonstrate in the following section, the logic of the generic allows one to reformulate the universality implied by this verse: "We are nothing, now let's be not-all."

Hence, in the context of Algeria, one finds that the revolutionary collective that for Fanon is also the nation in action—"[a] nation born of the concerted action of the people"—is formed via a political choice open to all, instead of on identitarian grounds.[92] In addition to the evident example of Fanon himself, a black non-Muslim from Martinique who becomes Algerian after joining the anticolonial struggle, *A Dying Colonialism* contains numerous such examples.[93] Thus is the testimony of Charles Geromini, a member of the European minority in Algeria, who counts himself among the "European students . . . [that] have finally chosen in this war to be Algerians."[94] "I had some fear that I might not be welcomed," Geromini confides at the end of his testimony: "My fear was unfounded. I was welcomed like any other Algerian. For the Algerians I am no longer an ally. I am a brother, simply a brother, like the others."[95] By means of his choice to participate in the fight against colonialism, he ceases to be someone who merely supports the struggle in its overlap with his own position, inclinations, or interests (i.e., an ally), and becomes part of a collective (the Algerian nation), wherein his particular identity as a European minority becomes a matter of indifference with regard to his belonging. Though the reference to brotherhood certainly signals the existence of affect, and the form of sociality it presupposes suggests a masculine homosocial and perhaps even a patriarchal figuration of nation, Fanon shows that notions of brotherhood, gender, and family are also critically reevaluated and transformed through the process of struggle.

Geromini's insistence that his experience is "in no way exceptional" is borne out by the numerous other cases that Fanon mentions, where those usually relegated to the side of the enemy in the nationalist conception are shown to be active supporters of the Algerian cause.[96] Beginning with the surprising declaration that "the most important backing given by Algeria's Europeans to the people's struggle has been and remains that of the settlers," Fanon proceeds to reference the participation of European doctors, nurses, young people, families, politicians, civil servants, and even police officers.[97] He demonstrates that the collective that drives the revolution is composed of a cross section of society. Since it cuts across identitarian categories, it cannot be circumscribed by any particular identitarian designation within the Algerian nation. All one can say is that it is a generic subset of the set/nation called Algeria. As an indistinct subset to which belongs a bit of everything of the nation—one that embodies "the being of the situation as such"—one can say that it *is* the nation in movement.[98] To be "Algerian," then, is to live in "Algeria," but it is also to belong to the generic subset that fights for Algeria's independence and egalitarian transformation.[99] "Algeria" is thus both a set—a given territorial space—*and*, in its revolutionary mode, a generic subset that transforms the set's organizational coordinates. The revolutionary process constitutive of generic nation can therefore be defined as "the collective consciousness in motion of the entire people."[100]

This process also advances through unbinding. Under the signifier not only of independence but of revolution, social relations, as well as relations with technology, science, and even language, are reevaluated and reconfigured according to their implications for egalitarian struggle. From the radio to modern medicine, both of which were previously associated with colonial domination and rejected accordingly, the revolutionary movement appropriates technology and science insofar as they serve the fight and lay the bases for future society.[101] Even the French language— the "language of occupation, a vehicle of the oppressing power [that] seemed doomed for eternity to judge the Algerian in a pejorative way"— acquires new values and is "liberate[d] . . . from its historic meanings."[102]

Fanon's focus on the family with regard to unbinding is particularly significant due to its usual function as a basic unit of sociality and as a site where the social bond tends to be strongest.[103] Thus, simultaneous with the shift from reform to revolution, the "attitude [of the militant son] toward his father and the other members of the family frees itself of everything that proves unnecessary and detrimental to the revolutionary situation. . . . The old stultifying attachment to the father melts in the sun of the Revolution."[104] Even the most immediate social relations are tested for their consistency with the revolutionary project: "The measured and ritual relations of the pre-war period give way to totally new relations."[105] The traditional authority ascribed to the older brother in his relation to the younger one breaks down and both relate to each other beyond previously "automatic ways of behavior."[106] The unconscious compulsion to repeat patterns of behavior that functioned as the basis for old forms of sociality is interrupted in the course of a process that brings into being a new order.[107] Hence, with the participation of young women, "the woman-for-marriage progressively disappeared, and gave way to the woman-for-action."[108] With the daughter involved in assignments that entail "relinquishing the veil, putting on makeup, going out at all hours heaven knew where," and sometimes even having to leave her family to seek safety among the maquis, "the parents no longer dared protest. . . . [The father's] old fear of dishonor had become altogether absurd."[109] Even when confronted by his own lingering concerns, "these questions that were still present to [the father's] mind revealed themselves to be inappropriate and irrelevant."[110] Sexual relations are also transformed as a result of the growing involvement of women in the revolution.[111] Reestablished upon the basis of revolutionary struggle, "[the] couple is no longer an accident but something rediscovered, willed, and built."[112]

The heteronomous and indistinct status of the revolutionary collective against the colonialist state places the effects of the former at the margins of representation and intelligibility.[113] Like the voice from the radio, "the Revolution [is] present 'in the air' in isolated pieces, but not objectively."[114] While the collective is subtracted from representation—which is why it can be referred to as being indistinct—it constantly runs up against culture and knowledge as it strives to transform them. Some degree of intelligibility can emerge at the point where revolutionary politics impinges upon its historical context's linguistic, cultural, and epistemological sources of meaning. "Decolonization, we know, is an historical process," stresses Fanon: "[I]t can only be understood, it can only find its significance and become self-coherent insofar as we can discern the history-making movement which gives it form and substance."[115] What Fanon suggests here is the need for some form of ideology. Decolonization is a historical process in that it occurs in a given place and time and "makes history" in its transformation of one form of order into another. The submission to knowledge of the nature of this transformation, moreover, depends upon the attribution of at least minimal intelligibility to the *direction* in which the process is headed.

Yet it is also apparent how easily the search for intelligibility can again adopt the form of fantasy, especially given people's own anxiety to know what is going on. In the Algerian case, this was exacerbated by the biased nature of official news outlets and the subsequent self-censorship of other, previously trusted, news agencies. Remarkably, it was in the analysis of official accounts that, according to Fanon, Algerians first attempted to gauge the progress of anticolonial struggle. Reading symptomatically, "[i]t was the defenses of the occupier, his reactions, his resistances, that underscored the effectiveness of national action and made that action participate in a world of truth. . . . *Because it avowed its own uneasiness, the occupier's lie became a positive aspect of the nation's new truth.*"[116] Posited retroactively, anticolonial action was determined as the absent cause of the occupier's reaction. Nevertheless, the absence of explicit information continued to produce anxiety in the Algerian people, causing a shift from reading symptomatically to producing their own symptom. As a kind of reaction formation, "[t]he Algerian, . . . especially if he lived in the rural areas, supplemented his absence of news by an absolutely irrational overestimation," explains Fanon: "Reactions occurred at that time which were so disproportionate to objective reality that to an observer they assumed a pathological character."[117]

It is in this context that the radio grew in importance as an alternative source of information. The French authorities, however, quickly caught on and readjusted their tactics by jamming the airwaves. Given the disruption and further fragmentation of the flow of information, it again fell to the listeners to "compensate for the fragmentary nature of the news by an autonomous creation of information."[118] Confronted by content riddled with gaps, the listeners began to fill these gaps with either "the assumed point of view of the political directorate" or with imagined occurrences, such that "[f]rom one village to the next, from one shack to the next, the *Voice of Algeria* would recount new things, tell of more and more glorious battles, picture vividly the collapse of the occupying power."[119] Thus, for these listeners, the task consisted not only in attaching decisive meaning to fragmentary reports, but in "making a deliberate choice . . . between the enemy's congenital lie and the people's own lie, which suddenly acquired a dimension of truth."[120] In this way an "Algerian political idea" was formed and inscribed into "a vast epic" of national struggle.[121] This political idea and the epic of national liberation within which it was put to work were the imaginary and symbolic responses to the anxiety produced by the real of armed conflict.

As with nation, however, Fanon's work reveals another example of an attempt to endow a political sequence with some intelligibility without adopting the same fantasy-form. Indeed, I maintain that this example can be found at the level of Fanon's own discourse, a discourse that precisely does ideological work—with "ideology" conceived in a second sense as that which provides the support that enables people to consist in their capacity as a collective subject. Contrary to nationalist ideology, revolutionary ideology is not a counterfantasy insofar as its function is precisely to maintain an opening toward a future yet to be fully determined, to maintain open the gap in the structure, even as it serves to make coherent some of the future's anticipated contours. What Fanon teaches is that revolutionary ideology, if it is to avoid falling back on reactionary or dogmatic formulations, must endeavor to give some coherence to the irruption and trajectory of antagonism at the same time that it too remains open to and conditioned by it.

Revolutionary ideology must remain open to the real (of) politics that functions as both its own cause and source of (in)consistency. This, I argue, is the form of Fanon's discourse. It endows the contours and trajectory of a revolutionary process with some intelligibility by inserting them within a discourse oriented by the idea of a new humanism, itself built upon a revolutionary national culture. His discourse is open at both ends, however. National culture for him is not the source of an "authentic" national(ist) character, but is rather a nonessentialist material in movement from which a new society is formed under the idea of a new and emancipatory humanism. National culture is the historico-symbolic "material" reconfigured and transformed by the torsion of the revolutionary process.[122] "The liberation struggle does not restore to national culture its former values and configurations," Fanon declares: "This struggle, which aims at a fundamental redistribution of relations between men, cannot leave intact either the form or substance of the people's culture. After the struggle is over, there is not only the demise of colonialism, but also the demise of the colonized."[123] Hence, and again evincing a logic that cuts across colonial Manichaeanism, "[i]n order to achieve this liberation, the inferiorized man brings all his resources into play, all his acquisitions, the old and the new, his own and those of the occupant."[124]

Sexuation, the Party, and "Ideology 2"

> [M]ale and female, like being, are not predicates, which means
> that rather than increasing our knowledge of the subject,
> they qualify the mode of the failure of our knowledge.
>
> JOAN COPJEC, *Read My Desire*

———

IN LIGHT OF THE CENTRALITY given by Freud to "love relationships" in group formation, I would like in this final section to formalize, by means of Lacan's formulas of sexuation, the conception of nonidentitarian revolutionary politics for which I've been arguing throughout.[125] If "love" is assumed to be that through which a multiplicity of individuals or social groups is able to form the One of a collective, Lacan's formulas enable us to productively see the limits of such a conception, while simultaneously offering an alternative formulation of a nonidentitarian collective that is both universal *and* nontotalizable. It is important to note that sexual difference here refers neither to biology nor to the expression of gendered identities, but rather to two ways of thinking a stumbling block or failure immanent to the symbolic.[126]

My approach to the formulas is to read them as ontological formulations that do not relate strictly to sexual difference per se, but that think the limit and failure of structure in different and incompatible ways.[127] On each side is a set of two statements, each of which proposes a particular logic with regard to the constitution of a collective in light of a structural law and its limits (see figure 5.1). Taken together, the statements that make up each side appear to contradict one another. The left side, which Lacan designates as the "male" side, states (1) there exists an element

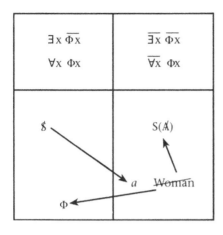

Figure 5.1. Lacan's Formulas of Sexuation; adapted from Jacques Lacan, *Encore, The Seminar of Jacques Lacan Book XX.*

that is not submitted to the phallic function (i.e., to castration, to the law of language that splits the subject, or, for our current purposes, to structural determination), while simultaneously adding that (2) all elements are submitted to the phallic function. Similarly, the right side, which Lacan designates as the "female" side, states (1) there does not exist an element that is not submitted to the phallic function, while adding that (2) not-all elements are submitted to the phallic function.[128]

In stating that all elements are submitted to the law of the structure while adding that there exists an element that is not, the male side posits a collective held together by an exceptional element, one whose jouissance is unrestrained due to its exception from castration. This position is homologous to that of the primal father in Freud. The primal father is the source of law yet is himself free to enjoy without restriction, while the rest of the horde is subjected to the law and its prohibitions.[129] It is thus also homologous to the position of the sovereign, or of God. Lacan associates the logic of the male side, moreover, with that of semblance and meaning. "What analytic discourse brings out is precisely the idea that . . . meaning is based on semblance," he explains: "If analytic discourse indicates that . . . meaning is sexual, that can only be by explaining its limit."[130] Since only the male side designates a determinate limit (as I will show), then to the extent that meaning (and also knowledge) is constituted through the determination of limits, it is constituted through a masculine logic. Semblance, meaning, and knowledge side with the male and are made possible by the same fantasy structure. This is why underneath, $ appears in relation to *a*, essentially reproducing the formula of fantasy ($ ◊ *a*), where *a* is the object through which the subject attempts to fill his lack. Accordingly, the male side aligns itself with the constitution of the fantasy of presence. The exceptional element that escapes determination is in this way accounted for from within the law in a way that completes the latter by means of this very exception.[131] The male side expresses the logic of identity, furthermore, to the extent that the latter is constituted via the fantasy of completeness.

The female side proposes a different logic through which to think the lack of structural determination. The second statement on this side tells us that not-all elements are submitted to the law of the structure, while the first tells us that there does not exist an element that is not submitted to this law. Contrary to the male side, which posits the limit as determinate exception, the female side posits it as indeterminacy and subtraction. This is why for Lacan "Woman" as such does not exist, as is expressed in the graph by placing her under erasure (~~Woman~~), and her inexistence is correlated to both the lack in the Other, S(Ⱥ)—that is, to the fact that the structure is incomplete—and to the signifier of the phallus (Φ) as a signifier without a signified.[132]

It is important, however, to delve more deeply into why the negation of the universal quantifier on the female side ($\sim\forall x\ \Phi x$) does not necessarily imply the affirmation of a negative existential ($\exists x\ \sim\Phi x$). I quote Lacan at length:

In [Aristotelian] logic, on the basis of the fact that one can write "not-every (*pas-tout*) x is inscribed in Φx," one deduces by way of implication that there is an x that contradicts it. But that is true on one sole condition, which is that, in the whole or the not-whole in question, we are dealing with the finite. Regarding that which is finite, there is not simply an implication but a strict equivalence. . . . The not-whole becomes the equivalent of that which, in Aristotelian logic, is enunciated on the basis of the particular. There is an exception. But we could, on the contrary, be dealing with the infinite. Then it is no longer from the perspective of extension that we must take up the not-whole (*pas-toute*). . . .

Now, as soon as you are dealing with an infinite set, you cannot posit that the not-whole implies the existence of something that is produced on the basis of a negation or contradiction. You can, at a pinch, posit it as an indeterminate existence. But, as we know from the extension of mathematical logic, that mathematical logic which is called intuitionist, to posit a "there exists," one must also be able to construct it, that is, know how to find where that existence is.[133]

For Lacan, then, the collective on the female side is infinite. The reason that the statement "not-all elements are submitted to the structural function" does not imply that "there exists an element that is not submitted to said function," is because as an infinite collective, it can be taken in a nonextensional manner. In other words, rather than implying that since not-all apples are red, there exists an apple that is not red (which would be the consequence if one takes it in extension), it should be read as implying either that no apple is completely red *or* that there exists at least one apple that is not completely red.[134] To say that not-all elements are submitted to the law of the structure is thus to acknowledge that the law is incomplete, that it is "not-all." As the example demonstrates, moreover, the limit of this infinite set, unlike the male side that sets its limit through a definite (even if inaccessible) exception, is indeterminate. The collective on the female side is "without perimeter."[135]

Yet it is precisely with Lacan's conception of the infinite that Badiou takes issue. He reads the infinity posited by Lacan on the female side in its (non)relation to the male side. "The infinite prohibits the relation between the two enjoyments from being dialectical, from being the unity of contraries, and ultimately from being a relation. The infinite is here a power of dissymmetry," Badiou explains: "The impossible relation of the for-all of man and the feminine not-all is inscribed in the division of enjoyment: neither can be actualized as the negation of the other, because actually the infinite is by no means the negation of the finite. It is its *inaccessible* determination."[136] Indeed, in the final sentence of the preceding excerpt, Lacan seems to point out that according to intuitionist logic, for the existence of the infinite to be affirmed it must be shown to be constructible—one must be able to reach it through an operation that enables a jump from the finite to the infinite. But such a jump is impossible. The infinite is nonconstructible, which is why intuitionist logic rejects the existence of actual infinity and settles for its conception as inaccessible horizon or "negative virtuality within the finite."[137] Hence, in Badiou's reading, Lacan turns to the infinite only to effectively do away with it by reducing it to a fiction within the realm of the finite, thus exhibiting a pre-Cantorian conception of infinity.[138] Badiou concludes from this that

"Lacan had no concept of the infinite other than in terms of operational inaccessibility."[139]

Alenka Zupančič, on the other hand, suggests that while one can indeed find a conception of infinity as inaccessible limit in Lacan, one can also find an axiomatic (and thus post-Cantorian) conception of actual infinity as well. The former sides with the "male," while the latter, with the "female" side of the formulas. Thus when Lacan gives the example of Achilles and the tortoise, wherein Achilles can catch up with the tortoise only at an infinite limit beyond reach, it is clear that he is referring to the male's mode of enjoyment.[140] The tortoise is "the incarnated consequence . . . of the exception to the function of castration. The tortoise is not Woman but *a*," Zupančič rightly insists.[141] She goes on to propose that in at least two instances Lacan does affirm the existence of actual infinity. One of those instances is found in the same extended excerpt, where the statement "as soon as you are dealing with an infinite set" can be taken as an axiomatic affirmation of infinity associated with the not-all.[142] "But it is the second step which is crucial," insists Zupančič: "In it, Lacan does not deny every existential consequence (or implication) of the not-all; what he denies is the existential consequence of an *exception* at the level of this set that he calls the not-all. It is not the existence of the not-all that is at stake, but the existence of an exception to the not-all."[143] In this way, it is not the existence of actual infinity that he denies, but rather the determinate existence of an exception. The final sentence, then, rather than suggest an overriding intuitionist conception of infinity that denies actual infinity, can instead be read as breaking with intuitionist infinity to the extent that the indeterminate existence implied by the not-all is nonconstructible. "This indetermination," explains Lacan, "is suspended between $\exists x$ and $\sim\exists x$, between an existence that is found by affirming itself and woman insofar as she is not found."[144] In its suspension between existence and nonexistence, this indetermination can be said to "inexist." Indeterminacy is attributed both to the limit and to the set, since without a determinate limit the set itself is indeterminate. And the positing of an indeterminate and nonconstructible set does not imply a return to a notion of infinity as inaccessible horizon of the finite because we are axiomatically already at the level of the infinite. Furthermore, it is "possible to show that Badiou's notion of the universal as universal singularity is very close to Lacan's notion of the not-all," argues Zupančič: "They both include a certain 'for all' [*pour tous*] (in Lacan's case, in the negative form of: 'there is no x which would be exempt from the function Φx') and, at the same time, they exclude any notion of totality."[145] Indeed, given that Badiou's universal singularity corresponds to the generic set, Zupančič's point is borne out by the fact that Badiou chooses ♀ as the symbol for the generic set itself.[146]

One can thus read the male and female sides as posing two different and incompatible formulations of universality. The male side strives to construct an all-encompassing universal, a universal that is meaningfully intelligible. Yet it also demonstrates the exception as its condition of (im)possibility. The exception is that through which totalization is established—it allows for its completion by internally accounting for its limit—yet this very exception simultaneously posits an element that is excluded from the universal class and thus signals an existence that precisely undermines this universality; this, I would note, is the paradoxical status of both the sovereign *and* "blackness" with which I began this chapter. This is why "all fantasies are dual, organized like a Möbius strip, containing both a hypothesis as to what must be gained in order to surmount lack *and* a hypothesis as to what caused the loss of that object which would complete him."[147] The fantasy, via the various objects that come to stand in for *objet a*, posits both what is necessary to complete the structure and why order continues to be plagued by inconsistency—that stubborn remainder that it incessantly tries, but constantly fails, to fully exclude. It is on the female side, rather, that we get a universality without a determinate exception, one that remains nontotalizable. "[I]t is only on the right (female) side of the formulas that the function of castration becomes universal, while losing at the same time every reference to totality, to all," Zupančič asserts.[148]

The universal on the right side is established from the perspective of the indeterminacy of limits, from the not-all that is the condition for the new. And here one can return to Freud's suggestion regarding the "dictatorship of reason" as a means to unite a collective even in the absence of libidinal bonds among its members. At first glance Freud's suggestion seems to go against his main discovery: the unconscious as that which undermines the very subject of reason. But, as Dolar argues, "Freud never described [the unconscious] as something simply opposed to reason, but rather as a glitch of reason, its slip, its inner torsion."[149]

"Reason is ambiguously described not simply in terms of the agency of repression," Dolar continues elsewhere, "but rather in terms of the repressed: as that which will always make itself heard, however much we try to suppress it."[150] Thus, the unconscious is not "unreasonable," but marks the site of an agency that inheres back upon conscious reason. The glitch makes evident that conscious reason is not-all and is the condition necessary for another reason—a dictatorship of reason like the dictatorship of the proletariat—to emerge through a torsion initiated from its very site.

This is why, in the context of politics, "it is from [the gap of the] nonrelation that politics as such, which is to say mass politics, is born."[151] The indistinct mass or crowd is the evental condition for revolutionary politics. Revolutionary politics as such is mass politics because the reason it produces as it traverses the situation is conditioned on the masses' evental appearance. And here it might do well to recall that Freud's "group" psychology can also be translated as "mass" psychology. In placing the emphasis on the "mass" instead of on the "group," one can counter the spontaneous reading of Freud—which simply places the mass at the origin of an artificial group—by instead highlighting how the mass itself evinces the unbinding of groups necessary for political change.[152] Thus, if one supplements Lacan's formulas with an event, the trace of which could very well be the Φ in the lower portion as the only mark left by the event after it has vanished, then one can designate the place of the not-all as the site from which a new order, a new reason, can be made to consist.[153] Further, one can designate the process that brings into being this new consistency as an act of will.[154] It is *because* we are universally castrated—that is, because there does not exist an x that is not castrated, and thus because we are all split, at the same time that the mode of this split is not totalizable under the rule of structure—that we can will. Far from disavowing the split of castration, the will inheres in this very split.

In "Fanon and Political Will," Peter Hallward asserts that "[p]olitical will is thought through: it subsumes a 'spontaneous' enthusiasm or rebellion in an organized mobilization or disciplined campaign."[155] Indeed, organization is necessary since the "passionate outburst in the opening phase, disintegrates if it is left to feed on itself," Fanon warns.[156] He is clear that rebellion cannot sustain itself without some form of structure, and especially so given the inevitability of the colonialist backlash.[157]

"The leaders of the insurrection realize that any peasant revolt, even on a grand scale, needs control and guidance," he insists: "They, therefore, must transform the movement from a peasant revolt into a revolutionary war. They discover that in order to succeed the struggle must be based on a clear set of objectives, a well-defined methodology and above all, the recognition by the masses of an urgent timetable."[158] Along these lines, Fanon declares: "A country which really wants to answer to history . . . must possess a genuine party."[159] The requirements of structure in the form of leadership, guidance, and discipline, which are necessary for the outburst to consist as process, bring with them a logic that leans toward the "male" side. For the revolutionary transformation of social relations to continue during the anticolonial struggle and after independence, "there must be a concept of man, a concept about the future of mankind," Fanon stresses.[160]

Yet the party that Fanon envisions is radically open, "decentralized to the limit," and must avoid becoming one with the state.[161] While the party plays an important role in educating the people, "[f]or the people the party is not the authority but the organization whereby they, the people, exert *their* authority and will."[162] The party and the people thereby constitute themselves and each other in their mutual determination. Though for all the influence that the party exerts over the people, for all the necessary structure the former provides the latter, it is the latter in its capacity for mass action that exerts a stronger determination over the former. "The party must be the direct expression of the masses," Fanon argues: "In order to arrive at this notion of party we must first and foremost rid ourselves of the very Western, very bourgeois, and hence very disparaging, idea that the masses are incapable of governing themselves."[163] If the party is the most organized part of the collective held together by the trace of mass revolt—which is to say that it is the most organized part of the revolutionary nation—one can also say that it too is punctured by the masses and must endeavor to maintain the gap open *within itself* as much as its very reason for being is to maintain open the breach made evident by the mass revolt in the first place.[164] The initial trace of the masses lives in the gap in the party, a gap through which the masses continue to inhere upon the party's own trajectory and the postevental trajectory altogether. Mass action is thus the real as both absent cause of the party and the persistent source of its own (in)consistency. Against the inertia toward closure from the masses that often comes with institutionalization, the masses continuously demonstrate that the party, too, is "not-all." That the party must remain open to the masses means that it must remain open to its own conditions, conditions that continue to inhere back upon the party, forcing it to continually change and adjust.[165] Revolutionary will thus comes to be in the precarious disjunction between organizational structure and mass action. Consequently, one must posit the Two as the numericality of the (non) relation between the masses and the party.[166]

The politics of a revolutionary nation proceeds in the disjunction between the masses in movement (the agency of the not-all) and the party (the organizational structure that leans toward the "male" in its logic). The masses' intervention is not carried out in the name of a future potential, however, but on the basis of the actuality of their "infinite humanity."[167] They puncture a hole in the party like revolutionary politics punctures a hole in fantasy and truth in knowledge: "The combat waged by a people for their liberation leads them . . . either to reject or to explode the so-called truths sown in their consciousness by the colonial regime, military occupation, and economic exploitation," Fanon declares.[168] To the extent that these "so-called truths" are central to the way in which the police logic of the colonial state organizes the field of meaning, Fanon registers the effects of revolutionary politics upon this field when he notes: "What we have witnessed is a radical transformation of the means of perception, of the very world of perception."[169] In this way, the concept of man and of the future of mankind is not simply the creation of another fantasy. Basing itself on the actuality of "infinite humanity," it does not posit knowledge that will be in the future, but anticipates knowledge that will have been in the now. The latter can be thought of as "ideology 2 (torsion-coherence)" that pierces the fantasy-form of "ideology 1 (totality-repetition)."[170] Undermining the fantasy structure of knowledge that ensures the repetition of existing forms of social relations, revolutionary ideology aids the advent of a new consistency through a torsion initiated from the site of the not-all, a torsion through which we can create what will have been, and can do so from within a process very much in formation. Hence, one can also note the importance of the ideological work of the party in preventing people themselves from falling back upon fantasy in the face of their own anxious encounter with the real, as was seen in the case of the Algerian people's reaction to the lack of reliable information.

Thus, as evinced with Fanon's own discourse, a discourse can exist that brings some consistency to the antagonistic trajectory of revolutionary politics in its torsion against existing order, knowledge, and meaning. Badiou indicates a similar function for Marxism and psychoanalysis. "The Marxist analysis in terms of class is isomorphous with the Lacanian analysis in terms of truth," he argues: "Both cases require torsion, since the truth cannot be said all. . . . This means that it must be said not-all. That is, it must be said in the guise of the subject: hysteric for the one, revolutionary for the other. 'Proletariat' is the political name of the truth that is not-all."[171] Marxism and psychoanalysis can then only half-say the truth of which they speak, not just because language itself fails to capture it "all," but because truth as such is not-all—it resists totalization.

Along similar lines, Lacan himself stresses "the maintenance, within analysis, of a conflict situation, necessary to the very existence of analysis," especially against ego psychology's attempt to reduce analysis to the reconciliation of the ego with its environment, and thus to the fantasy of complementarity.[172] Indeed, "[i]f Marxism and psychoanalysis can still be called scientific against all odds, it is not because of the objective delimitation of a specific and empirically verifiable instance or domain of the social order," argues Bosteels, "but because they link a category of truth onto a delinking, an unbinding, or a coming-apart of the social bond in moments of acute crisis."[173] Neither Marxism nor psychoanalysis, then, can be said to constitute a "worldview" that aims to merely explain a given state of affairs.[174] Rather, as "doctrines of the intervening subject," they attempt to bring consistency to a thought/practice that inheres in the place of disjunction.[175] Fanon's Algerian writings, along with Julia de Burgos's "To Julia de Burgos" and Oscar "Zeta" Acosta's *The Revolt of the Cockroach People*, should be read in the same register.

I now return to the Black Lives Matter movement and its capacity to produce a collective politics around the fact that not-all lives matter. This would not deny the systemic racism that exposes black lives and the lives of other people of color to a heightened threat of death. To the contrary, it would fight this very system from the perspective of its universalizable limits: "blackness" not as counteridentity, but as universalizable nonidentity. Rather than functioning as a new empty signifier capable of producing a new identitarian hegemony, "blackness" can index the indistinction proper to a politics of the not-all, a politics that has and can once again deserve the name of universal citizenship. This would enable us to avoid falling back into a logic of addition where to black lives would be progressively added Latina/o lives, Native American lives, LGBTQ lives, (undocumented) immigrant lives, Muslim lives, nonhuman lives, and so on, in the hope that once counted, all lives would matter. The time has come to revive the existence of a generic revolutionary nation and a universalism of the not-all built on an egalitarian logic that cuts through, unbinds, and transforms the structures that produce social order as we strive to create a postcapitalist present.

NOTES

1. Derrida, *Beast and Sovereign*, 31.
2. Freud, *Civilization*, 83; Derrida, *Beast and Sovereign*, 31.
3. Freud, *Civilization*, 83.
4. Viego, *Dead Subjects*, 58.
5. Ruda, "Remembering," 151.
6. I analyze Lacan's formulas of sexuation in chapter 5.
7. Dolar, "Freud," 22.
8. Dolar, "Freud," 22.
9. For a critique of the "democratic drive" in favor of "communist desire," see Jodi Dean, *Communist Horizon*. While I agree with Dean's critique of the drive as a model for political subjectivity (see chap. 1 of this text), I also seek to distance myself from desire as an adequate alternative, at least to the degree that it is constituted through fantasy.
10. Zupančič, *Odd*, 47.
11. Zupančič, *Odd*, 49–50.
12. Ruda, "Remembering," 146.
13. Arendt, "Decline," 299.
14. Arendt, "Decline," 291–292.
15. Arendt, "Decline," 293.
16. Arendt, "Decline," 297.
17. For a few examples of different theorizations of citizenship, see the essays included in Oboler, *Latinos and Citizenship*; Torres, Mirón, and Inda, *Race, Identity, and Citizenship*; Rocco, *Transforming Citizenship*; Ong, *Flexible Citizenship*.
18. Rosaldo, "Cultural Citizenship," 37.
19. Rosaldo, "Cultural Citizenship," 27; Flores, "Citizens," 258.

20. Flores, "Citizens," 276.

21. Flores, "Citizens," 265.

22. Flores, "Citizens," 262.

23. Flores, "Citizens," 267.

24. Flores, "Citizens," 268.

25. Flores, "Citizens," 268.

26. Flores, "Citizens," 263–264. Indeed, "undocumented" in Flores's essay is synonymous with "Mexicano."

27. Flores, "Citizens," 267 (my emphasis).

28. Flores, "Citizens," 276 (my emphasis).

29. Flores, "Citizens," 268, 273.

30. Flores, "Citizens," 262.

31. Zupančič, *Odd*, 60.

32. Zupančič, *Odd*, 59.

33. Moreiras, *Exhaustion*, 4.

34. Bosteels, "Antagonism," 149.

35. Moreiras, *Exhaustion*, 268 (emphasis in the original).

36. Althusser, "Ideology," 116.

37. Moreiras, *Exhaustion*, 292; Laclau, "Empty Signifiers," 38.

38. Moreiras, *Exhaustion*, 293.

39. G. Williams, *Other Side*, 149. Yet with the publication of *Posthegemony: Political Theory and Latin America*, it is Jon Beasley-Murray who has probably become the theorist primarily identified with this term. Beasley-Murray, however, begins by distancing himself from the deconstructive "labor of the negative" characteristic of the mode of posthegemony proposed by Williams and Moreiras, opting rather for habit, affect, and multitude as a way out of the game of hegemony and subalternity (*Posthegemony*, xiv). While I share Beasley-Murray's insistence on an affirmative project that requires a new figure of a collective subject, universal citizenship as I formulate it entails a rupture with habit stemming from the flight of thought rather than of affect (cf. *Posthegemony*, 228). On the other hand, while the multitude also undoes distinctions between identity and difference, Beasley-Murray's likening of the multitude to Spinoza's Substance seems to make of it a godlike figure, which is very different from the thought of being that guides my project: being as the radical dissemination of the One (Beasley-Murray, *Posthegemony*, 234–235; G. Williams, "Subalternist"; Hallward, *Badiou*, 6–10, 62, 149).

40. G. Williams, *Other Side*, 149; G. Williams, "Subalternist." More recently, Abraham Acosta has proposed "illiteracy" as a concept and mode of analysis that also aims to bring to the fore the radically democratic implications of deconstructive subalternist thought. In reading moments of unintelligibility in the social text and theorizing the democratic effects that obtain when such moments suspend

the administrative logics of political reason, Acosta can be seen as a more direct heir to the continued theorization of the strand of posthegemony first proposed by Williams and Moreiras—even while Acosta does not articulate his project in terms of "posthegemony" and Williams and Moreiras have themselves turned to the notion of "infrapolitics." In Acosta's formulation, "illiteracy" neither refers simply to the inability to read and write nor aims to privilege speech or orality over writing (A. Acosta, *Illiteracy*, 9–10). Illiteracy, rather, "is what emerges when a regime of sensibility encounters 'zones of indistinguishability' between identity and difference, inside and outside, proper and improper, truth and error," explains Acosta: "[It] names what must be excluded . . . in order for reading to happen" (11). Illiteracy is thus the name for what occurs when the conceptual and categorical distinctions constitutive of a given order break down, an occurrence that must be prohibited as the very condition for meaningful signification to take place. In line with deconstructive accounts of subalternity and posthegemony, illiteracy is the short circuit that results from "the return of the constitutive repression that makes knowledge possible" (11). It is in this way that illiteracy, too, is situated at the limits of knowledge and representation.

41. Beverley, *Latinamericanism*, 27.

42. Beverley, *Latinamericanism*, 110, 30–31, 40–41.

43. Beverley, *Latinamericanism*, 59 (emphasis in the original).

44. Bosteels, "Antagonism," 155.

45. Moreiras, *Exhaustion*, 284–285. This underlying consensus that nevertheless sustains their theoretical and political differences thus creates a certain inverse symmetry between both positions, to the degree that Moreiras and Williams argue for subalternity and posthegemony and Beverley for hegemony and postsubalternism (Beverley, *Latinamericanism*, 8–9, 111).

46. For other recent works that bring Badiou into dialogue with Latina/o studies see Michael Dowdy's *Broken Souths* and Joanna Swanger's *Radical Social Change*.

47. Gallego, *Chicana/o Subjectivity*, 4.

48. Gallego, *Chicana/o Subjectivity*, 32–33.

49. Gallego, *Chicana/o Subjectivity*, 27.

50. Badiou, *Being and Event*, 432. See also Žižek, *Sublime Object*, 77.

51. Badiou, *Being and Event*, 386.

52. Badiou, *Being and Event*, 339 (emphasis in the original).

53. Badiou, *Being and Event*, 339 (emphasis in the original).

54. Badiou, *Theoretical Writings*, 124–125. It is this aspect of Badiou's framework that Gallego ignores when he states, "Badiou's theory of the subject begins with a truth made evident by an event that defies the laws of its situation" (*Chicana/o Subjectivity*, 30). In reducing the notion of truth to the void itself, Gallego threatens to overlook the function of the generic procedure and

the constitution of the generic multiple, both of which I consider to be Badiou's most important contributions to postidentity theory.

55. Badiou, *Theoretical Writings*, 127. For a more thorough explanation of why a generic subset is indiscernible, see Badiou, *Being and Event*, 367–371.

56. Badiou, *Theory of the Subject*, 128. Badiou also addresses his relationship to Marxism and the Marxist critique of capitalism in *Rebirth*, chap. 1, "Capitalism Today."

57. Badiou, *Theory of the Subject*, 129; Badiou, *Ethics*, 105–106.

58. Badiou, *Theory of the Subject*, 48; Bosteels, *Badiou and Politics*, 330.

59. Quoted in Bosteels, *Badiou and Politics*, 330.

60. See Harvey, *Seventeen Contradictions*, 35, 51; Karatani, *Transcritique*, 23–25, 298–301.

61. Hallward puts forth a similar critique in *Badiou*, 283–284. Gavin Walker does an excellent job of tracing Badiou's rejection of "economic" Marxism to the critique conducted in the 1970s by the Union des Communistes de France Marxiste-Léniniste (UCFML, to which Badiou belonged) against the adherence of the French Communist Party (PCF) to state-monopoly capitalism theory, which held, among other things, that a transition to socialism would result from within the development of capitalism itself and placed the regulatory state at the center of politics (Walker, "Field of Operation," 53–55, 57). While Badiou rejects these two tenets, he nevertheless seems to ignore the fact that the UCFML's own political line, which also privileged politics over economics, was itself informed by economic analysis. Indeed, according to the UCFML's Groupe Yenan-Économie, their objective was "to scientifically destroy the revisionist theory of the structural crisis of so-called state-monopoly capitalism, but also the ultra-left theory in which the crisis is *solely* political" (quoted in Walker, "Field of Operation," 56; emphasis in the original). Thus in too severely separating economics from politics Badiou risks mirroring the PCF's mistake from the other side. That is, while the PCF focused on the economy at the expense of a heterogeneous politics, Badiou risks focusing on the latter at the expense of a sustained analysis of the former.

62. Badiou, *Ethics*, 27.

63. Badiou, *Sarkozy*, 66–69.

64. Badiou, *Being and Event*, 148.

65. Badiou, *Metapolitics*, 76.

CHAPTER 1: CAUSE AND CONSISTENCY

1. Badiou, *Metapolitics*, 78.

2. Habermas, "Citizenship," 258; Hobsbawm, *Nations*, 19–20.

3. Beiner, "Introduction," 3; Rocco, *Transforming Citizenship*, 16; Shafir, *Citizenship Debates*; Bellamy, *Citizenship*, 71.

NOTES TO PAGES 25–29   197

4. Žižek, *Sublime Object*, 81; Kymlicka and Norman, "Return," 304.

5. Badiou, *Theory of the Subject*; Bosteels, *Badiou and Politics*, 87, chap. 8; Bosteels, "Nonlaw," 1908–1909, 1912–1913.

6. Badiou, *Theory of the Subject*, 262.

7. Badiou, *Theory of the Subject*, 133.

8. Of which the interval between terms is both the mark of the absent cause that gave rise to them and the place of the subject (Badiou, *Theory of the Subject*, 134).

9. Bosteels, *Badiou and Politics*, 84.

10. Bosteels, *Badiou and Politics*, 85; Badiou, *Theory of the Subject*, 184.

11. Badiou, *Theory of the Subject*, 136.

12. Badiou, *Theory of the Subject*, 127.

13. Evident here is the way in which Badiou anticipates Žižek in distinguishing between an earlier and a later Lacan, in emphasizing the dialectical mode of Lacan's thought, and in understanding the Lacanian real in political terms—in this latter case also anticipating Ernesto Laclau and Chantal Mouffe's conception of antagonism as the real in *Hegemony and Socialist Strategy* (Bosteels, "Translator's Introduction," xiv–xv; Bosteels, *Badiou and Politics*, 68–69, 86; Badiou, *Theory of the Subject*, 114–115, 133, 136, 226–227).

14. Badiou, *Theory of the Subject*, 24.

15. To put this more concretely, Alenka Zupančič points out that "capitalist production (also in its social dimension) is a constant production of otherness, and a constant valorization of this otherness, of its transformation into value," in a way that makes the demand for the recognition of otherness and the inclusion of difference perfectly compatible with the structures of domination and exploitation that must be dismantled (Zupančič, "Surplus Enjoyment," 174).

16. Badiou, *Theory of the Subject*, 24. Cf. Frantz Fanon with regard to the final outcome of anticolonial struggle: "After the struggle is over, there is not only the demise of colonialism, but also the demise of the colonized" (Fanon, *Wretched*, 178).

17. Badiou, *Theory of the Subject*, 228 (emphasis in the original).

18. Badiou, *Theory of the Subject*, 232.

19. Badiou, *Theory of the Subject*, 231.

20. At worst, one can hear in Lacan's logic echoes of the claim that any attempt to change society will only end in reinforcing the forces of oppression, and at best (though still problematic), that communism can be the outcome of the inner workings of capitalism.

21. Balibar, "Philosophy," 313, 318–319. The first tension Balibar points out stems from the "duality of interpretations of the idea of a democratic constitution of rights, expressed in the competition between the notions of fundamental rights . . . and that of popular sovereignty or legislative and constituent 'general will'" (313). This tension is thus the result of competing interpretations of the democratic establishment of a sociopolitical order founded on modern rights,

where the first side understands the inaugural democratic act as instituting a set of rights grounded upon a substantive pre- or extrapolitical source (be it God, Nature, Man, or a moral sphere), while the second understands rights to be the prescriptive outcome of the democratic act itself as an act of autolegislation. The notion of fundamental rights here tends to side with the liberal tradition of natural rights, while the notion of popular sovereignty—with its nod to Rousseau's notion of "general will"—tends to side with the civic republican tradition (316). Consequently, each contending vision provides an equally contending perspective on "how a continuous 'foundation' and consequently a *guarantee* for the democratic constitutional order can be provided" (314; emphasis in the original). The second tension that Balibar identifies, which also tends to coincide with the liberal/republican distinction, is that "man," upon being constituted as the ultimate foundational reference, "is immediately *divided* into two opposing significations": man as *proprietor* and man as *communitarian* man (314; emphasis in the original). This split indeed seems to derive from the first tension to the extent that the liberal notion of rights takes them to be a God-given or natural attribute of the individual, while the republican notion of popular sovereignty takes rights to be predicated on the collective will of the community—furthermore, Balibar suggests that we refer to the liberal and republican conception of man respectively as "individual" and "subject" (314).

22. Balibar, "Philosophy," 314 (emphasis in the original).

23. Balibar, "Philosophy," 314 (emphasis in the original).

24. See also Žižek, "Robespierre," vii–xxxix.

25. Žižek, *Lost Causes*, 417.

26. Along these lines, Žižek argues, "'Dictatorship' does not mean the opposite of democracy, but democracy's own underlying mode of functioning—from the very beginning, the thesis on the 'dictatorship of the proletariat' involved the presupposition that it is the opposite of other form(s) of dictatorship, since the entire field of state power is that of dictatorship. When Lenin designated liberal democracy as a form of bourgeois dictatorship . . . [w]hat he meant is that the very *form* of the bourgeois-democratic state, the sovereignty of its power in its ideologico-political presuppositions, embodies a 'bourgeois' logic. One should use the term 'dictatorship' in the precise sense in which democracy is also a form of dictatorship, that is, as a purely *formal* determination" (Žižek, *Lost Causes*, 412; emphasis in the original).

27. Žižek, *Lost Causes*, 416 (emphasis in the original).

28. Žižek, *Lost Causes*, 416.

29. Žižek, *Lost Causes*, 413.

30. I think it worth emphasizing again that even though in this text Žižek's emphasis is indeed on violence, here and in the discussion that follows, I use the word "force" instead of "violence" in order to suggest that while force can

certainly express itself through violence, the former is more encompassing of other "noncommunicational" forms of confrontation that are nonetheless not violent in the strict sense of the term. An example can be seen in the case of Egypt in 2011, where, in its early phase, the largely nonviolent tactics used by the revolutionaries were nevertheless an expression of force that was able to overthrow Mubarak and (albeit temporarily) change the relationship between the people and the military, while refusing to "communicate" or "negotiate" with the government on the government's own terms. A similar example of force, I believe, was evident in the Occupy movement's unwillingness to immediately present a series of demands upon which a dialogue with the government or the traditional political class could commence. While the movement was certainly not devoid of guiding principles, the unwillingness to formulate demands and negotiate with the authorities followed from the fact that its most significant aspect was its experimentation with new modes of organization. These experiments, moreover, were not up for "debate" with the authorities—which is not to say that negotiation and debate did not take place *within* the movement itself.

31. Žižek, *Lost Causes*, 415.

32. Žižek, *Lost Causes*, 413.

33. Žižek, *Lost Causes*, 413. The universality associated with the "part of no part" is also evident when Rancière explains that "it is through the existence of this part of those who have no part, of this nothing that is all, that the community exists as a political community" (Rancière, *Disagreement*, 9).

34. On feminine sexuation and the "not-all" see Lacan, *SXX*. I analyze this in more detail in chapter 5.

35. Balibar, "Philosophy," 316.

36. Habermas quoted in Balibar, "Philosophy," 316.

37. Balibar, "Philosophy," 316 (emphasis in the original). Rocco makes a similar point with regard to Habermas (Rocco, *Transforming Citizenship*, 30).

38. Rancière, *Disagreement*, xi (my emphasis).

39. I. Young, "Group Difference," 272.

40. I. Young, "Group Difference," 272.

41. Bosniak, "Universal Citizenship," 969.

42. I. Young, "Group Difference," 264 (my emphasis).

43. I. Young, "Group Difference," 276. At best, she relegates the existence of antagonism to the past when "[d]uring [the] angry, sometimes bloody, political struggle in the nineteenth and twentieth centuries, many among the excluded and disadvantaged thought that winning full citizenship status, that is, equal political and civil rights, would lead to their freedom and equality" (264). What she fails to acknowledge is that many of these angry and sometimes bloody struggles did not simply seek inclusion into full citizenship rights, but actually sought to transform the very foundations of bourgeois legality.

44. Cf. Marx, "Jewish Question."

45. I. Young, "Group Difference," 277.

46. I. Young, "Group Difference," 276.

47. Badiou, *Theory of the Subject*, 184.

48. Hobsbawm, *Nations*, 10.

49. B. Anderson, *Imagined Communities*, 36.

50. D. Miller, *Nationality*, 35. Though Miller is quick to insist that to say a nation is imaginary is not to say it does not exist or that one has been fooled into believing in the existence of one (10). In other words, even though nation is a construct, this category nevertheless exhibits a degree of effectivity in continuing to function as a primary category around which contemporary societies are meaningfully organized. It continues to influence collective and individual action, and thus continues to be a valuable category of analysis. See Balibar, "Nation Form," where he makes a similar point regarding "fictive ethnicity."

51. D. Miller, *Nationality*, 22.

52. Hobsbawm, *Nations*, 9–10; Habermas, "Citizenship," 257.

53. Hobsbawm, *Nations*, 18 (emphasis in the original).

54. Hobsbawm, *Nations*, 18–19.

55. D. Miller, *Nationality*, 28–29. See also Keitner, *Paradoxes of Nationalism*, 47–55, on earlier political uses of "nation" in France.

56. Habermas, "Citizenship," 257.

57. Habermas, "Citizenship," 257.

58. Laclau, "Empty Signifiers," 37.

59. Laclau, "Empty Signifiers," 37.

60. Laclau, "Empty Signifiers," 37.

61. Laclau, "Empty Signifiers," 39.

62. Laclau, "Empty Signifiers," 37.

63. Laclau, "Empty Signifiers," 37. A neutral limit would constitute a weak difference since, as Laclau insists, continuity is maintained between what is on either side of the limit, and the limit merely works to designate a difference between terms internal to the system. Thus, changes involving a neutral limit would simply entail a change of places, rather than the transformation of the system as such—that is, it would remain within the differential logic of the structure. An exclusion, however, points to a radical difference whose irruption into the system would affect the system in its entirety—it would make "impossible" the continuation of the system as it previously was. Likewise, such an exclusion *is* the impossibility inherent to the very system; it is what must remain impossible for the system to continue to exist as it is.

64. Laclau, "Empty Signifiers," 38.

65. Laclau, "Empty Signifiers," 39.

66. Lacan, "Subversion," 681.

67. Žižek, *Sublime Object*, 109.

68. Žižek, *Sublime Object*, 110.

69. Žižek, *Sublime Object*, 106.

70. Žižek, *Sublime Object*, 106.

71. Žižek, *Sublime Object*, 106.

72. Habermas, "Citizenship," 258.

73. Habermas, "Citizenship," 258.

74. Habermas, "Citizenship," 257.

75. Eagleton, "Nationalism," 28.

76. Balibar, "Nation Form," 86.

77. B. Anderson, *Imagined Communities*, 195.

78. B. Anderson, *Imagined Communities*, 195. See also Stavrakakis on the role of the notion of a lost golden age in romantic nationalist conceptions ("Enjoying the Nation," 199).

79. Habermas, "Citizenship," 258 (emphasis in the original).

80. For the first conception see also Bellamy, *Citizenship*, 71.

81. Hobsbawm, *Nations*, 19.

82. Hobsbawm, *Nations*, 19–20.

83. Hallward, *Postcolonial*, 127 (emphasis in the original).

84. Balibar, "Rights of Man," 51–52.

85. Hobsbawm, *Nations*, 22.

86. Hobsbawm, *Nations*, 102. Keitner, however, dates the first use of "nationalism" in French to a 1798 history of Jacobinism written by an exiled priest, Jacques Barruel (Keitner, *Paradoxes of Nationalism*, 85). At this point one must note that there is also an anticolonialist tradition that takes nation as a basis for revolutionary politics, as exemplified in mid-twentieth-century national liberation movements. I analyze the case of Algeria's anticolonial struggle through the writings of Fanon in chapter 5, showing that there, too, is evidence of a conception of generic revolutionary nation similar to the one described here.

87. Stavrakakis, "Enjoying the Nation," 200.

88. In Žižek's words, "the impossible 'square of the circle' of symbolic and/ or imaginary identification never results in the absence of any remainder, there is always a leftover which opens the space for desire and makes the Other (the symbolic order) inconsistent, with fantasy as an attempt to overcome, to conceal this inconsistency, this gap in the Other" (*Sublime Object*, 139). While both my presentation of the two levels of ideology and Žižek's own remark here suggest a linear progression of the function of ideology from the discursive level to that of fantasy (to the extent that fantasy deals with the remainder that escapes the initial process of interpellation), in other places Žižek reverses the order, beginning first with fantasy as the precondition for the subject's interpellation at the symbolic level. For example, Žižek also states that "before being caught in

the identification, in the symbolic recognition/misrecognition, the subject ($) is trapped by the Other through a paradoxical object-cause of desire in the midst of it (*a*), through this secret supposed to be hidden in the Other: $ ◊ *a*—the Lacanian formula of fantasy" (*Sublime Object*, 43–44). Thus, rather than entailing a linear progression, it may be best to think the relationship between both levels as one of overdetermination. This remainder, furthermore, is the Lacanian subject. On this point, see Dolar, who argues that "the psychoanalytic subject is the failure to become an Althusserian one" (Dolar, "Interpellation," 78).

89. Žižek, *Sublime Object*, 140.

90. Žižek, *Sublime Object*, 123.

91. Žižek, *Sublime Object*, 123–124; Evans, *Dictionary*, 55.

92. On Lacan's graph of desire see Lacan, "Subversion," 671–702; and Žižek, *Sublime Object*, 95–144.

93. Žižek, *Sublime Object*, 132.

94. Žižek, *Sublime Object*, 136–137.

95. Žižek, *Sublime Object*, 137–138.

96. $ ◊ *a* is Lacan's formula for fantasy, with *a* (the *objet petit a*) being the object-cause of desire.

97. It is this aspect that a mere discursive analysis of ideology fails to grasp. As a consequence, discursive analyses are unable to account for the stubbornly captivating force behind such ideologically abject figures as the Jew, the "illegal" immigrant, the criminal, and so forth.

98. Stavrakakis, "Enjoying the Nation," 191.

99. Stavrakakis, "Enjoying the Nation," 197.

100. Žižek, *Sublime Object*, 141; Stavrakakis, "Enjoying the Nation," 193.

101. Cf. Žižek, *Sublime Object*, 143.

102. Weber, *Myth*, 33.

103. Popper, Lang, and Popper, "Maps to Myth," 91–92; Bonazzi, "Frontier Thesis," 151; Mitchell, "Whose West," 499; Redding, "Mythographies," 314.

104. Popper, Lang, and Popper, "Maps to Myth," 92.

105. Popper, Lang, and Popper, "Maps to Myth," 92. Mitchell, however, is quick to point out the many exclusions that also structured Turner's text. Citing recent critiques of Turner, he argues that "his thesis ignores Native Americans, Hispanics, Chinese, African Americans, women, even that group of Anglo-Saxon males untransformed by Turner's mystical process" (Mitchell, "Whose West," 500).

106. Turner, *Frontier*, 1.

107. Bonazzi, "Frontier Thesis," 151.

108. Bonazzi, "Frontier Thesis," 151.

109. Turner, *Frontier*, 30.

110. French Constitution of 1793, quoted in Marx, "Jewish Question," 42.

111. French Constitution of 1793, quoted in Marx, "Jewish Question," 42.

112. Marx, "Jewish Question," 42 (my emphasis).

113. One cannot help but see strong parallels between this conception and the conception of democracy promoted by today's libertarians—a form of democracy limited to reducing the presence of the government in order to secure the private interests of capital against any social concerns.

114. Turner, *Frontier*, 302–303.

115. I return to this theme in chapter 2.

116. R. Williams, *Loaded Weapon*. This also points to the racialization of the American nation-state and of American citizenship. I analyze the racialization of American citizenship in more detail in chapter 2.

117. R. Williams also cites this excerpt in *Loaded Weapon*, 39.

118. R. Williams, *Loaded Weapon*, 33.

119. R. Williams, *Loaded Weapon*, 39 (my emphasis).

120. R. Williams, *Loaded Weapon*, 43.

121. Turner, *Frontier*, 3–4.

122. See Inda, *Targeting Immigrants*, for an analysis of the way the figure of the "illegal" immigrant has been a primary one against which the rearticulation of American citizenship has occurred during the latter half of the twentieth century.

123. Žižek, *Sublime Object*, 79.

124. Žižek, *Sublime Object*, 79.

125. Žižek, *Sublime Object*, 80.

126. Žižek, *Sublime Object*, 80.

127. Žižek, *Sublime Object*, 81.

128. Žižek, *Sublime Object*, 81.

129. Žižek, *Sublime Object*, 81.

130. Žižek, *Sublime Object*, 139 (emphasis in the original).

131. Žižek, *Sublime Object*, 138.

132. Hallward, *Badiou*, 144.

133. See also Bosteels, "Nonlaw," 1917–1918, on this point.

134. Bosteels, *Badiou and Politics*, 87. Bosteels has formulated a similar criticism of Žižek and made the case that such a stance is characteristic of much contemporary theory more generally. See especially Bosteels, "In Search of the Act," in *Actuality of Communism*; and Bosteels, *Badiou and Politics*, chap. 8. Cf. Hallward, *Badiou*, 150–151.

135. Žižek, *Sublime Object*, 141.

136. Badiou refers to this as "that which, in lack itself, survives the lacking" (*Theory of the Subject*, 140).

137. Bosteels, "Nonlaw," 1918. Thus, from his early work in *Theory of the Subject*, Badiou already notices a basic problem with the theoretical stance represented by psychoanalysis, which is reproduced by many of the theories that draw

from it: "namely, its difficulty to register the making of a new consistent truth beyond the exposure and acknowledgement of the structural lack, or void, that is only the vanishing cause, no matter how sublime or obscene" (Bosteels, *Badiou and Politics*, 75).

138. Hallward, *Badiou*, 125.

139. My point is not to dismiss Lacan or psychoanalysis, as will be evident from the chapters that follow, but to specify an impasse, of which the contribution of Badiou's philosophy is to make into a pass. Dolar himself notices this impasse when he states: "Analysis stops at a threshold—it cannot pass a certain threshold without ceasing to be analysis—but it circumscribes a locus in which a step should be made; but this circumscribing a place is itself a political gesture, a political opening, the opening of a door through which we must make a step" (Dolar, "Freud," 29). Badiou's philosophy takes this step. His thought, moreover, is conditioned by the historical episodes in which this kind of step has also been taken in politics.

140. Bosteels, *Badiou and Politics*, 75.

141. Hallward, *Badiou*, 144.

142. Badiou, *Metapolitics*, 73.

CHAPTER 2: ETHNICS OF THE REAL

1. Huerta said this in the midst of the 2006 mobilizations against HR 4437, a Republican-led federal bill that would have made it a crime to be in the country without authorization and to provide nonemergency assistance to an undocumented person, among other measures. I discuss this bill and the 2006 immigration marches in chapter 3.

2. See Horne, "Open Letter," 1, where he claims that his opposition to ethnic studies is motivated by Martin Luther King Jr.'s "I Have a Dream" speech, during which King famously said that he dreamt of a nation where his children would be judged by the content of their character rather than by the color of their skin. I return to this at the end of the chapter.

3. See the characterization of the program by the subsequent state superintendent of public instruction, John Huppenthal, in an appearance on *Democracy Now!* where he stresses that those who designed the curriculum "were going to . . . racemize [*sic*] the classes. And in racemizing [*sic*] the classes, there is a philosopher in South America, controversial philosopher, because—it's strictly right in his books—he uses a Marxist structure to his thinking and his philosophy, that—and Marx, of course, said that the entire history of mankind was a struggle between the classes. So the designers of the Mexican American Studies classes explicitly say in their journal articles that they're going to construct Mexican American Studies around this Marxian framework. . . . [In Paulo

Freire's] *Pedagogy of the Oppressed*, that word 'oppressed' is taken right out of . . . *The Communist Manifesto*" (*Democracy Now!*, "Debating Tucson School District's Book Ban"). See also on the representation of the Mexican American studies program as "alien," Orozco, "Racism and Power," 51–54.

4. A. Acosta, "Hinging on Exclusion," 104.

5. A. Acosta, "Hinging on Exclusion," 104; Huppenthal, "Notice of Noncompliance," 1, 5–6.

6. Horne, "Open Letter," 1 (my emphasis).

7. Horne, "Open Letter," 1–2 (emphasis in the original).

8. See Cole, *Enemy Aliens*, 131, 136–137.

9. Horne, "Open Letter," 4.

10. Horne, "Open Letter," 4 (my emphasis).

11. Quoted in C. Acosta, "Dangerous Minds," 3.

12. Soto and Joseph, "Neoliberalism," 48.

13. Poblete, "Introduction," x.

14. Cabrera et al., "Missing," 1102; Ochoa O'Leary et al., "Assault," 106–107.

15. C. Acosta, "Dangerous Minds," 8–9, 14; Acuña et al., *Amici Curiae*, 21; Soto and Joseph, "Neoliberalism," 46; C. Ramírez, "Learning," 1066; M. Anderson, "Ongoing Battle."

16. C. Ramírez, "Learning," 1062.

17. Quoted in C. Ramírez, "Learning," 1062. Indeed, Grijalva continues: "This country celebrates and acknowledges its diversity—in this respect, Mexican Americans are no different from Italian Americans or Polish Americans. We're all Americans, and our families all came from somewhere." Ramírez further identifies the assimilationist thrust of Grijalva's statement in the implicit racial politics behind his choice to link Mexican Americans to Italian Americans and Polish Americans. After all, the latter two are examples of ethnic groups the integration of which was correlated with their recognition as white, which entailed their simultaneous distancing from other people of color, like African Americans, Mexicans, and Chinese (C. Ramírez, "Learning," 1064–1065). Read in this way, Grijalva's statement also taps into a troubling historical tendency within the Mexican American community to challenge their discrimination by claiming white status. Historically, this enabled Mexican Americans to legally dispute their position within a segregated social order, but without challenging the institution of segregation itself. On this point, see also Haney López, *Racism on Trial*; Foley, "Becoming Hispanic," 53–70.

18. I use the male pronoun on purpose here since, as I argue in chapter 5, this "unalienated" identitarian subject employs a "masculine" logic according to Lacan's formulas of sexuation.

19. Viego, *Dead Subjects*, 16.

20. Viego, *Dead Subjects*, 5. Lacan, for example, acerbically denounces the "mistaken proposal to strengthen the ego in a type of treatment diverted thereafter

towards successful adaptation—a phenomenon of mental abdication tied to the aging of the psychoanalytic group in the Diaspora owing to the war, and the reduction of an eminent practice to a *Good Housekeeping* seal of approval attesting to its suitability to the 'American way of life'" (Lacan, "Subversion," 685).

21. Danto, "Redbaiting," 213–231.

22. Viego, *Dead Subjects*, 245; Lacan, *SXI*, 142.

23. Quoted in C. Acosta, "Dangerous Minds," 10. Along explicitly social psychological lines, Ochoa O'Leary et al. make the point that discriminatory legislation like HB 2281 has historically "encumbered the coping capacity of young adults" ("Assault," 110). Among the benefits of Mexican American studies, the authors identify "significantly less depression and higher self-esteem" for the students (110). See also Villanueva, "Teaching as a Healing Craft," 23–40.

24. Aparicio, "Latino Cultural Studies," 13.

25. Viego, *Dead Subjects*, 127–129. As Éric Laurent stresses, for Lacan, "[t]here is no way to define a subject as self-consciousness" (Laurent, "Alienation," 22).

26. Lacan, *SXI*, 205.

27. Gallego, *Chicana/o Subjectivity*, 22.

28. Laclau, "Subject of Politics," 52.

29. Honig, *Foreigner*, 108.

30. Quoted in Smith, *Freedom's Fetters*, 12.

31. Cole, *Enemy Aliens*, 91.

32. Smith, *Freedom's Fetters*, 94.

33. Quoted in Smith, *Freedom's Fetters*, 438 (emphasis in the original).

34. One can thus not fail to notice the irony in the fact that Horne, Huppenthal, and many of the supporters of HB 2281 themselves belong to a party that bears one of the original marks of political "foreignness" in the United States.

35. Quoted in Smith, *Freedom's Fetters*, 441.

36. Cole, *Enemy Aliens*, 91.

37. Cole, *Enemy Aliens*, 107.

38. Cole, *Enemy Aliens*, 108.

39. Cole, *Enemy Aliens*, 108.

40. Wiecek, "Domestic Anticommunism," 387.

41. Preston, *Aliens and Dissenters*, 210; Cole, *Enemy Aliens*, 116.

42. Cole, *Enemy Aliens*, 118.

43. Cole, *Enemy Aliens*, 7–8.

44. Preston, *Aliens and Dissenters*, 216, 220.

45. Preston, *Aliens and Dissenters*, 221.

46. Cole, *Enemy Aliens*, 118. Despite this episode's many failures—among them, the cancellation by acting secretary of labor Louis Post of most of the deportation orders and the highly critical *Report upon the Illegal Practices of the*

United States Department of Justice, published by the American Civil Liberties Union and signed by some of the most prominent lawyers and law professors of the time (Cole, *Enemy Aliens*, 122–125; Wiecek, "Domestic Anticommunism," 390–391)—it was nevertheless important in setting up a general blueprint for the antiradical campaigns that would ensue in subsequent decades. It did this by establishing four pillars of future campaigns. The first pillar was its preventive approach; it "sought to neutralize all persons who it thought might pose a potential *future* threat" (Cole, *Enemy Aliens*, 126; emphasis in the original). The second was the targeting of noncitizens as a way to avoid checks on governmental authority that would be in force in the case of citizens. Third was the use of administrative rather than criminal venues to bypass due process protections afforded by the latter—for example, a public trial, protection against self-incrimination, the right to a lawyer, the presumption of innocence, and the right to confront evidence against one. The fourth pillar was the theory of guilt by association, which enabled arrests based on membership—and even mere suspicion of membership—in radical organizations, and which sought to punish *ideas* over actions (Cole, *Enemy Aliens*, 125–127).

47. For an account of the early twentieth-century imbrication of anti-Asian racism with antiradicalism and immigration policy, see Sohi, *Echoes of Mutiny*, especially chapter 3, "Anarchy, Surveillance, and Repressing the 'Hindu' Menace."

48. Alicia Schmidt Camacho highlights the imbrication of race, nation, and immigration law throughout US history, whereby "U.S. nationhood and white supremacy [have] reinforced each other, so that immigration policy [has] served political leaders as an instrument for fixing the figurative and material limits of the national body" (*Migrant Imaginaries*, 28). Mae Ngai also notes how "[t]wo major elements of twentieth-century American racial ideology evolved from the genealogy of the racial requirement to citizenship: the legal definition of 'white' and the rule of racial unassimilability" (*Impossible Subjects*, 37).

49. Smith, *Freedom's Fetters*, 440; Cole, *Enemy Aliens*, 92.

50. Cole, *Enemy Aliens*, 95. Of the 120,000 interned, about two-thirds were US citizens (Ngai, *Impossible Subjects*, 175).

51. Quoted in Cole, *Enemy Aliens*, 95. Although people of German and Italian descent were also placed under suspicion, they were selected and investigated on an individual basis. Meanwhile, anti-Asian racial animus led to the overwhelming and blanket targeting of Japanese Americans en masse (Ngai, *Impossible Subjects*, 175).

52. The historical presumption of Asian inassimilability has led Lisa Lowe to make a similar claim as the one I put forth in this chapter with regard to the political potential of the "alien." "The racialization of Asian Americans in relation to the state locates Asian American culture as a site for the emergence of another kind of political subject, one who has a historically 'alien-ated' relation

to the category of citizenship," Lowe argues: "That historical alienation situates the Asian American political subject in critical apposition to the category
of the citizen, as well as to the political sphere of representative democracy that
the concept of the citizen subtends" (*Immigrant Acts*, 12). What I would add to
Lowe's analysis, among other considerations, is that any ethnic minority culture
is also always alienated from itself, and that it is also from this location—from
the acultural cut of a given (minority) culture—that the emergence of another
kind of political subject must be thought.

53. Quoted in Irwin, *Bandits*, 42.

54. Indeed, the imbrication of race and foreignness can also be seen at work
in the mass deportations of Mexicans during the 1930s and again in the 1950s
when many US citizens of Mexican descent were deported as well. See Schmidt
Camacho, *Migrant Imaginaries*, 29–30; J. García, *Operation Wetback*; Balderrama
and Rodríguez, *Decade of Betrayal*.

55. Compare this with my discussion in chapter 1 of the figure of the Indian
in Frederick Jackson Turner's "frontier thesis."

56. Saldaña-Portillo, "Wavering," 148.

57. See Articles VIII and IX of the Treaty of Guadalupe Hidalgo.

58. Griswold del Castillo, *Guadalupe Hidalgo*, 66.

59. Saldaña-Portillo, "Wavering," 147.

60. Saldaña-Portillo, "Wavering," 147–148.

61. And thus one once again sees the dynamic whereby the inclusion of some
hinges on displacing violence and dispossession onto others.

62. Griswold del Castillo, *Guadalupe Hidalgo*, 69–70.

63. Cf. Laclau, "Empty Signifiers," 39. On discourses regarding Mexican
inassimilability during the early twentieth century, see Nevins, *Operation Gatekeeper*, 105.

64. Cf. also Laclau, *Populist Reason*, 96, on the constitution of equivalential
relations. I analyze this in more detail in chapter 5.

65. See Prashad, "Ethnic Studies," 157–176.

66. Žižek, *Sublime Object*, 221 (emphasis in the original).

67. Wiecek, "Domestic Anticommunism," 406, 429.

68. Quoted in Cole, *Enemy Aliens*, 130.

69. Moloney, *National Insecurities*, 249; Cole, *Enemy Aliens*, 133.

70. Wiecek, "Domestic Anticommunism," 424. Denaturalization refers to
the annulment of the citizenship of individuals who have been naturalized. This
should be distinguished from denationalization, which refers to the revocation of
the citizenship of natural born citizens.

71. Cole, *Enemy Aliens*, 131.

72. Wiecek, "Domestic Anticommunism," 402.

73. Cole, *Enemy Aliens*, 145–148.

74. Schmidt Camacho, *Migrant Imaginaries*, 117–118; Ngai, *Impossible Subjects*, 234–239.

75. Schmidt Camacho, *Migrant Imaginaries*, 26.

76. Ruiz, "Una Mujer," 2–4.

77. Ruiz, "Una Mujer," 1.

78. Ruiz, "Una Mujer," 7–14; Larralde and Griswold del Castillo, "Luisa Moreno," 287–288; M. García, *Memories*, 117.

79. Ruiz, "Una Mujer," 2.

80. Schmidt Camacho, *Migrant Imaginaries*, 38.

81. Gutiérrez, *Walls and Mirrors*, 110–114.

82. M. García, *Memories*, 108–112.

83. Moreno, "Non-Citizen Americans," 47. This speech is also alternatively known as "Caravans of Sorrow."

84. Moreno, "Non-Citizen Americans," 47.

85. Moreno, "Non-Citizen Americans," 51.

86. Moreno, "Non-Citizen Americans," 50.

87. Moreno, "Non-Citizen Americans," 51.

88. Ruiz, "Una Mujer," 12.

89. Cf. Burt Corona, who recalls the ideological effects of the inaugural meeting of El Congreso: "Above all, the congregation of so many Spanish-speaking people stamped in my mind, and in the minds of many others, that we were a *national minority* and not just a regional one" (M. García, *Memories*, 111; my emphasis).

90. Moreno, "Non-Citizen Americans," 51. It is consistent, however, with the immigration privileges given by the United States to countries of the Western Hemisphere throughout most of the twentieth century. I touch on this in chapter 3.

91. Larralde and Griswold del Castillo, "Luisa Moreno," 287; Ruiz, "Una Mujer," 7.

92. Ruiz, "Una Mujer," 7–8.

93. Ruiz, "Una Mujer," 8.

94. I must emphasize that Ruiz's discussion of Moreno's name change is largely speculative. Contrary to Ruiz's claim, Larralde and Griswold del Castillo argue that Moreno changed her name to avoid bringing "embarrassment" upon the family name, especially since her family disagreed with her politics. Her choice of name, these authors contend, was meant to honor a well-known Mexican labor organizer, Luis Moreno (Larralde and Griswold del Castillo, "Luisa Moreno," 285). Ruiz, on the other hand, suggests that "Luisa" could have been chosen in honor of Luisa Capetillo, another female organizer in Florida, who had preceded Moreno by about twenty years (Ruiz, "Una Mujer," 8).

95. Schmidt Camacho, *Migrant Imaginaries*, 116.

96. Schmidt Camacho, *Migrant Imaginaries.*

97. Quoted in Larralde and Griswold del Castillo, "Luisa Moreno," 299. The book to which she refers is probably Milton R. Konvitz, *The Alien and the Asiatic in American Law,* published in 1946.

98. It is clear that Moreno is also making reference to the Declaration of the Rights of Man and of the Citizen, and noting that as radically foreign, she is being excluded from such rights. Her alienation from these supposedly "inalienable" rights is precisely conditioned on her exclusion from the nation. She is alienated from the rights of "man and citizen" because of her positioning as the alien embodied.

99. Larralde and Griswold del Castillo, "Luisa Moreno," 295.

100. See Cole, *Enemy Aliens,* 132–136, for an account of the lengths to which the US government went to try to deport Bridges.

101. Quoted in Larralde and Griswold del Castillo, "Luisa Moreno," 296; Ruiz, "Una Mujer," 19; Schmidt Camacho, *Migrant Imaginaries,* 116.

102. "For the conventions of testimony are nothing less than the conventions of citizenship," argues Litvak: "HUAC's rules of testimonial etiquette rule over the performance of Americanness itself" (*Un-Americans,* 8).

103. Larralde and Griswold del Castillo, "Luisa Moreno," 295.

104. Larralde and Griswold del Castillo, "Luisa Moreno," 300; Ruiz, "Una Mujer," 19. After leaving the United States, Moreno would go to Guatemala and become involved in activities in support of Jacobo Árbenz's progressive government before the US backed coup in 1954, and would spend time as an English translator for revolutionary Cuba's new education system in 1960 (Larralde and Griswold del Castillo, "Luisa Moreno," 300, 302–303).

105. Lyon, *Brecht in America,* 314.

106. Lyon, *Brecht in America,* 314.

107. Lyon, *Brecht in America,* 324.

108. Soon after these hearings, Thomas would be investigated for corruption and sent to prison for "putting nonworkers on the Government payroll and appropriating their salaries to himself" (Lardner, "My Life," 190). Even so, he would end up serving less time than some of the House Un-American Activities Committee witnesses jailed for contempt (Lardner, "My Life," 190).

109. Bently, *Treason,* 209. In the following discussion I reference Brecht's testimony as it appears in written form in Bentley, *Thirty Years of Treason,* and in audio form in Bentley, *Bertolt Brecht before the Committee on Un-American Activities.* In cases in which I combine or correct the transcript with material from the audio recording, I include both the page number from the transcript and the time from the recording.

110. As Bentley notes, however, some of the translations were in fact closer to the original than Brecht made out (*Bertolt Brecht,* track 2, 20:21).

111. Litvak, *Un-Americans*, 8. Here and in what follows I would like to complicate the claim that the hearing highlighted "the political and ideological aspects of Brecht's 'un-Americanness'" in any kind of direct way (Mews, "'Un-American' Brecht," 8).

112. Lyon, *Brecht in America*, 309.

113. Bentley, *Treason*, 209.

114. Brecht, "Unread Statement," 221–222.

115. The committee was well aware that such public hearings could backfire. This appears to be the reason that Richard Nixon, then a first-term congressman from California who was also on the committee during this time, "disappeared" when it came time to question the "Hollywood nineteen," the designation given to the group of those subpoenaed who intended to not cooperate with the committee (Lyon, *Brecht in America*, 324).

116. Bentley, *Treason*, 209.

117. Bentley, *Treason*, 214; Bentley, *Bertolt Brecht*, track 2, 00:09:33–00:10:26.

118. Lyon, *Brecht in America*, 313.

119. It is thus no coincidence that Eric Bentley, an expert on Brecht and theater, is also the editor of *Thirty Years of Treason*, which is composed primarily of transcripts from the House Un-American Activities Committee hearings. In *Are You Now or Have You Ever Been*, Bentley even arranges the transcripts into the form of a play. Besides this, it is also evident that the dialogic form of the hearings and the physical arrangement of the space in which they took place (audience included) coincide in many ways with the characteristics of theater.

120. Lyon, *Brecht in America*, 323.

121. Lyon, *Brecht in America*, 323.

122. Bentley, *Bertolt Brecht*, track 2, 00:32:04–00:32:09. Lyon also notes that while in New York, Brecht "added [the cigar] to a routine he was still rehearsing" (Lyon, *Brecht in America*, 326).

123. Brecht, *Brecht on Theatre*, 143.

124. Brecht, *Brecht on Theatre*, 95.

125. Brecht, *Brecht on Theatre*, 91.

126. Brecht, *Brecht on Theatre*, 136.

127. By this I do not mean to imply that Brecht was the only one to be suspected of "putting on an act." See Bentley, *Are You Now*, xvii–xix, and Litvak, *Un-Americans*, 9–10, for other examples, and specifically with regard to the testimony of the actor Lionel Stander.

128. Viego, *Dead Subjects*, 59.

129. This is at least part of the logic that compelled post–World War II organizations like LULAC to anchor their rights claims on their own claims to whiteness.

130. Lacan, "Subversion," 673.

131. Viego, *Dead Subjects*, 69.

132. Lacan, "Freudian Thing," 335.

133. Though a more inclusive multicultural articulation of nationalism is certainly more preferable to a strictly white-supremacist one, if true change remains our objective, then we must move beyond both, given that at bottom their form remains the same. I propose such an alternative in chapter 5.

134. This is why, as I have demonstrated at several points in this chapter, the inclusion of some groups often occurs in tandem with the exclusion and denigration of others. For other examples, see Cacho, *Social Death*; Prashad, "How the Hindus Became Jews," 586–587.

135. Viego, *Dead Subjects*, 133.

136. This does not mean that a hysteric will always speak in the hysteric's discourse, for example, or an analyst in the analyst's discourse, and so on (Fink, *Lacanian Subject*, 129–130).

137. Viego, *Dead Subjects*, 133. See also Fink, *Lacanian Subject*, 131.

138. In arguing for the hysteric's discourse, Viego is also drawing from Alberto Moreiras, who makes a similar argument with regard to Latin American studies. See Moreiras, *Exhaustion*, 81–82. Demonstrating the continued theoretical overlap between debates in Latina/o and Latin American studies, Moreiras has more recently responded to John Beverley's critique (which I address in the introduction of this book) by arguing that it bases itself on a form of "ego Latinamericanism" (Moreiras, "Fatality," 217–221).

139. Viego, *Dead Subjects*, 134.

140. Lacan, *SXVII*, 176.

141. Fink, *Lacanian Subject*, 134–135.

142. Lacan, *SXVII*, 94; Zupančič, "Surplus Enjoyment," 163–164. I use the male pronoun here because in exempting himself from castration, the master adheres to the masculine logic in Lacan's formulas of sexuation. See chapter 5.

143. Badiou, *Century*, 47.

144. On ego psychology as master's discourse, see Lacan, *SXVII*, 73.

145. Fink, *Lacanian Subject*, 131.

146. Zupančič, "Surplus Enjoyment," 166.

147. Zupančič, "Surplus Enjoyment," 166.

148. Zupančič, "Surplus Enjoyment," 166.

149. This translation is based on Jack Agüeros's translation, though I have made substantial modifications. See Julia de Burgos, "To Julia de Burgos," in *Song of the Simple Truth: The Complete Poems of Julia de Burgos*, 3, 5. I would like to thank Northwestern University Press for permission to reprint this poem.

150. I refer to a second layer of inscription because the "social" existence of Burgos already implies the alienating effects of a previous inscription at the level of the social/symbolic—a previous moment of alienation that is the condition

of possibility for poetic creation itself since it constitutes her entrance into language.

151. I discuss the concept of the evental site in chapter 3.

152. For a political reading of the horizon as a figure of the real, see Dean, *Communist Horizon*, 1–3.

153. Lacan formulates the place of the divisor as the site of repression when he states: "If, in fact, one wished to preserve the possibility of a handling of a fractional type, one would place the signifier that has disappeared, the repressed signifier, below the principal bar, in the denominator" (*SXI*, 249).

154. Bosteels, *Marx and Freud*, 236.

155. Horne, "Open Letter," 1.

156. Indeed, Joy James also points out that by this time, "Birmingham city officials had declared the NAACP a 'foreign corporation' and criminalized its activities" ("Martin Luther King, Jr.," 32).

157. King, "Letter from Birmingham Jail," 35. This resonates strongly with Frantz Fanon's earlier claim that for the FLN in Algeria, *"every individual living in Algeria is an Algerian"* (*Dying Colonialism*, 152; emphasis in the original). I analyze the implications that Fanon's statement holds for rethinking the concept of "nation" in chapter 5.

158. King, "Newly Discovered 1964 MLK Speech."

CHAPTER 3: CRIMINALIZATION AT THE EDGE OF THE EVENTAL SITE

1. Quoted in Dowling and Inda, "Introduction," 6.

2. Quoted in Dowling and Inda, "Introduction," 6.

3. Quoted in Dowling and Inda, "Introduction," 6.

4. Inda, *Targeting Immigrants*, 67–68.

5. E. Young, *Alien Nation*, 130. For a brief overview of Asian exclusion measures see Lowe, *Immigrant Acts*, 13, 180n14.

6. Carter, Green, and Halpern, "Immigration Policy," 148.

7. Immigration Act of 1917, Pub. L. No. 301, 39 Stat. 874 (1917); Inda, *Targeting Immigrants*, 68; Ngai, *Impossible Subjects*, 37.

8. Inda, *Targeting Immigrants*, 68; Ngai, *Impossible Subjects*, 37; Nevins, *Operation Gatekeeper*, 101.

9. Inda, *Targeting Immigrants*, 68. After 1891, unauthorized immigrants could only be deported if they were discovered within a year of entry. The 1917 act extended the statute of limitation to five years (69).

10. Inda, *Targeting Immigrants*, 69.

11. Inda, *Targeting Immigrants*, 69.

12. Ngai, *Impossible Subjects*, 58; Schmidt Camacho, *Migrant Imaginaries*, 29.

13. De Genova, "Mexican/Migrant 'Illegality,'" 76 (my emphasis).

14. De Genova, "Mexican/Migrant 'Illegality,'" 63.

15. De Genova, "Mexican/Migrant 'Illegality,'" 63–64; Ngai, *Impossible Subjects*, 50.

16. De Genova, "Mexican/Migrant 'Illegality,'" 75.

17. De Genova, "Mexican/Migrant 'Illegality,'" 75.

18. See Agamben, *Homo Sacer.*

19. From 1973 to 1980, for example, the *New York Times* increased its average number of annual articles on undocumented immigration by 650 percent when compared with its coverage from 1970 to 1972 (Nevins, *Operation Gatekeeper*, 112).

20. Nevins, *Operation Gatekeeper*, 113. It thus bears emphasizing that the language we use does not merely reflect reality, but rather helps construct it. The categories that we use and their connotations exert an influence over the way we conceptualize that of which we speak.

21. Santa Ana et al., "May to Remember," 216.

22. Inda, "Subject to Deportation," 296. Yet, given the predominant association of undocumented people with Mexicans, analysis of the conceptual link between undocumented people and criminality must also take into account the ways in which it draws on previous racist discourses that represent Mexicans as inherently violent and criminal.

23. Immigration Reform and Control Act of 1986, Pub. L. No. 99–603, 100 Stat. 3359 (1986).

24. And it even remained central to efforts by the Obama administration to provide relief to some undocumented people through executive actions. As I will demonstrate, one of the problems with reform efforts, such as those under Obama, that justify relief for some undocumented people by distinguishing them from "criminal aliens" is that they reify this category at the same time that they overlook how the criminalization of noncitizen behavior in general has cast a wider net subsuming a larger number of people within it. Against this reification, it is the very production of criminality that must be questioned, opposed, and overturned. The consequences of the continued reification of the category of "criminal alien" under the Obama administration, in fact, can be directly seen in the way this same category structures the more aggressive rhetoric and actions of immigration enforcement under the Trump administration.

25. Meissner et al., *Immigration Enforcement*, 98; Weissbrodt and Danielson, *Immigration Law*, 284.

26. Inda, "Subject to Deportation," 300; Weissbrodt and Danielson, *Immigration Law*, 284; Miller, *Border Patrol Nation*, 222.

27. On the human costs of and legal challenges to the often-retroactive determination of aggravated felonies, see Bernstein, "Those Deported"; and Kanstroom, *Aftermath.* The retroactive determination of criminality for deportation

purposes is the latest iteration of a longer history where retroactive violations have been used to safeguard "national security." In *Galvan v. Press* (1954), for example, the US Supreme Court "ruled that Congress could deport permanent resident aliens for having been members of the Communist Party at a time when membership was legal" (Cole, *Enemy Aliens*, 136). What one can see with "aggravated felonies" is the displacement of the threat of radical politics by "criminality."

28. Morawetz, "Deportation Laws," 1939. Thus Morawetz refers to the "Alice-in-Wonderland-like definition of the term 'aggravated felony,'" where "a crime need not be either aggravated or a felony" for it to count as an aggravated felony (1939).

29. Weissbrodt and Danielson, *Immigration Law*, 285–286.

30. Weissbrodt and Danielson, *Immigration Law*, 287.

31. Davis, *Prisons Obsolete*, 28.

32. Davis, *Prisons Obsolete*, 32. On the similar use of legislation to target and proletarianize Mexicans in California after the Mexican-American War, see Nevins, *Operation Gatekeeper*, 108.

33. James, "Introduction," xii.

34. My intention in connecting the production of migrant illegality to the legacies of slavery is not to collapse them together in a way that overlooks the historical specificity of each. Rather, it is to highlight the way in which criminalization has functioned and continues to function as a disciplinary mechanism meant to secure a discriminatory social order and facilitate the exploitation of a particular social group, even if the difference between the explicit racial framework of the Black Codes and the seemingly race-neutral language of recent immigration legislation could be said to make those affected by the latter a more heterogeneous group.

35. De Genova, "Mexican/Migrant 'Illegality,'" 82 (emphasis in the original).

36. Bacon, *Illegal People*, 17–19. This is done in disregard of explicit US Immigration and Customs Enforcement policy instructing its agents to make sure employers do not use workplace raids to interfere with the right of workers to organize (Dowling and Inda, "Introduction," 21; Bacon, *Illegal People*, 17). Cf. Cole, who also demonstrates how anti-anarchist provisions in immigration law were used to target and deport the largely foreign-born membership of the Industrial Workers of the World during the first decades of the twentieth century (*Enemy Aliens*, 110).

37. Alexander, *New Jim Crow*, 18. Operation Streamline, a Bush administration program begun in 2005, has been a driving factor in making convictions for unauthorized entry a source of mass incarceration. Under this program, undocumented border crossers are subjected to federal criminal charges—a misdemeanor resulting in up to six months in prison for a first violation, and a felony punishable by up to twenty years in prison for reentry after deportation—and

processed en masse in expedited proceedings (Lin, "Operation Streamline," 1). "During the Bush Administration, the annual count of federal criminal prosecutions for immigration offenses more than quadrupled while federal prosecutions of other crimes substantially decreased," notes Lin: "Alternatively, nearly 80,000 immigration prosecutions were filed in fiscal year 2008, compared to 39,458 in the previous year and 16,310 in fiscal year 2001" (1–2). Operation Streamline continued under the Obama administration, and can be credited with around 750,000 convictions from 2005 to 2016 (Miller, "Bigger Problem"). Similarly, Customs and Border Protection has become the largest federal law enforcement agency in the country, and funding for border and immigration enforcement has reached a level higher than all other federal law enforcement agencies combined (Miller, "Bigger Problem"). As these numbers show, even if recent legal decisions and measures, such as *Brown v. Plata* and the approval of Proposition 47 in California, may be optimistically interpreted as having begun to turn the tide on mass incarceration, they will prove inadequate if the criminalization of immigration is not also overturned—though I write this at the beginning of Trump's presidency, which has given new life to a rabid "law-and-order" agenda.

38. Jameson, *Representing Capital*, 148.

39. Benanav, "Misery and Debt," 29 (emphasis in the original).

40. Beltrán, *Trouble with Unity*, 138.

41. See Foucault, *Society Must Be Defended*.

42. Gilmore, *Golden Gulag*, 113.

43. Gilmore, *Golden Gulag*, 95. By "criminalization" of immigration, I refer both to efforts to bring immigration violations under the purview of criminal law—like the example of HR 4437, to which I will turn later in this chapter—and to the way in which the discourse of criminal law and a preoccupation with "criminality" have become central to the management of immigration. Important to note is how the criminalization of immigration coincides with a larger trend, a more generalized governing tactic that some have designated as "governing through crime," which can be understood as the administrative counterpart to contemporary neoliberalism (Simon, *Governing through Crime*, 4; Dowling and Inda, *Governing Immigration through Crime*; Harvey, *Brief History of Neoliberalism*, 2–3).

44. Gilmore, *Golden Gulag*, 110.

45. Gilmore, *Golden Gulag*, 96.

46. Alexander, *New Jim Crow*, 142, 1–2.

47. Gilmore, *Golden Gulag*, 77.

48. Dowling and Inda, "Introduction," 27.

49. Foucault, *Security, Territory, Population*, 200.

50. Foucault, *Security, Territory, Population*, 201.

51. Dowling and Inda, "Introduction," 27.

52. See Inda, *Targeting Immigrants*.

53. Dowling and Inda, "Introduction," 27 (my emphasis).

54. Isin, "Acts of Citizenship," 16.

55. Isin, "Acts of Citizenship," 18.

56. Isin, "Acts of Citizenship," 24.

57. Isin, "Acts of Citizenship," 25.

58. Isin, "Acts of Citizenship," 25.

59. Isin, "Acts of Citizenship," 27.

60. Isin, "Acts of Citizenship," 34.

61. Much of the terminology in this section is drawn from set theory, which Badiou considers to be ontology insofar as it alone constitutes a discourse capable of presenting being qua being—that is, of presenting being insofar as it *is*, without predicates. See Badiou, *Being and Event*, 5. Besides Badiou's own work, the best introduction in English that highlights the role of mathematics in Badiou's philosophy remains Hallward, *Badiou*. "Situation" is the general designation for the "place" where presentation occurs. It is largely synonymous with "set" yet allows Badiou to extend the basic notion of set to other, nonmathematical (and thus nonontological) contexts.

62. Badiou, *Being and Event*, 97, 175.

63. Inda, *Targeting Immigrants*, 74.

64. Hoefer, Rytina, and Baker, *Unauthorized Immigrant Population 2011*, 2. See also Baker and Rytina, *Unauthorized Immigrant Population 2012*, 1–2; and Passel, Cohn, and Gonzalez-Barrera, *Population Decline of Unauthorized Immigrants*, 3.

65. Hoefer, Rytina, and Baker, *Unauthorized Immigrant Population 2011*, 6–7.

66. Inda, *Targeting Immigrants*, 78.

67. Arendt, "Decline of the Nation-State," 267–302; Hallward, *Badiou*, 118.

68. Felon disenfranchisement laws vary by state, with most states restoring a felon's right to vote upon the end of the incarceration term, or after completion of parole or probation (see https://www.aclu.org/map/map-state-criminal -disfranchisement-laws).

69. On recent cases where citizens have been deported by Immigration and Customs Enforcement, see Stevens, "Thin ICE."

70. In Badiou's words: "Being Other than it, such a multiple guarantees the set's immanent foundation, since 'underneath' this foundational multiple, there is nothing which belongs to the initial set. Therefore, belonging cannot infinitely regress: this halting point establishes a kind of original finitude" (*Being and Event*, 186).

71. Badiou, *Being and Event*, 175–176.

72. Cacho, *Social Death*, 5 (emphasis in the original).

73. Badiou, *Being and Event*, 187.

74. Badiou, *Being and Event*, 329.

75. Badiou, *Being and Event*, 181.

76. Badiou, *Being and Event*, 329.

77. Badiou, *Being and Event*, 197.

78. Badiou, *Being and Event*, 209–210, 230.

79. Badiou, *Logics of Worlds*, 53.

80. Isin, *Citizens without Frontiers*, 149.

81. Isin, *Citizens without Frontiers*, 149.

82. Isin, *Citizens without Frontiers*, 151 (emphasis in the original). In passing, one can notice that here Isin articulates citizenship as action and conduct (thus as practice), which demonstrates a shift in his focus toward what comes after an "act" of citizenship. In Badiou's framework, one could liken this to the shift from event to generic procedure.

83. Badiou, *Theoretical Writings*, 127.

84. Badiou, *Theoretical Writings*, 109 (emphasis in the original).

85. Beltrán, *Trouble with Unity*, 130; Bloemraad, Voss, and Lee, "Protests," 3–7; L. Chavez, *Latino Threat*, 154–166; Pallares and Flores-González, "Introduction," xv; Santa Ana et al., "May to Remember," 214–215.

86. Cisneros, "(Re)Bordering," 254; Bloemraad, Voss, and Lee, "Protests," 4.

87. Wang and Winn, "Groundswell," 45. Among its other provisions were included "substantial investment in border security, including almost seven hundred miles of double-layer fencing, increasingly high-tech document control, more cooperation between the Department of Homeland security [*sic*] and local law enforcement, and stiffer penalties for employers hiring illegal migrants" (Bloemraad, Voss, and Lee, "Protests," 6).

88. Cisneros, "(Re)Bordering," 254.

89. See R. Gonzales, "Left Out," 272; L. Chavez, *Latino Threat*, 156; Beltrán, *Trouble with Unity*, 192n5; and the essays contained in two recent anthologies analyzing the protests: *Rallying for Immigrant Rights*, edited by Kim Voss and Irene Bloemraad; and *¡Marcha!*, edited by Amalia Pallares and Nilda Flores-González. Alfonso Gonzales provides the best genealogy of the marches by tracing the participation of many of its organizers to previous organizational efforts dating back to the Chicano Movement in the 1960s and 1970s, the Central American peace and sanctuary movement in the 1980s, and Latina/o migrant activism in California in the 1990s (*Reform without Justice*, 53–55).

90. Far from dismissing these organizational networks in favor of a form of *absolute* spontaneity or contingency, which Badiou often seems to attribute to his notion of the event, I regard these networks as important in aiding the possibility for such an event to happen, even if the essence of an event is to exceed them.

91. Cisneros, "(Re)Bordering," 256; Santa Ana et al., "May to Remember," 215; L. Chavez, *Latino Threat*, 155; Beltrán, *Trouble with Unity*, 130, 137; Betancur and Garcia, "Immigration Mobilizations," 32.

92. Betancur and Garcia, "Immigration Mobilizations," 21.

93. Isin, "Acts of Citizenship," 18; Beltrán, *Trouble with Unity*, 131.

94. Beltrán, *Trouble with Unity*, 132.

95. Arendt quoted in Beltrán, *Trouble with Unity*, 136. See also Arendt, "What is Freedom," 151.

96. Butler and Spivak, *Who Sings the Nation-State*, 65.

97. Beltrán, *Trouble with Unity*, 132.

98. Arendt, *Human Condition*, 8.

99. Arendt, *Human Condition*, 176 (emphasis in the original).

100. Arendt, *Human Condition*, 178–179.

101. Arendt, *Human Condition*, 179.

102. Arendt, *Human Condition*, 179.

103. Beltrán, *Trouble with Unity*, 141, 155.

104. Beltrán, *Trouble with Unity*, 140, 133.

105. Beltrán, *Trouble with Unity*, 141.

106. Beltrán, *Trouble with Unity*, 155.

107. Badiou, *Theory of the Subject*, 263.

108. Badiou, *Rebirth*, 56.

109. Badiou, *Pocket Pantheon*, 130; Badiou, *Logics of Worlds*, 321–324.

110. Cisneros, "(Re)Bordering," 254.

111. L. Chavez, *Latino Threat*, 168.

112. Betancur and Garcia, "Immigration Mobilizations," 21; Beltrán, *Trouble with Unity*, 130–131.

113. Pallares and Flores-González, "Introduction," xvi–xvii.

114. Beltrán, *Trouble with Unity*, 146, 148.

115. Badiou, *Rebirth*, 77.

116. Badiou, *Rebirth*, 73; Inda, *Targeting Immigrants*.

117. Badiou, *Rebirth*, 71.

118. Regarding this tactic, Cacho warns: "When we distinguish ourselves from unlawful and outlawed status categories, we implicitly insist that these socio-categories are not only necessary but should be reserved and preserved for the 'genuinely' lazy (welfare recipients), 'undoubtedly' immoral (marrying for citizenship), and 'truly' dangerous (gang violence). . . . They work only if a sympathetic public already accepts that discrimination against non-valued others is legitimate and necessary" (*Social Death*, 18).

119. Cf. Badiou, *Metapolitics*, 118; Rancière, *Disagreement*, 118.

120. Quoted in Pulido, "Day without Immigrants," 3.

121. Quoted in L. Chavez, *Latino Threat*, 155.

122. Sassen, "U.S. Immigration Policy," 375. Sassen has demonstrated the ways in which the neoliberal restructuring of production has also produced transnational labor migrations. Challenging common assumptions that vast

poverty, high population growth, and economic stagnation are the determining causes of immigration, she tracks surges in immigration to the United States to patterns of foreign investment in export-oriented production in developing countries, including but not limited to Mexico, that have become some of the primary sources of immigrants (373). She notes that, while investment in production for export does create jobs, a seeming contradiction arises from the fact that the places where these jobs are created are also the ones that have begun to send a growing number of people. The reason for this is that the reorganization of production in such places has also had a disrupting impact on existent work structures by "uproot[ing] people and creat[ing] an urban reserve of wage laborers" (375). While this phenomenon is consistent with the effects of capitalist accumulation in general, production for export also adds to this "the development of economic, cultural, and ideological connections with the industrialized countries" that operate as the sources of investment and as the sites of consumption (377). Moreover, since production for export tends to favor the employment of women, the organization of domestic reproductive work has also been affected, at the same time that women's entrance into the labor market has contributed to male unemployment (376). Given these effects, surplus workers have increasingly activated and relied on the multifarious relations that have been established with wealthier countries in order to sell their labor power abroad. While Mexico's close economic and cultural relations with the United States have a longer history comprising different migratory fluxes, Mexican immigration to the United States since the mid-1960s is nevertheless motivated in large part by the same kind of neoliberal economic restructuring outlined by Sassen with reference to Caribbean and Asian migration (379). This is epitomized in Mexico's case by the Border Industrialization Program, which was established in 1965 with the aim of creating jobs to compensate for the end of the Bracero Program the previous year. Adhering to the patterns of neoliberal production, the Border Industrialization Program allowed "US-owned, labor-intensive assembly plants (maquiladoras) to operate in a virtual free-trade zone along the US border" and had the effect of further attracting workers to the border region (De Genova, "Mexican/Migrant 'Illegality,'" 69). To the extent that these workers were not able to be absorbed into the border labor market, the result was the intensification of migration to the United States. With the coming into effect of the North American Free Trade Agreement in 1994, restrictions were further reduced for the international flow of money and goods, but not for labor. Echoing the earlier effects of the Border Industrialization Program, Schmidt Camacho notes that "[e]ven the expansion of the manufacturing sector and the growth of the maquiladoras in the wake of the trade agreement did not offset the displacement of workers in both agriculture and industry" (*Migrant Imaginaries*, 288). The inability of both Mexican agriculture and Mexican industry to compete with their northern counterparts again swelled the ranks of surplus workers and triggered emigration (289).

123. Santa Ana et al., "May to Remember," 224; Cisneros, "(Re)Bordering," 261.

124. Pulido, "Day without Immigrants," 1–2; L. Chavez, *Latino Threat*, 166. Pulido points to a split between moderate and radical elements around the question of amnesty. According to her, "[t]he vast majority of immigrants are very clear on what they need: full amnesty. And while segments of the grassroots leadership have no trouble saying so, the more mainstream and moderate leadership does. Indeed, in a television interview Los Angeles mayor Antonio Villaraigosa explained that the protestors were marching for a 'bi-partisan agreement' that would protect US borders as well as the rights of immigrants. Talk about a translation crisis! As often happens, the middle-class leadership, in this case, Chicano and Latino politicians, are repackaging the demands of the working class into a form that they feel will be acceptable to the establishment—and in the process, selling out the people. No elected official is demanding amnesty" ("Day without Immigrants," 2). Varsanyi has also demonstrated the ways through which undocumented workers exert an influence and participate in the political process by having an impact on the political endorsements of their unions, by attending political rallies, and by volunteering in "get out the vote" drives. One of Varsanyi's examples is precisely the participation of undocumented people in Antonio Villaraigosa's 2001 mayoral campaign ("Getting Out the Vote," 229). The limitations of Varsanyi's focus on electoral politics, however, are evident in Pulido's account of the disconnect between the majority of participants' more radical demands in the 2006 marches, and the middle-class political leadership whose more moderate stance not only downplayed calls for amnesty but reiterated support for border security, which is today synonymous with the militarization of the border. While the form of participation that Varsanyi describes is certainly important and can have significant impacts over workers' material conditions, the 2006 mobilizations, in my estimation, also exceeded representation by mainstream political brokers (including elected officials) in participants' refusal to have their demands determined by what the political class deemed politically "feasible."

125. Beltrán, *Trouble with Unity*, 152–153.

126. Beltrán, *Trouble with Unity*, 154. While Arendt herself distinguishes between "work" and "labor," Beltrán does not strictly abide by the conceptual distinctions that Arendt confers upon them (152–154). Accordingly, and given the additional reasons that (1) the productive activity of the undocumented actually straddles Arendt's distinction between labor and work; (2) the reorganization of work under neoliberalism is producing what, in Arendtian terms, we could call the "laboring of work" in its reconfiguration of work with the attributes of

labor; and (3) both labor and work, for Arendt, fall short of the political, in the analysis that follows I also do not strictly adhere to the conceptual distinctions Arendt establishes between these terms, even while, again following Beltrán, I focus more on her conception of labor.

127. Beltrán, *Trouble with Unity*, 149 (emphasis in the original).

128. Beltrán, *Trouble with Unity*, 150, 152.

129. Beltrán is well aware of this tension, which has also been emphasized by other queer and feminist theorists (Beltrán, *Trouble with Unity*, 133–134). My contention is that her analysis is unable to overcome the depoliticizing tendencies in Arendt's framework, despite Beltrán's efforts to do so.

130. Butler and Spivak, *Who Sings the Nation-State*, 23.

131. Butler and Spivak, *Who Sings the Nation-State*, 16.

132. Rancière, *Disagreement*, 118.

133. Badiou, *Pocket Pantheon*, 4. "However," Badiou argues elsewhere, "in a certain 'objective' Marxism, and under the name 'working class,' that word ['proletariat'], because it designated a component of social analysis as leadership of the revolutionary movement . . . also represented the possibility of an identitarian instrumentalization. The great revolutionaries were always careful to block any identitarian drift in the word" (Badiou, *Rebirth*, 79).

134. Badiou, *Rebirth*, 79.

CHAPTER 4: OSCAR "ZETA" ACOSTA AND GENERIC POLITICS

1. Muñoz, *Youth, Identity, Power*, 76. "Chicano," as I employ it, designates participation in or identification with the Chicano Movement. It supposes the politicized articulation of Mexican American ethnic/racial identity as distinct. As a previous "term of disparagement for working-class Mexican Americans," the choice of the term "Chicano" itself signals the political revalorization of Mexican American identity (Allatson, *Key Terms*, 61). "Mexican American" refers to "people of Mexican descent born and[/or] raised in the United States" (Muñoz, *Youth, Identity, Power*, 27).

2. Muñoz, *Youth, Identity, Power*, 93.

3. Chabram Dernersesian, "Chicana! Rican?," 269–295; Saldívar-Hull, *Feminism on the Border*; Moraga, *Loving in the War Years*; Rodríguez, "Carnal Knowledge," 113–140; A. García, *Chicana Feminist Thought*.

4. Dean, *Solidarity of Strangers*, 8.

5. Gallego, *Chicana/o Subjectivity*, 27.

6. Badiou, *Being and Event*, 56.

7. Badiou, *Ethics*, 73.

8. Badiou, *Being and Event*, 35–36.

9. Gallego, *Chicana/o Subjectivity*, 170.

10. Haney López, *Racism on Trial*, 16–17; Acuña, *Occupied America*, 258.

11. Acuña, *Occupied America*, 259; Haney López, *Racism on Trial*, 20–21; Muñoz, *Youth, Identity, Power*, 79–80.

12. Muñoz, *Youth, Identity, Power*, 80.

13. Haney López, *Racism on Trial*, 1.

14. McCurdy, "1,000 Walk Out"; *Los Angeles Times*, "Board Will Hear Demands."

15. Acuña, *Occupied America*, 260; Torgerson, "Start of a Revolution."

16. García and Castro, *Blowout!*, 177, 184; McCurdy, "Venice High Youths"; McCurdy, "1,000 Walk Out."

17. Haney López, *Racism on Trial*, 24–27; O. Acosta, *Uncollected Works*, 8; Rosales, *Chicano!*, 193.

18. Moore, *Love and Riot*, 13; Haney López, *Racism on Trial*, 4.

19. Haney López, *Racism on Trial*, 31; O. Acosta, "East L.A. 13," 14.

20. Haney López, *Racism on Trial*, 4–5.

21. Haney López, *Racism on Trial*, 41–42. On the importance of *Hernández v. Texas* in the history of Mexican American civil rights struggles, as well as critical analyses of the racial politics and various legacies of the defense's regard of Mexican Americans as white, see Haney López, *Racism on Trial*, 76–77; Olivas, *"Colored Men" and "Hombres Aquí"*; Foley, "Becoming Hispanic," 53–70; I. García, *White but Not Equal*.

22. Mendoza, *Historia*, 206.

23. O. Acosta, "East L.A. 13," 14.

24. O. Acosta, "East L.A. 13," 14.

25. Haney López, *Racism on Trial*, 43.

26. Haney López, *Racism on Trial*, 43.

27. Haney López, *Racism on Trial*, 91, 105.

28. Haney López, *Racism on Trial*, 40.

29. By this, however, I do not mean to suggest that these cases were the *only* or *initial* source of the development of Chicano nationalism. Gómez-Quiñones identifies the ascendancy of such ideological tendencies in the United Mexican American Students as early as 1967. See Gómez-Quiñones, *Mexican Students*, 25. Nor can one ignore the influence of politico-cultural works like the "Plan Espiritual de Aztlán" (1969) in the development of Chicano nationalism, or the influence of strains within the African American civil rights movement in the United States and national liberation movements abroad in articulating oppositional politics in nationalist terms. As Haney López has demonstrated, "commonsense" notions of difference outside the courtroom also influenced Acosta and the defendants' conceptions of group distinction (Haney López, *Racism on Trial*). Instead of implying a relation of unidirectional influence between the courtroom and the

movement beyond it, Chicano nationalism appears as overdetermined. Nevertheless, the law has historically been a privileged terrain for both contesting and affirming group difference, with a high degree of influence over popular imaginaries (Gross, *What Blood Won't Tell*, 12).

30. Hobsbawm, *Nations*, 46.

31. E. Chávez, *"¡Mi Raza Primero!,"* 5, 42.

32. Anaya and Lomelí, *Aztlán.*

33. Rancière, *Disagreement*, 29 (emphasis in the original).

34. Rancière and Badiou's work share much in common, from conceptualizing the function of the state as the counting of parts, to critiquing identity politics and communicative models of democracy, to situating political subjectivation with regard to a gap in the social, among other points. Rancière's account of subjectivation, however, tends to remain at the level of the democratic irruption and leaves under-theorized the function of politics as process—the theorization of which, as I have argued, is one of the main advantages I find in Badiou's framework.

35. O. Acosta, *Uncollected Works*, 284–285.

36. Rancière, *Disagreement*, 30.

37. See Pulido, *Black, Brown, Yellow, and Left.*

38. Holloway, *Change the World*, 141.

39. Adams, "Hipsters and *Jipitecas*," 69; Tatum, *Chicano and Chicana Literature*, 102; Kowalczyk, "Oscar Zeta Acosta," 200; A. Ramírez, "Reseñas," 49; Saldívar, *Chicano Narrative*, 96; Mendoza, *Historia*, 203.

40. Aldama, *Postethnic Narrative Criticism*, 64; Kowalczyk, "Oscar Zeta Acosta," 199.

41. Kowalczyk, "Oscar Zeta Acosta," 199.

42. Aldama, *Postethnic Narrative Criticism*, 65.

43. See Kowalczyk, "Oscar Zeta Acosta," 203, on this point; and Aldama, *Postethnic Narrative Criticism*, 67, on a slightly different formulation of it.

44. O. Acosta, *Revolt*, 14.

45. González, *Chicano Novels*, 93–94; Gallego, *Chicana/o Subjectivity*, 165–166. These two critics, however, are not the only ones to point out Acosta's critical reflections on Chicano nationalism. Carrasquillo argues that Acosta "disavows nationalism or nativism . . . as false consciousness" ("Oscar 'Zeta' Acosta's American Odyssey," 78), and Hames-García maintains that Acosta exposes the naïveté behind essentialist claims to cultural authenticity ("Dr. Gonzo's Carnival," 465–466). Yet, while these critics understand Acosta's critique to consist in pointing out the insufficiency of Chicano nationalism as a fixed, stable, or well-founded identitarian category, Gallego and González argue that Acosta actually questions the adequacy of Chicano nationalism as a *political* category.

46. O. Acosta, *Revolt*, 186.

47. O. Acosta, *Revolt*, 188.

48. O. Acosta, *Revolt*, 189.

49. Gallego, *Chicana/o Subjectivity*, 167.

50. González, *Chicano Novels*, 106.

51. Gallego, *Chicana/o Subjectivity*, 167.

52. O. Acosta, *Revolt*, 27.

53. O. Acosta, *Revolt*, 27.

54. O. Acosta, *Revolt*, 28.

55. O. Acosta, *Revolt*, 28 (ellipsis in the original).

56. O. Acosta, *Revolt*, 31.

57. O. Acosta, *Revolt*, 29.

58. Saldaña-Portillo, *Revolutionary Imagination*, 264.

59. Cf. Saldaña-Portillo, *Revolutionary Imagination*, 267.

60. Indeed, notwithstanding her critique of developmentalist models of revolutionary subjectivity, Saldaña-Portillo also refuses to give up on the notion of futurity geared toward progressive change, as is made clear when she states: "[W]e should not respond by, in turn, uncritically privileging identity, tradition, and antiprogressive models of futurity. For if one continues to recognize the need for revolutionary change . . . if one's sympathies continue to lie with the revolutionary movements committed to challenging capitalist development, as mine do . . . then one accepts that some model of progress pertains" (*Revolutionary Imagination*, 6).

61. Gallego, *Chicana/o Subjectivity*, 170–171.

62. Gallego, *Chicana/o Subjectivity*, 171.

63. O. Acosta, *Revolt*, 135.

64. Gallego, *Chicana/o Subjectivity*, 171.

65. O. Acosta, *Revolt*, 17.

66. Saldívar, *Chicano Narrative*, 95.

67. Mendoza also gestures toward this additional function of Cockroach when he remarks that besides being "an umbrella term for the dispossessed, oppressed, and colonized people . . . [i]t also refers to those who would resist domination, including white allies of Chicanas/os" (*Historia*, 211).

68. O. Acosta, *Revolt*, 60.

69. O. Acosta, *Revolt*, 168.

70. For a more thorough explanation of the concept of the generic collective, see my introduction and chapter 3.

71. González, *Chicano Novels*, 103.

72. O. Acosta, *Revolt*, 196–197. I have bracketed my own ellipses in this extract.

73. González, *Chicano Novels*, 103.

74. González, *Chicano Novels*, 102.

75. O. Acosta, *Revolt*, 89–93.

76. O. Acosta, *Revolt*, 106.

77. O. Acosta, *Revolt*, 118.

78. O. Acosta, *Revolt*, 112.

79. O. Acosta, *Revolt*, 126–128.

80. O. Acosta, *Revolt*, 123, 136.

81. Though it seems plausible, and even likely, that Acosta himself was involved in at least some bombings in real life, to date no conclusive evidence has emerged to confirm this (Haney López, *Racism on Trial*, 234–235).

82. O. Acosta, *Revolt*, 201.

83. O. Acosta, *Revolt*, 204.

84. O. Acosta, *Revolt*, 207–208 (emphasis in the original).

85. Rancière, *Disagreement*, xi.

86. O. Acosta, *Revolt*, 212 (ellipses in the original).

87. O. Acosta, *Revolt*, 213.

88. O. Acosta, *Revolt*, 213.

89. O. Acosta, *Revolt*, 213.

90. O. Acosta, *Revolt*, 213.

91. O. Acosta, *Revolt*, 213 (emphasis and ellipsis in the original).

92. O. Acosta, *Revolt*, 235 (ellipses in the original).

93. O. Acosta, *Revolt*, 238.

94. Roland Zanzibar is a Mexican American reporter who is killed by the police the day of the Chicano Moratorium. The police claim that they received information from an unidentified source during the riots that there was someone with a gun in the Silver Dollar Bar. After arriving at the bar, the police shot a tear gas projectile to clear the building. The projectile hit Zanzibar in the head and ultimately killed him. Since Zanzibar had been critical of the police, the militants believe that his death had not been accidental.

95. O. Acosta, *Revolt*, 247–249 (emphasis in the original). I have bracketed my own ellipses in this extract.

96. O. Acosta, *Revolt*, 237–238.

97. This is the actual spelling of his name. In the novel, Acosta spells it with one *t*.

98. Houston and Smith, "Mexican-American Observers."

99. The following exchange is found in Houston and Smith's news article "Mexican-American Observers":

When Pittluck asked attorneys representing the district attorney's office and the Salazar family if they had any further questions for the videotape commentator Wallace, an attorney among the observers, Oscar Acosta, arose and said, "Yes, I do."

"Mr. Acosta," said Pittluck, forcefully, "you're a member of the bar and you know that you're not here today . . ."

Acosta interrupted brusquely, "You're a disgrace to your profession, you and the attorneys sitting at (the counsel table). You are prejudicing the jury by showing this film. It is totally irrelevant." (p. 3, col. 2)

Here is a similar exchange from another article by the same authors that took place during the questioning of Thomas Wilson, the deputy who fired the shot that killed Salazar:

At one point in the questioning, Pittluck asked Wilson, "What were you aiming at?" on the first shot.

Before Wilson could reply, Mexican-American attorney Oscar Acosta, frequently an outspoken critic of sheriff's witnesses, jumped to his feet and shouted:

"He was aiming at Ruben Salazar, that's the one he was aiming at. This is an obscenity, Mr. Pittluck. We are sick of it. This room is polluted with perjury and you know it."

Acosta then led a walkout of about 25 Chicano militants. (Houston and Smith, "Deputy Says He Did Not Know," p. 21, col. 1)

100. Houston and Smith, "Mexican-American Observers"; E. Chávez, "¡Mi Raza Primero!," 71.

101. This is not to say that the Fernandez inquest as it appears in the novel was totally made up. Indeed, at the beginning of 1970, Acosta had also participated in a coroner's inquest into the death of Richard Lupe Hernandez as the attorney representing the family. Like Fernandez, Hernandez was found dead in his cell by hanging. See Drummond, "Noguchi Makes Rare Move."

102. O. Acosta, *Revolt*, 216.

103. O. Acosta, *Revolt*, 230.

104. O. Acosta, *Revolt*, 249 (emphasis and ellipsis in the original).

105. Cf. Mendoza, *Historia*, 223.

106. O. Acosta, *Revolt*, 254.

107. O. Acosta, *Revolt*, 256.

108. Cf. O. Acosta, *Revolt*, 104.

109. O. Acosta, *Revolt*, 257–258.

110. González, *Chicano Novels*, 110–111.

111. Cf. González, *Chicano Novels*, 111–112.

CHAPTER 5: BETWEEN CROWD AND GROUP

1. Butler and Yancy, "What's Wrong with 'All Lives Matter'?"

2. Bosteels, "Antagonism," 154.

3. Indeed, Keeanga-Yamahtta Taylor identifies as one of the most powerful effects of the Black Lives Matter movement the way it has shifted attention back upon institutional and systemic factors in the production of racism and inequality, thus making such structural factors the necessary object of critique and the target of militant action (Taylor, *#BlackLivesMatter*, chap. 6).

4. Since the mid-1990s, the official strategy of border enforcement in the southern US border has been to rechannel border crossers toward the most dangerous and inhospitable environments in order to make death itself function as a deterrent, a strategy known as "prevention through deterrence." The dramatic increase in migrant deaths that subsequently occurred—one conservative estimate puts the number of deaths at 5,596 between 1998 and 2012—was thus an entirely foreseen and accepted consequence of this policy, making it plain that for the Border Patrol and the US government, migrant lives do not matter either. On this policy and the rate of migrant deaths, see De León, *Land of Open Graves*, 36. Black Lives Matter, however, has also expanded to organize against anti-black violence and discrimination in immigration enforcement and detention. See Garza, "Herstory of the #BlackLivesMatter Movement"; and Black Alliance for Just Immigration, http://blackalliance.org.

5. Bosteels, "Antagonism," 155.

6. Wilderson, "Prison Slave," 22.

7. My emphasis.

8. Hallward, *Damming the Flood*, 378n45.

9. Laclau, *Populist Reason*, ix.

10. Nye, *Origins of Crowd Psychology*, 23–29; Laclau, *Populist Reason*, 36–37; Pick, "Freud's *Group Psychology*," 55–56.

11. Le Bon, *Crowd*, 32.

12. Freud, *Group Psychology*, 8–9.

13. Freud, *Group Psychology*, 9.

14. Freud, *Group Psychology*, 14.

15. Freud, *Group Psychology*, 14.

16. Freud, *Group Psychology*, 14.

17. Given that the German title of Freud's book is *Massenpsychologie und Ich-Analyse*, it can also be translated as "mass psychology" rather than "group psychology." In Spanish, for example, it is usually translated as *psicología de masas* (mass psychology). On this point see Bosteels, *Marx and Freud*, 19n33.

18. Freud, *Group Psychology*, 4.

19. McDougall, *Group Mind*, 67–70.

20. Freud, *Group Psychology*, 14–15. Freud is citing McDougall, *Group Mind*, 33.

21. McDougall, *Group Mind*, 68.

22. McDougall, *Group Mind*, 69.

23. Žižek, *Sublime Object*, 132.

24. Freud, *Group Psychology*, 21–22.

25. Freud also briefly considers the existence of leaderless groups that may be more advanced and able to endure a lesser degree of completeness by substituting "an idea, an abstraction," for the leader (*Group Psychology*, 29).

26. Freud, *Group Psychology*, 44 (emphasis in the original).

27. The common object stands at a variable distance from the members and occupies a limit position internal to the group itself. In the case of groups constituted around a leader, where the original distance between the ego and the ego ideal is not very large, Freud suggests that the leader "need only possess the typical qualities of the individuals concerned in a particularly clearly marked and pure form, and need only give an impression of greater force and of more freedom of libido; and in that case the need for a strong chief will often meet him half-way and invest him with a predominance to which he would otherwise perhaps have had no claim" (*Group Psychology*, 57). Anticipating my analysis of the masculine side of Lacan's formulas of sexuation, one could say that this kind of leader functions more as an "example" than as an "exception." As we will see later, Laclau's theory of hegemony follows a similar logic. On the logic of the example versus the exception, see also Agamben, *Homo Sacer*, 21–22.

28. I also turn to Laclau because of his ontological formulation of the subject—a "subject of the political [that] exists . . . apart from subject positions on the ontic plane of the social" (Marchart, "Name of the People," 11)—and his theorization of the political implications of psychoanalytic theory. His proximity to Badiou, moreover, enables me to tease out what I consider to be slight but significant differences between them. My engagement with Laclau focuses mainly on *On Populist Reason* because of this book's own engagement with Freud's *Group Psychology* and crowd theory, and, relatedly, because of his more sustained focus on affect and the social bond.

29. Laclau, *Populist Reason*, ix–x.

30. Laclau, *Populist Reason*, 107–108 (emphasis in the original).

31. Laclau, *Populist Reason*, 116.

32. Laclau, *Populist Reason*, 93.

33. Laclau, *Populist Reason*, 108.

34. Laclau, *Populist Reason*, 108 (emphasis in the original). See Marchart, "Name of the People," 7–10, for a more detailed analysis of the logic of naming in Laclau.

35. Laclau, *Populist Reason*, 97, 95.

36. Laclau, *Populist Reason*, 95.

37. Laclau, *Populist Reason*, 96. He continues: "[I]n an equivalential relation, demands share nothing positive, just the fact that they all remain unfulfilled. So there is a specific negativity which is inherent to the equivalential link" (96).

38. Laclau, *Populist Reason*, 105.

39. Laclau, *Populist Reason*, 93.

40. The attention that Laclau gives to the role of affect in his later work is at least in part a response to criticism that his earlier ontologico-rhetorical theorization of political articulation tended to minimize or ignore this dimension. See Stavrakakis, "Antinomies of Formalism," 264–265.

41. This is clear when elsewhere Laclau describes how the particular demands of undocumented people attain a level of universality: "So how can some kind of universality emerge out of them? Only insofar as people excluded from many other sites within a situation . . . perceive their common nature as excluded and live their struggles—in their particularity—as part of a larger emancipatory struggle" ("Ethics," 131).

42. Laclau, *Populist Reason*, 77.

43. Rousseau, "Social Contract," 155.

44. Laclau, *Populist Reason*, 106.

45. Laclau, *Populist Reason*, 116.

46. Laclau, *Populist Reason*, 115.

47. Along these lines, Simon Critchley explains Laclau's notion of hegemony thusly: "beginning from a position of emptiness, a particular group posits the fullness of the universal and hegemonically articulates that universality in political action, thereby becoming a political subject" (*Infinitely Demanding*, 104).

48. Žižek, *Sublime Object*, 128.

49. To return to the example of Black Lives Matter with which I began, it would imply the production of other lives (the lives of "real criminals" or the undocumented) as constitutively devaluated.

50. Benjamin Arditi notes that the question of fullness in Laclau's theory also implies the creation of a split within the populist formation between the intellectual/political leaders that know it to only ever be mythical and the rest of the people that take it to be a real possibility. Thus, "[o]n the one hand, we have something that resembles . . . a subject supposed to know. . . . Whether it is the theorist or leader, this is a subject perceived to misrecognize nothing because s/he is fully aware that there is no chance for a reconciled society actually materializing," Arditi points out, while "[o]n the other hand, we find the masses, who embark in a project of plentitude that is presented to them as a space of inscription for all social demands and as a scenario where those demands will actually be fulfilled" ("Populism," 496). For another thorough critique of Laclau—this time with regard to his (lack of) theorization of the state, discourse, and representation—see the first chapter of Beasley-Murray, *Posthegemony*.

51. Badiou, *Metapolitics*, 76–77.

52. Badiou, *Metapolitics*, 75.

53. Badiou, *Metapolitics*, 72.

54. Badiou, *Metapolitics*, 73.

55. Badiou, *Metapolitics*, 77.

56. For a more thorough exposition of his treatment of contending affects, see Badiou, *Logics of Worlds*, 76, 86–88. Affects in these pages, while not unrelated to the consistency of a political process, are defined primarily through the kinds of postures that such a process can adopt with regard to the treatment of continuity and discontinuity. Compare this with Badiou's earlier theorization of the four subject-effects in part VI of *Theory of the Subject*.

57. This should not be taken to imply that participants themselves will not experience a series of affects, which depending on circumstances can range from trauma and terror to extreme joy, in the very process of unbinding. See Beasley-Murray, *Posthegemony*, 140–141, for an example in the context of the guerrilla movement in El Salvador.

58. Dolar, "Freud," 20.

59. Freud and Einstein, "Why War?," 13. I return to this suggestion by Freud in this chapter's final section.

60. I present a more detailed exegesis of the logic of the generic procedure in the introduction and in chapter 3.

61. Badiou, *Being and Event*, 339; Badiou, *Theoretical Writings*, 127.

62. Badiou, *Ethics*, 53–56.

63. Badiou, *Ethics*, 54–55.

64. More recently, however, Badiou has begun insisting on the notion of the "Idea" as a necessary category in his philosophy, and on the "communist" Idea in politics. Though present in a different form in his earlier work, his current conception of the Idea is developed around the problematic that concerns *Logics of Worlds*, the sequel to *Being and Event*, which supplements the earlier ontological formulation of his philosophy with a phenomenology. The Idea is like a Borromean knot that ties together a singular politics, its historical inscription, and a subjective figure (Badiou, *Communist Hypothesis*, 235–238). The Idea is not what holds the members of the generic collective together, as identitarian fantasy does for "the people" in Laclau's conception. It is not that on which the consistency of the subject depends, but is that which enables the individual to consist in his/her subjective capacity—it is what helps that part of the subject that remains an individual to continue with the process (*Communist Hypothesis*, 239).

65. Gibson, *Fanon*, 11–12; Sekyi-Otu, *Fanon's Dialectic*, 40–46.

66. Fanon, *Wretched*, 14, 94.

67. Sekyi-Otu, *Fanon's Dialectic*, 34, 35 (emphasis in the original). Similarly, Gibson insists that Fanon's whole project is to get beyond colonial and anticolonial Manichaeanism (Gibson, *Fanon*, 6–7).

68. Karatani, *Transcritique*, 47.

69. Žižek, *Parallax View*, 20.

70. Fanon, *Dying Colonialism*, 120.

71. Cf. Freud: "We have seen that with an army and a church this contrivance [by which a group is held together] is the illusion that the leader loves all of the individuals equally and justly. But this is simply an idealistic remodeling of the state of affairs in the primal horde, where all of the sons knew that they were equally persecuted by the primal father, and feared him equally" (*Group Psychology*, 53).

72. Laclau, *Populist Reason*, 97.

73. Fanon, *Wretched*, 10.

74. Fanon, *Wretched*, 105.

75. Fanon, *Wretched*, 100.

76. Fanon, *Wretched*, 103.

77. Fanon, *Wretched*, 105.

78. Fanon, *Wretched*, 103.

79. Fanon, *Wretched*, 83.

80. Fanon, *Wretched*, 98–99.

81. Fanon, *Wretched*, 106.

82. Fanon, *Wretched*, 110–111.

83. Fanon, *Dying Colonialism*, 32.

84. Fanon, *Dying Colonialism*, 152 (emphasis in the original). Compare this with Martin Luther King Jr.'s declaration that "[a]nyone who lives inside the United States can never be considered an outsider anywhere within its bounds" ("Letter from Birmingham Jail," 35). I analyze this remark at the end of chapter 2.

85. One must also note that, though considered Algerian, Fanon and many other FLN militants were living in exile. While this does not undermine the claim that everyone living in Algeria is Algerian, it suggests that living in Algeria is not the *only* determination of belonging.

86. Thus identitarian distinction begins to be undermined: "Once we embrace a fully extensional theory of set (whereby a set is defined solely by what belongs to it), there is no obvious sense in which a set retains any distinctive unity at all" (Hallward, *Badiou*, 336).

87. Briefly, Georg Cantor, the father of modern set theory, first attempted to define the abstract notion of "set" as "the grouping into a totality of quite distinct objects of our intuition or thought" (quoted in Badiou, *Being and Event*, 38). "Without exaggeration," explains Badiou, "Cantor assembles in this definition every single concept whose decomposition is brought about by set theory: the concept of totality, of the object, of distinction, and that of intuition" (38). Cantor's definition was clearly inadequate, since it involved a series of concepts that ran counter to the very implications of set theory. In consequence, the notion of "intuition of objects" was reformulated "such that [a set] could only be thought as the extension of a concept, or of a property expressed in a . . . formalized

language" (39). In this way, a set was redefined as the counting-as-one of all the terms that possessed a formally, rigorously specified property. "[T]he naïve optimism shown by Cantor concerning the power of intuition to totalize its objects," Badiou continues, "is transferred here to the security that can be guaranteed by a well-constructed language" (39). Yet this "intensional" thesis, held by Gottlob Frege, which was based on the "speculative proposition . . . that nothing of the multiple can occur in excess of a well-constructed language, and therefore that being, inasmuch as it is constrained to present itself to language as the referent-multiple of a property, cannot cause a breakdown in the architecture of this language if the latter has been rigorously constructed," was itself proven false by the existence of certain sets that caused this language to fall into paradox (40). Among the consequences of the inability to define a set by means either of intuition or language was the necessity of "abandon[ing] all hope of explicitly defining the notion of set. . . . By consequence, it is of the very essence of set theory to only possess an implicit mastery of its 'objects' (multiplicities, sets): these multiplicities are deployed in an axiom-system in which the property 'to be a set' does not figure. . . . Axiomatization is required such that the multiple, left to the implicitness of its counting rule, be delivered *without concept*" (43; emphasis in the original).

88. For other readings of Fanon that draw on Badiou, see Mellino, "Notes from the Underground," 61–73; Farred, "Wretchedness," 159–172; Neocosmos, "Nation and Its Politics," 187–199; Pithouse, "Fidelity to Fanon," 225–234.

89. Hallward, *Badiou*, 333. The resonance of the FLN's prescriptive statement on national belonging with Badiou's own political practice with the Organisation Politique in France against the persecution of the *sans-papiers* (undocumented workers) in recent decades can be gauged by the organization's insistence that "everyone who is here [in France] is from here" (quoted in Hallward, *Badiou*, 233). Despite the advantages of this axiomatic definition of belonging, however, when it comes to immigration it is clear that it must also be supplemented by a position that maintains an openness toward the cross-border movement of people, at the same time that it targets the root causes of labor and other types of migration (in both sending and receiving countries), if such a definition is to avoid becoming compatible with a reactionary hardening and militarization of national borders. After all, the assertion that everyone in France (or the United States) is from there is not by itself incompatible with arguments seeking to impede *new* arrivals from coming into the country. This would imply inscribing politics within a more transnational frame, which entails pushing beyond the boundaries of Badiou's own conceptual framework. Among other things, it would imply placing different national situations in relation to each other both with regard to capitalism as world-system and with regard to a politics capable of traversing them. It is this kind of traversality—virtually

ignored in Badiou's work—that Isin suggests when he includes in his definition of traversal citizenship "the right to act across or against frontiers" (Isin, *Citizens without Frontiers*, 149). Thomas Nail also underscores the importance of an "extra-territorial" approach to organizing in his critical reading of Badiou's philosophy and activism as it pertains to undocumented immigration (Nail, "Sans-Papiers," 124).

90. Fanon, *Dying Colonialism*, 157.

91. Badiou, *Rebirth*, 57.

92. Fanon, *Wretched*, 179.

93. Fanon's becoming Algerian can thus also be compared to Ernesto "Che" Guevara's becoming Cuban through his participation in the Cuban Revolution.

94. Quoted in Fanon, *Dying Colonialism*, 163.

95. Quoted in Fanon, *Dying Colonialism*, 176.

96. Fanon, *Dying Colonialism*, 163.

97. Fanon, *Dying Colonialism*, 157, 161–162.

98. Badiou, *Being and Event*, 339.

99. And remembering that many FLN members were in exile, including Fanon at the time of writing his Algerian texts, to be Algerian could mean to participate in the process through which Algeria as revolutionary nation is brought into being, even if this entails not being physically present in "national" space. This can also open up the notion of belonging to other determinations that can remain out of view of a strictly set-theoretical conception based solely on location.

100. Fanon, *Wretched*, 144.

101. Fanon, *Dying Colonialism*, 121.

102. Fanon, *Dying Colonialism*, 89.

103. Fanon, *Wretched*, 18.

104. Fanon, *Dying Colonialism*, 101.

105. Fanon, *Dying Colonialism*, 110.

106. Fanon, *Dying Colonialism*, 110.

107. Fanon, *Dying Colonialism*, 78. Significantly, however, Fanon also rejects the idea that such a break with compulsion is either easy, clean, or final: "no revolution can, with finality and without repercussions, make a clean sweep of well-nigh instinctive modes of behavior" (*Dying Colonialism*, 113).

108. Fanon, *Dying Colonialism*, 108.

109. Fanon, *Dying Colonialism*, 108. For critical feminist readings of Fanon, see Helie-Lucas, "Women, Nationalism, and Religion," 271–282 (critiques Fanon's account of women's liberation as mythical); McClintock, "Fanon and Gender Agency," 283–293 (argues that, notwithstanding Fanon's acute understanding of the dynamics of colonial power and gender, he falls back on masculine tropes to depict women's agency, at the same time that the latter is made

derivative of the agency of men); Fuss, "Interior Colonies," 294–328 (critiques Fanon for fetishizing the veil much like the European colonizers do, for disregarding black women's subjectivity, for ignoring the role of sexual violence against black women in colonialism, and for designating homosexuality as culturally white); Sharpley-Whiting, "Fanon's Feminist Consciousness," 329–353 (argues that Fanon displays a protofeminist consciousness).

110. Fanon, *Dying Colonialism*, 109.

111. Fanon, *Dying Colonialism*, 109.

112. Fanon, *Dying Colonialism*, 114. It is important to note that colonialism also effects its own form of unbinding: "The tactic [of internment] adopted by French colonialism . . . has had the result of separating the people from each other, of fragmenting them, with the sole objective of making any cohesion impossible" (118). This instance of colonialist unbinding, moreover, also develops in relation to the signifier of revolution, yet does so in both a reactionary mode (by arguing that what is going on is not a revolution but is the work of a criminal few) and an obscurantist mode (which justifies colonization and the ideological integrity of the French nation by reference to the event of the French Revolution). It aims to counter revolutionary unbinding by disrupting its process, a revolutionary process that also entails the reconstitution of transformed social relations on new principles. Colonialism seeks to unbind, but with the ultimate goal of reconstituting social relations as they once were—hence its parallel efforts to "organize the tribes and religious brotherhoods into parties" (Fanon, *Wretched*, 72)—and in a way that makes them more easy to govern.

113. Fanon, *Dying Colonialism*, 78.

114. Fanon, *Dying Colonialism*, 87.

115. Fanon, *Wretched*, 2.

116. Fanon, *Dying Colonialism*, 76 (emphasis in the original).

117. Fanon, *Dying Colonialism*, 77.

118. Fanon, *Dying Colonialism*, 86.

119. Fanon, *Dying Colonialism*, 86.

120. Fanon, *Dying Colonialism*, 87.

121. Fanon, *Dying Colonialism*, 84.

122. Compare this with Bosteels's reading of Bolívar Echeverría's notion of "national substance" (Bosteels, "Estado, comuna, comunidad," 50–70).

123. Fanon, *Wretched*, 178.

124. Fanon, *African Revolution*, 43. Along these lines, Gibson notes that for Fanon, "the end of colonialism would be truly expressed in the reformation and recreation of a vibrant national culture which had its basis in revolutionary transformation rather than ethnic identity, with a future constructed by all who wanted to play a positive part" (Gibson, *Fanon*, 13).

125. Freud, *Group Psychology*, 22.

126. Renata Salecl underscores that "[t]he reassertion of sexual difference in Lacanian psychoanalysis is thus not a return to biology but a way to stress that what we call 'sexual difference' is first and above all the name for a certain fundamental *deadlock* inherent in the symbolic order. Lacan's 'formulas of sexuation' provide the logical matrix of this deadlock" (Salecl, "Introduction," 2; emphasis in the original). See also Bryant, *Democracy of Objects*, 251.

127. Bryant does something similar in *Democracy of Objects*. See also Cutrofello, "Ontological Status," 141–170. Badiou's own positing of mathematics as ontology is inspired by Lacan's appreciation of pure logic as the "science of the real," remembering that for Lacan the real is precisely the impasse of formalization (Badiou, *Being and Event*, 4–5; Badiou, *Theory of the Subject*, 23, 154).

128. For a brief and accessible explanation of the conventions of first-order logic, see Badiou, *Being and Event*, 49–51.

129. Freud, *Group Psychology*, 52. Lacan also designates as the "father function" the exception that negates the phallic function (*SXX*, 79). Interestingly, it seems that while Fanon distinguishes the colonial master from the master in Hegel's dialectic in that the former, unlike the latter, does not require recognition from the slave, it is the exceptional figure of the primal father that more closely resembles the colonial master, as when Freud states, "His intellectual acts were strong and independent even in isolation, and his will needed no reinforcement from others" (Fanon, *Black Skin, White Masks*, 220; Freud, *Group Psychology*, 52).

130. Lacan, *SXX*, 79.

131. Lacan, *SXX*, 79–80.

132. Lacan, *SXX*, 80–81.

133. Lacan, *SXX*, 102–103.

134. Grigg, "Lacan and Badiou," 57.

135. Badiou, "Subject and Infinity," 218.

136. Badiou, "Subject and Infinity," 218 (emphasis in the original).

137. Badiou, "Subject and Infinity," 219, 220.

138. Badiou, "Subject and Infinity," 224.

139. Badiou, "Subject and Infinity," 219.

140. Zupančič, "Perforated Sheet," 291; Lacan, *SXX*, 8.

141. Zupančič, "Perforated Sheet," 292.

142. The first is when Lacan adds that while Achilles can never catch up to the tortoise, he can nevertheless *pass* it (Lacan, *SXX*, 8; Zupančič, "Perforated Sheet," 293–294).

143. Zupančič, "Perforated Sheet," 294 (emphasis in the original).

144. Lacan, *SXX*, 103.

145. Zupančič, "Perforated Sheet," 295.

146. "Due to a predilection whose origin I will leave the reader to determine," Badiou states in *Being and Event*, "I will choose the symbol ♀ for this

inscription. This symbol will be read 'generic multiple,' 'generic' being the adjective retained by mathematicians to designate the indiscernible, the absolutely indeterminate" (356). Tracy McNulty, however, is critical of Badiou's linking of woman to universality—indeed, Lacan himself restricted the universal to the male side (McNulty, "Feminine Love," 206; Lacan, *SXX*, 80). By reading together Badiou's *Saint Paul* and "What Is Love?," McNulty suggests that Badiou figures "feminine" or "maternal" love as the exception to the law of castration within a male fantasy (McNulty, "Feminine Love," 202), thereby turning it into another object that "gives consistency to the One of the universal totality" (204). Thus, even when she concedes that Badiou acknowledges the inability of overcoming castration by means of an object, McNulty maintains that, for him, "it seems important that woman's way of supplementing the sexual nonrelation—or of denying castration—be retained, and made the support for a universal totality" (207). Ironically, it seems that McNulty's critique of Badiou mirrors Badiou's critique of Lacan, which I noted before with regard to virtual infinity. What Badiou fails to see in Lacan (an account of actual infinity on the female side), McNulty fails to see in Badiou (a conception of the universal, also on the female side, that is not based on fantasy). Badiou takes Lacan's notion of infinity to be nothing more than the *objet a* of a finitist fantasy, while McNulty sees in Badiou's notion of feminine love the *objet a* of the fantasy of a universal totality. What McNulty seems to disregard is that for Badiou, the "universal totality" that he designates as the humanity function, and that the feminine position sustains, itself appears to be incomplete—hence its visual representation as both open and marked by a dotted line (Badiou, "What Is Love?," 197).

147. Bryant, *Democracy of Objects*, 256 (emphasis in the original).

148. Zupančič, "Perforated Sheet," 295.

149. Dolar, "Freud," 21.

150. Dolar, *Voice*, 92.

151. Badiou, *Theory of the Subject*, 128.

152. Dolar, "Freud," 26.

153. It is thus perhaps no coincidence that the crowd has frequently been associated with femininity (Pick, "Freud's *Group Psychology*," 45, 57).

154. Cf. Hallward, "Will of the People," 17–29; and Hallward, "Fanon and Political Will," 213–224.

155. Hallward, "Fanon and Political Will," 215.

156. Fanon, *Wretched*, 89.

157. Fanon, *Wretched*, 84.

158. Fanon, *Wretched*, 86.

159. Fanon, *Wretched*, 127.

160. Fanon, *Wretched*, 143.

161. Fanon, *Wretched*, 128.

162. Fanon, *Wretched*, 128 (my emphasis).

163. Fanon, *Wretched*, 130.

164. On this latter point, compare with Jodi Dean's statement that "[t]he crowd's breach of the predictable and given creates the possibility that a political subject might appear. The party steps into that breach and fights to keep it open for the people" (*Crowds and Party*, 5–6).

165. It is obvious that historical conditions also influence the trajectory of the party, yet mass action continues to push politics forward against the friction of historical constraints.

166. This differs from Badiou's own designation of the numericality of politics (*Metapolitics*, 150–151). On the other hand, inasmuch as for Badiou the Two is also that by which the truth of love is produced, it may allow us to once again bring the logic of "love" back into politics, but in a way that evacuates this category of the fantasy of union. That is, while I have been arguing against the conception of a political collective held together by libidinal bonds (love), for Badiou love names the way in which a subject consists in the irreparable disjunction between two people. It is this kind of love consisting in disjunction rather than in synthesis that characterizes a revolutionary collective. The Two of which I speak, however, does not reference two people, but two logics. This may also imply that one must break the strict separation between philosophy's conditions.

167. Fanon, *Wretched*, 221. Indeed, while at times Fanon places the creation of a "new man" in the future (*Wretched*, 239), at other times he affirms its actuality. Thus, in *A Dying Colonialism*, he affirms that the Algerian Revolution "has [already] produced a new humanity and no one must fail to recognize this fact" (28).

168. Fanon, *Wretched*, 220.

169. Fanon, *Dying Colonialism*, 96. Fanon's description resonates with Rancière, according to whom politics effects a change upon the distribution of the sensible.

170. Badiou, *Theory of the Subject*, 169.

171. Badiou, *Theory of the Subject*, 173.

172. Lacan, *SXI*, 127.

173. Bosteels, *Marx and Freud*, 16.

174. Freud, "Question of a *Weltanschauung*," 195–225; Lacan, *SXX*, 30.

175. Bosteels, *Marx and Freud*, 17.

BIBLIOGRAPHY

Acosta, Abraham. "Hinging on Exclusion and Exception: Bare Life, the US/ Mexico Border, and *Los que nunca llegarán.*" *Social Text* 30, no. 4 (Winter 2012): 103–123.

————. *Thresholds of Illiteracy: Theory, Latin America, and the Crisis of Resistance.* New York: Fordham University Press, 2014.

Acosta, Curtis. "Dangerous Minds in Tucson: The Banning of Mexican American Studies and Critical Thinking in Arizona." *Journal of Educational Controversy* 8, no. 1 (2014): 1–18.

Acosta, Oscar "Zeta." *The Autobiography of a Brown Buffalo.* New York: Vintage Books, 1989 [1972].

————. "The East L.A. 13 vs. the L.A. Superior Court." *El Grito* 3, no. 2 (Winter 1970): 12–18.

————. *Oscar "Zeta" Acosta: The Uncollected Works.* Edited by Ilan Stavans. Houston: Arte Público, 1996.

————. *The Revolt of the Cockroach People.* New York: Vintage Books, 1989 [1973].

Acuña, Rodolfo. *Occupied America: A History of Chicanos.* 6th ed. New York: Pearson Longman, 2007.

Acuña, Rodolfo, Bill Bigelow, Richard Delgado, and Jean Stefancic. *Amici Curiae for Maya Arce v. Huppenthal.* November 25, 2013.

Adams, Rachel. "Hipsters and *Jipitecas*: Literary Countercultures on Both Sides of the Border." *American Literary History* 16, no. 1 (2004): 58–84.

Agamben, Giorgio. *Homo Sacer: Sovereign Power and Bare Life.* Translated by Daniel Heller-Roazen. Stanford, CA: Stanford University Press, 1998.

Aldama, Frederick Luis. *Postethnic Narrative Criticism: Magicorealism in Oscar "Zeta" Acosta, Ana Castillo, Julie Dash, Hanif Kureishi, and Salman Rushdie.* Austin: University of Texas Press, 2003.

Alexander, Michelle. *The New Jim Crow: Mass Incarceration in the Age of Color-blindness.* 2nd ed. New York: New Press, 2012.

Allatson, Paul. *Key Terms in Latino/a Cultural and Literary Studies.* Malden, MA: Blackwell, 2007.

Althusser, Louis. "Ideology and Ideological State Apparatuses: Notes towards an Investigation." In *Lenin and Philosophy and Other Essays,* translated by Ben Brewster, 85–126. New York: Monthly Review Press, 2001.

Anaya, Rudolfo A., and Francisco Lomelí, eds. *Aztlán: Essays on the Chicano Homeland.* Albuquerque: University of New Mexico Press, 1989.

Anderson, Benedict. *Imagined Communities: Reflections on the Origin and Spread of Nationalism.* Rev. ed. New York: Verso, 2006.

Anderson, Melinda D. "The Ongoing Battle over Ethnic Studies." *Atlantic.* March 7, 2016. https://www.theatlantic.com/education/archive/2016/03/the-ongoing-battle-over-ethnic-studies/472422/.

Aparicio, Frances. "Latino Cultural Studies." In *Critical Latin American and Latino Studies,* edited by Juan Poblete, 3–31. Minneapolis: University of Minnesota Press, 2003.

Arditi, Benjamin. "Populism Is Hegemony Is Politics? On Ernesto Laclau's *On Populist Reason.*" *Constellations* 17, no. 3 (2010): 488–497.

Arendt, Hannah. "The Decline of the Nation-State and the End of the Rights of Man." In *The Origins of Totalitarianism,* 267–302. New York: Harvest Books, 1968.

———. *The Human Condition.* 2nd ed. Chicago: University of Chicago Press, 1998.

———. "What Is Freedom?" In *Between Past and Future: Six Exercises in Political Thought,* 143–171. New York: Viking, 1961.

Bacon, David. *Illegal People: How Globalization Creates Migration and Criminalizes Immigrants.* Boston: Beacon, 2008.

Badiou, Alain. *Being and Event.* Translated by Oliver Feltham. London: Continuum, 2006.

———. *The Century.* Translated by Alberto Toscano. Malden, MA: Polity, 2007.

———. *The Communist Hypothesis.* Translated by David Macey and Steve Corcoran. New York: Verso, 2010.

———. *Ethics: An Essay on the Understanding of Evil.* Translated by Peter Hallward. New York: Verso, 2001.

———. *Logics of Worlds: Being and Event II.* Translated by Alberto Toscano. London: Continuum, 2009.

———. *The Meaning of Sarkozy.* Translated by David Fernbach. New York: Verso, 2008.

———. *Metapolitics.* Translated by Jason Barker. New York: Verso, 2006.

———. *Pocket Pantheon: Figures of Postwar Philosophy*. Translated by David Macey. New York: Verso, 2009.

———. *The Rebirth of History*. Translated by Gregory Elliott. New York: Verso, 2012.

———. "The Subject and Infinity." In *Conditions*, translated by Steven Corcoran, 211–227. London: Continuum, 2008.

———. *Theoretical Writings*. Translated by Alberto Toscano and Ray Brassier. London: Continuum, 2006.

———. *Theory of the Subject*. Translated by Bruno Bosteels. London: Continuum, 2009.

———. "What Is Love?" In *Conditions*, translated by Steven Corcoran, 179–198. London: Continuum, 2008.

Baker, Bryan, and Nancy Rytina. *Estimates of the Unauthorized Immigrant Population Residing in the United States: January 2012*. Washington, DC: Department of Homeland Security, Office of Immigration Statistics, 2013.

Balderrama, Francisco E., and Raymond Rodríguez. *Decade of Betrayal: Mexican Repatriation in the 1930s*. Rev. ed. Albuquerque: University of New Mexico Press, 2006.

Balibar, Étienne. "Citizen Subject." In *Who Comes after the Subject?*, edited by Eduardo Cadava, Peter Connor, and Jean-Luc Nancy, 33–57. New York: Routledge, 1991.

———. "Is a Philosophy of Human Civic Rights Possible? New Reflections on Equaliberty." *South Atlantic Quarterly* 103, no. 2–3 (Spring/Summer 2004): 311–322.

———. "The Nation Form: History and Ideology." In *Race, Nation, Class: Ambiguous Identities*, edited by Étienne Balibar and Immanuel Wallerstein, translated by Chris Turner, 86–106. New York: Verso, 1991.

———. "'Rights of Man' and 'Rights of the Citizen': The Modern Dialectic of Equality and Freedom." In *Masses, Classes, Ideas: Studies on Politics and Philosophy before and after Marx*, 39–59. New York: Routledge, 1994.

Beasley-Murray, Jon. *Posthegemony: Political Theory and Latin America*. Minneapolis: University of Minnesota Press, 2010.

Beiner, Ronald. "Introduction." In *Theorizing Citizenship*, edited by Ronald Beiner, 1–28. New York: SUNY Press, 1995.

Bellamy, Richard. *Citizenship: A Very Short Introduction*. New York: Oxford University Press, 2008.

Beltrán, Cristina. *The Trouble with Unity: Latino Politics and the Creation of Identity*. New York: Oxford University Press, 2010.

Benanav, Aaron. "Misery and Debt: On the Logic and History of Surplus Populations and Surplus Capital." *Endnotes* 2 (2010): 20–51.

Bentley, Eric. *Are You Now or Have You Ever Been: The Investigation of Show Business by the Un-American Activities Committee, 1947–1958*. New York: Harper Colophon Books, 1972.

———. *Bertolt Brecht before the Committee On Un-American Activities: House of Representatives, 80th Congress, 1st Session, Oct. 20–30, 1947, an Historical Encounter*. New York: Folkways Records, 1963.

———, ed. *Thirty Years of Treason: Excerpts from Hearings before the House Committee on Un-American Activities, 1938–1968*. New York: Viking, 1971.

Bernstein, Nina. "For Those Deported, Court Rulings Come Too Late." *New York Times*. July 20, 2010.

Betancur, John J., and Maricela Garcia. "The 2006–2007 Immigration Mobilizations and the Community Capacity: The Experience of Chicago." *Latino Studies* 9, no. 1 (2011): 10–37.

Beverley, John. *Latinamericanism after 9/11*. Durham, NC: Duke University Press, 2011.

Black Alliance for Just Immigration. http://blackalliance.org.

Bloemraad, Irene, Kim Voss, and Taeku Lee. "The Protests of 2006: What Were They, How Do We Understand Them, Where Do We Go?" In *Rallying for Immigrant Rights: The Fight for Inclusion in 21st Century America*, edited by Kim Voss and Irene Bloemraad, 3–43. Berkeley: University of California Press, 2011.

Bonazzi, Tiziano. "Frederick Jackson Turner's Frontier Thesis and the Self-Consciousness of America." *Journal of American Studies* 27, no. 2 (1993): 149–171.

Bosniak, Linda. "Universal Citizenship and the Problem of Alienage." *Northwestern University Law Review* 94, no. 3 (2000): 963–982.

Bosteels, Bruno. *The Actuality of Communism*. New York: Verso, 2011.

———. *Badiou and Politics*. Durham, NC: Duke University Press, 2011.

———. "Estado, comuna, comunidad." *Bolivian Research Review / Revista Boliviana de Investigación* 11, no. 1 (2014): 50–70.

———. "Force of Nonlaw: Alain Badiou's Theory of Justice." *Cardozo Law Review* 29, no. 5 (2008): 1905–1926.

———. *Marx and Freud in Latin America: Politics, Psychoanalysis, and Religion in Times of Terror*. New York: Verso, 2012.

———. "Theses on Antagonism, Hybridity, and the Subaltern in Latin America." *Dispositio/n* 52, no. 25 (2005): 147–158.

———. "Translator's Introduction." In *Theory of the Subject*, by Alain Badiou, vii–xxxvii. London: Continuum, 2009.

Brecht, Bertolt. "Bertolt Brecht." In *Thirty Years of Treason: Excerpts from Hearings before the House Committee on Un-American Activities, 1938–1968*, edited by Eric Bentley, 207–220. New York: Viking, 1971.

————. *Brecht on Theatre*. Edited and translated by John Willett. New York: Hill and Wang, 1964.

————. "The Unread Statement." In *Thirty Years of Treason: Excerpts from Hearings before the House Committee on Un-American Activities, 1938–1968*, edited by Eric Bentley, 220–223. New York: Viking, 1971.

Bryant, Levi R. *The Democracy of Objects*. Ann Arbor, MI: Open Humanities Press, 2011.

Burgos, Julia de. "A Julia de Burgos / To Julia de Burgos." In *Song of the Simple Truth: The Complete Poems of Julia de Burgos*, compiled and translated by Jack Agüeros, 2–5. Willimantic, CT: Curbstone, 1997.

Butler, Judith, and Gayatri Chakravorty Spivak. *Who Sings the Nation-State? Language, Politics, Belonging*. London: Seagull Books, 2007.

Butler, Judith, and George Yancy. "What's Wrong with 'All Lives Matter'?" *New York Times*. January 12, 2015. https://opinionator.blogs.nytimes.com/2015/01/12/whats-wrong-with-all-lives-matter/?_r=0.

Cabrera, Nolan L., Jeffrey F. Milem, Ozan Jaquette, and Ronald W. Marx. "Missing the (Student Achievement) Forest for All the (Political) Trees: Empiricism and the Mexican American Studies Controversy in Tucson." *American Educational Research Journal* 51, no. 6 (December 2014): 1084–1118.

Cacho, Lisa Marie. *Social Death: Racialized Rightlessness and the Criminalization of the Unprotected*. New York: New York University Press, 2012.

Carrasquillo, Marci L. "Oscar 'Zeta' Acosta's American Odyssey." *MELUS* 35, no. 1 (Spring 2010): 77–97.

Carter, Bob, Marci Green, and Rick Halpern. "Immigration Policy and the Racialization of Migrant Labour: The Construction of National Identities in the USA and Britain." *Ethnic and Racial Studies* 19, no. 1 (1996): 135–157.

Chabram Dernersesian, Angie. "Chicana! Rican? No, Chicana-Riqueña! Refashioning the Transnational Connection." In *Multiculturalism: A Critical Reader*, edited by David Theo Goldberg, 269–295. Cambridge, MA: Blackwell, 1994.

Chávez, Ernesto. *"¡Mi Raza Primero!": Nationalism, Identity, and Insurgency in the Chicano Movement in Los Angeles, 1966–1978*. Los Angeles: University of California Press, 2002.

Chavez, Leo. *The Latino Threat: Constructing Immigrants, Citizens, and the Nation*. Stanford, CA: Stanford University Press, 2008.

Cisneros, Josue David. "(Re)Bordering the Civic Imaginary: Rhetoric, Hybridity, and Citizenship in *La Gran Marcha*." In *Governing Immigration through Crime: A Reader*, edited by Julie A. Dowling and Jonathan Xavier Inda, 253–268. Stanford, CA: Stanford University Press, 2013.

Cole, David. *Enemy Aliens: Double Standards and Constitutional Freedoms in the War on Terrorism*. New York: New Press, 2003.

Copjec, Joan. *Read My Desire: Lacan against the Historicists.* Cambridge, MA: MIT Press, 1994.

Critchley, Simon. *Infinitely Demanding: Ethics of Commitment, Politics of Resistance.* New York: Verso, 2007.

Cutrofello, Andrew. "The Ontological Status of Lacan's Mathematical Paradigms." In *Reading Seminar XX: Lacan's Major Work on Love, Knowledge, and Feminine Sexuality,* edited by Suzanne Barnard and Bruce Fink, 141–170. Albany, NY: SUNY Press, 2002.

Danto, Elizabeth Ann. "'Have You No Shame'—American Redbaiting of Europe's Psychoanalysts." In *Psychoanalysis and Politics,* edited by Joy Damousi and Mariano Plotkin, 213–231. New York: Oxford University Press, 2012.

Davis, Angela. *Are Prisons Obsolete?* New York: Seven Stories, 2003.

Dean, Jodi. *The Communist Horizon.* New York: Verso, 2012.

———. *Crowds and Party.* New York: Verso, 2016.

———. *Solidarity of Strangers: Feminism after Identity Politics.* Berkeley: University of California Press, 1996.

De Genova, Nicholas. "The Legal Production of Mexican/Migrant 'Illegality.'" In *Latinos and Citizenship: The Dilemma of Belonging,* edited by Suzanne Oboler, 61–90. New York: Palgrave Macmillan, 2006.

———. *Working the Boundaries: Race, Space, and "Illegality" in Mexican Chicago.* Durham, NC: Duke University Press, 2005.

De León, Jason. *The Land of Open Graves: Living and Dying on the Migrant Trail.* Oakland: University of California Press, 2015.

Democracy Now! "Debating Tucson School District's Book Ban After Suspension of Mexican American Studies Program." January 18, 2012. https://www.democracynow.org/2012/1/18/debating_tucson_school_districts_book_ban.

Derrida, Jacques. *The Beast and the Sovereign,* vol. 1. Edited by Michel Lisse, Marie-Louise Mallet, and Ginette Michaud. Translated by Geoffrey Bennington. Chicago: University of Chicago Press, 2009.

Dolar, Mladen. "Beyond Interpellation." *Qui Parle* 6, no. 2 (Spring/Summer 1993): 75–96.

———. "Freud and the Political." *Unbound* 4, no. 15 (2008): 15–29.

———. *A Voice and Nothing More.* Cambridge, MA: MIT Press, 2006.

Dowdy, Michael. *Broken Souths: Latina/o Poetic Responses to Neoliberalism and Globalization.* Tucson: University of Arizona Press, 2013.

Dowling, Julie A., and Jonathan Xavier Inda. "Introduction." In *Governing Immigration through Crime: A Reader,* edited by Julie A. Dowling and Jonathan Xavier Inda, 1–36. Stanford, CA: Stanford University Press, 2013.

Drummond, William J. "Noguchi Makes Rare Move in Calling Inquest: Coroner Breaks Tradition in Scheduling Inquiry on Death at Sheriff's Station." *Los Angeles Times.* January 24, 1970.

Eagleton, Terry. "Nationalism: Irony and Commitment." In *Nationalism, Colonialism, and Literature,* 23–39. Minneapolis: University of Minnesota Press, 1990.

Evans, Dylan. *An Introductory Dictionary of Lacanian Psychoanalysis.* New York: Routledge, 1996.

Fanon, Frantz. *Black Skin, White Masks.* Translated by Charles Lam Markmann. New York: Grove, 1967.

———. *A Dying Colonialism.* Translated by Haakon Chevalier. New York: Grove, 1965.

———. *Toward the African Revolution: Political Essays.* Translated by Haakon Chevalier. New York: Grove, 1967.

———. *The Wretched of the Earth.* Translated by Richard Philcox. New York: Grove, 2004.

Farred, Grant. "Wretchedness." In *Living Fanon: Global Perspectives,* edited by Nigel C. Gibson, 159–172. New York: Palgrave Macmillan, 2011.

Fink, Bruce. *The Lacanian Subject: Between Language and Jouissance.* Princeton, NJ: Princeton University Press, 1995.

Flores, William V. "Citizens vs. Citizenry: Undocumented Immigrants and Latino Cultural Citizenship." In *Latino Cultural Citizenship: Claiming Identity, Space, and Rights,* edited by William V. Flores and Rina Benmayor, 255–277. Boston: Beacon, 1997.

Foley, Neil. "Becoming Hispanic: Mexican Americans and the Faustian Pact with Whiteness." In *Reflexiones 1997: New Directions in Mexican American Studies,* edited by Neil Foley, 53–70. Austin: University of Texas Press, 1998.

Foucault, Michel. *Security, Territory, Population: Lectures at the Collège de France, 1977–1978.* Translated by Graham Burchell. New York: Palgrave Macmillan, 2007.

———. *Society Must Be Defended: Lectures at the Collège de France, 1975–1976.* Translated by David Macey. New York: Picador, 2003.

Freud, Sigmund. *Civilization and Its Discontents.* The Standard Edition. Edited and translated by James Strachey. New York: Norton, 1961.

———. *Group Psychology and the Analysis of the Ego.* Lexington, KY: Empire Books, 2012.

———. "The Question of a *Weltanschauung.*" In *New Introductory Lectures on Psycho-Analysis.* Translated by James Strachey, 195–225. New York: Norton, 1965.

Freud, Sigmund, and Albert Einstein. "Why War? An Exchange of Letters between Freud and Einstein." In *Freud and War,* edited by Marlène Belilos, 1–15. London: Karnac Books, 2016.

Fuss, Diana. "Interior Colonies: Frantz Fanon and the Politics of Identification." In *Rethinking Fanon: The Continuing Dialogue*, edited by Nigel C. Gibson, 294–328. New York: Humanity Books, 1999.

Gallego, Carlos. *Chicana/o Subjectivity and the Politics of Identity: Between Recognition and Revolution.* New York: Palgrave Macmillan, 2011.

García, Alma M., ed. *Chicana Feminist Thought: The Basic Historical Writings.* New York: Routledge, 1997.

García, Ignacio M. *White but Not Equal: Mexican Americans, Jury Discrimination, and the Supreme Court.* Tucson: University of Arizona Press, 2009.

García, Juan Ramon. *Operation Wetback: The Mass Deportation of Mexican Undocumented Workers in 1954.* Westport, CT: Greenwood, 1980.

García, Mario T. *Memories of Chicano History: The Life and Narrative of Bert Corona.* Berkeley: University of California Press, 1994.

García, Mario T., and Sal Castro. *Blowout! Sal Castro and the Chicano Struggle for Educational Justice.* Chapel Hill: University of North Carolina Press, 2011.

Garza, Alicia. "A Herstory of the #BlackLivesMatter Movement." *Feminist Wire.* October 7, 2014. http://www.thefeministwire.com/2014/10/blacklivesmatter-2/.

Gibson, Nigel C. *Fanon: The Postcolonial Imagination.* Malden, MA: Polity, 2003.

Gilmore, Ruth Wilson. *Golden Gulag: Prisons, Surplus, Crisis, and Opposition in Globalizing California.* Berkeley: University of California Press, 2007.

Gómez-Quiñones, Juan. *Mexican Students por La Raza: The Chicano Student Movement in Southern California 1967–1977.* Santa Barbara, CA: Editorial La Causa, 1978.

Gonzales, Alfonso. *Reform without Justice: Latino Migrant Politics and the Homeland Security State.* Oxford: Oxford University Press, 2014.

Gonzales, Roberto G. "Left Out but Not Shut Down: Political Activism and the Undocumented Student Movement." In *Governing Immigration through Crime: A Reader*, edited by Julie A. Dowling and Jonathan Xavier Inda, 269–284. Stanford, CA: Stanford University Press, 2013.

González, Marcial. *Chicano Novels and the Politics of Form: Race, Class, and Reification.* Ann Arbor: University of Michigan Press, 2009.

Grigg, Russell. "Lacan and Badiou: Logic of the *Pas-Tout.*" *Filozofski Vestnik* 26, no. 2 (2005): 53–65.

Griswold del Castillo, Richard. *The Treaty of Guadalupe Hidalgo: A Legacy of Conflict.* Norman: University of Oklahoma Press, 1990.

Gross, Ariela J. *What Blood Won't Tell: A History of Race on Trial in America.* Cambridge, MA: Harvard University Press, 2008.

Gutiérrez, David G. *Walls and Mirrors: Mexican Americans, Mexican Immigrants, and the Politics of Ethnicity.* Berkeley, CA: University of California Press, 1995.

Habermas, Jürgen. "Citizenship and National Identity: Some Reflections on the Future of Europe." In *Theorizing Citizenship*, edited by Ronald Beiner, 255–281. New York: SUNY Press, 1995.

Hallward, Peter. *Absolutely Postcolonial: Writing between the Singular and the Specific*. Manchester, UK: Manchester University Press, 2001.

———. *Badiou: A Subject to Truth*. Minneapolis: University of Minnesota Press, 2003.

———. *Damming the Flood: Haiti and the Politics of Containment*. New York: Verso, 2007.

———. "Fanon and Political Will." In *Living Fanon: Global Perspectives*, edited by Nigel C. Gibson, 213–224. New York: Palgrave Macmillan, 2011.

———. "The Will of the People: Notes towards a Dialectical Voluntarism." *Radical Philosophy* 155 (May–June 2009): 17–29.

Hames-García, Michael. "Dr. Gonzo's Carnival: The Testimonial Satires of Oscar Zeta Acosta." *American Literature* 72, no. 3 (September 2000): 463–493.

Haney López, Ian. *Racism on Trial: The Chicano Fight for Justice*. Cambridge, MA: Belknap, 2003.

Harvey, David. *A Brief History of Neoliberalism*. Oxford, UK: Oxford University Press, 2005.

———. *Seventeen Contradictions and the End of Capitalism*. Oxford, UK: Oxford University Press, 2014.

Helie-Lucas, Marie-Aimée. "Women, Nationalism, and Religion in the Algerian Liberation Struggle." In *Rethinking Fanon: The Continuing Dialogue*, edited by Nigel C. Gibson, 271–282. New York: Humanity Books, 1999.

Hobsbawm, Eric. *Nations and Nationalism since 1780: Programme, Myth, Reality*. 2nd ed. New York: Cambridge University Press, 1992.

Hoefer, Michael, Nancy Rytina, and Bryan Baker. *Estimates of the Unauthorized Immigrant Population Residing in the United States: January 2011*. Washington, DC: Department of Homeland Security, Office of Immigration Statistics, 2012.

Holloway, John. *Change the World without Taking Power: The Meaning of Revolution Today*. New ed. Ann Arbor, MI: Pluto, 2005.

Honig, Bonnie. *Democracy and the Foreigner*. Princeton, NJ: Princeton University Press, 2001.

Horne, Tom. "An Open Letter to the Citizens of Tucson." Tucson: Arizona Department of Education, June 11, 2007.

Houston, Paul, and Dave Smith. "Deputy Says He Did Not Know Kind of Missile." *Los Angeles Times*. September 30, 1970.

———. "Mexican-American Observers Walk Out of Salazar Inquest." *Los Angeles Times*. September 11, 1970.

Huppenthal, John. "Notice of Noncompliance." Tucson: Arizona Department of Education, Office of Superintendent John Huppenthal, January 2, 2015.

Inda, Jonathan Xavier. "Subject to Deportation: IRCA, 'Criminal Aliens,' and the Policing of Immigration." *Migration Studies* 1, no. 3 (March 2013): 292–310.

———. *Targeting Immigrants: Government, Technology, and Ethics.* Malden, MA: Blackwell, 2006.

Irwin, Robert McKee. *Bandits, Captives, Heroines, and Saints: Cultural Icons of Mexico's Northwest Borderlands.* Minneapolis: University of Minnesota Press, 2007.

Isin, Engin. *Citizens without Frontiers.* New York: Bloomsbury Academic, 2012.

———. "Theorizing Acts of Citizenship." In *Acts of Citizenship*, edited by Engin Isin and Greg Nielsen, 15–43. New York: Zed Books, 2008.

James, Joy. "Introduction." In *States of Confinement: Policing, Detention, and Prisons*, x–xvi. New York: St. Martin's, 2000.

———. "Martin Luther King, Jr." In *Imprisoned Intellectuals: America's Political Prisoners Write on Life, Liberation, and Rebellion*, 31–33. Lanham, MD: Rowman and Littlefield, 2003.

Jameson, Fredric. *Representing Capital: A Reading of Volume One.* New York: Verso, 2011.

Kanstroom, Daniel. *Aftermath: Deportation Law and the New American Diaspora.* New York: Oxford University Press, 2012.

Karatani, Kojin. *Transcritique: On Kant and Marx.* Translated by Sabu Kohso. Cambridge, MA: MIT Press, 2005.

Keitner, Chimène. *The Paradoxes of Nationalism: The French Revolution and Its Meaning for Contemporary Nation Building.* New York: SUNY Press, 2007.

King, Martin Luther, Jr. "Letter from Birmingham Jail." In *Imprisoned Intellectuals: America's Political Prisoners Write on Life, Liberation, and Rebellion*, edited by Joy James, 34–47. Lanham, MD: Rowman and Littlefield, 2003.

———. "Newly Discovered 1964 MLK Speech on Civil Rights, Segregation and Apartheid South Africa." *Democracy Now!* January 19, 2015. http:// www.democracynow.org/2015/1/19/exclusive_newly_discovered_1964 _mlk_speech.

Konvitz, Milton R. *The Alien and the Asiatic in American Law.* Ithaca, NY: Cornell University Press, 1946.

Kowalczyk, Kimberly. "Oscar Zeta Acosta: The Brown Buffalo and His Search for Identity." *Americas Review* 16, no. 3–4 (1988): 198–209.

Kymlicka, Will, and Wayne Norman. "Return of the Citizen: A Survey of Recent Work on Citizenship Theory." In *Theorizing Citizenship*, edited by Ronald Beiner, 283–322. New York: SUNY Press, 1995.

Lacan, Jacques. *Encore, The Seminar of Jacques Lacan Book XX: On Feminine Sexuality, The Limits of Love and Knowledge, 1972–1973.* Edited by Jacques-Alain Miller. Translated by Bruce Fink. New York: Norton, 1998.

———. "The Freudian Thing, or the Meaning of the Return to Freud in Psychoanalysis." In *Écrits*, translated by Bruce Fink, 334–363. New York: Norton, 2006.

———. *The Seminar of Jacques Lacan Book XI: The Four Fundamental Concepts of Psychoanalysis*. Edited by Jacques-Alain Miller. Translated by Alan Sheridan. New York: Norton, 1998.

———. *The Seminar of Jacques Lacan Book XVII: The Other Side of Psychoanalysis*. Edited by Jacques-Alain Miller. Translated by Russell Grigg. New York: Norton, 2007.

———. "The Subversion of the Subject and the Dialectic of Desire in the Freudian Unconscious." In *Écrits*, translated by Bruce Fink, 671–702. New York: Norton, 2006.

Laclau, Ernesto. "Ethics of Militant Engagement." In *Think Again: Alain Badiou and the Future of Philosophy*, edited by Peter Hallward, 120–137. New York: Continuum, 2004.

———. *On Populist Reason*. New York: Verso, 2007.

———. "Subject of Politics, Politics of the Subject." In *Emancipation(s)*, 47–65. New York: Verso, 2007.

———. "Why Do Empty Signifiers Matter to Politics?" In *Emancipation(s)*, 36–46. New York: Verso, 2007.

Lardner, Ring, Jr. "My Life on the Black List." In *Thirty Years of Treason: Excerpts from Hearings before the House Committee on Un-American Activities, 1938–1968*, edited by Eric Bentley, 189–194. New York: Viking, 1971.

Larralde, Carlos C., and Richard Griswold del Castillo. "Luisa Moreno: A Hispanic Civil Rights Leader in San Diego." *Journal of San Diego History* 41, no. 4 (1995): 284–311.

Laurent, Éric. "Alienation and Separation (I)." In *Reading Seminar XI: Lacan's Four Fundamental Concepts of Psychoanalysis*, edited by Richard Feldstein, Bruce Fink, and Maire Jaanus, 19–28. Albany, NY: SUNY Press, 1995.

Le Bon, Gustave. *The Crowd: A Study of the Popular Mind*. New York: Macmillan, 1947.

Lin, Joanne. "Operation Streamline Fact Sheet." Washington, DC: American Civil Liberties Union, Washington Legislative Office, July 21, 2009.

Litvak, Joseph. *The Un-Americans: Jews, the Blacklist, and Stoolpigeon Culture*. Durham, NC: Duke University Press, 2009.

Los Angeles Times. "Board Will Hear Demands from 4 East L.A. Schools." March 24, 1968.

Lowe, Lisa. *Immigrant Acts: On Asian American Cultural Politics*. Durham, NC: Duke University Press, 1996.

Lyon, James K. *Bertolt Brecht in America*. Princeton, NJ: Princeton University Press, 1980.

Marchart, Oliver. "In the Name of the People: Populist Reason and the Subject of the Political." *Diacritics* 35, no. 3 (Fall 2005): 3–19.

Marx, Karl. "On the Jewish Question." In *The Marx-Engels Reader*, 2nd ed., edited by Robert C. Tucker, 26–52. New York: Norton, 1978.

McClintock, Anne. "Fanon and Gender Agency." In *Rethinking Fanon: The Continuing Dialogue*, edited by Nigel C. Gibson, 283–293. New York: Humanity Books, 1999.

McCurdy, Jack. "1,000 Walk Out in School Boycott: Jefferson Teachers Quit Classes; 19 Juveniles, 1 Adult Arrested." *Los Angeles Times.* March 9, 1968.

———. "Venice High Youths, Police Clash: Crowd of 1,000 Clashes with Police at Venice High School." *Los Angeles Times.* March 13, 1968.

McDougall, William. *The Group Mind: A Sketch of the Principles of Collective Psychology and Some Attempt to Apply Them to the Interpretation of National Life and Character.* New York: G. P. Putnam's Sons, 1920.

McNulty, Tracy. "Feminine Love and the Pauline Universal." In *Alain Badiou: Philosophy and Its Conditions*, edited by Gabriel Riera, 185–212. Albany, NY: SUNY Press, 2005.

Meissner, Doris, Donald M. Kerwin, Muzaffar Chishti, and Claire Bergeron. *Immigration Enforcement in the United States: The Rise of a Formidable Machinery.* Washington, DC: Migration Policy Institute, 2013.

Mellino, Miguel. "Notes from the Underground, Fanon, Africa, and the Poetics of the Real." In *Living Fanon: Global Perspectives*, edited by Nigel C. Gibson, 61–73. New York: Palgrave Macmillan, 2011.

Mendoza, Louis Gerard. *Historia: The Literary Making of Chicana and Chicano History.* College Station: Texas A&M University Press, 2001.

Mews, Siegfried. "An 'Un-American' Brecht?" *German Politics and Society* 13, no. 3 (Fall 1995): 6–16.

Miller, David. *On Nationality.* New York: Oxford University Press, 1995.

Miller, Todd. *Border Patrol Nation: Dispatches from the Front Lines of Homeland Security.* San Francisco: City Lights Books, 2014.

———. "There's a Bigger Problem at the Border than Trump's Proposed Wall." *Nation.* August 23, 2016.

Mitchell, Lee Clark. "Whose West Is It Anyway? Or, What's Myth Got to Do with It? The Role of 'America' in the Creation of the Myth of the West." *American Review of Canadian Studies* 33, no. 4 (2003): 497–508.

Moloney, Deirdre M. *National Insecurities: Immigrants and U.S. Deportation Policy Since 1882.* Chapel Hill, NC: University of North Carolina Press, 2012.

Moore, Burton. *Love and Riot: Oscar Zeta Acosta and the Great Mexican American Revolt.* Mountain View, CA: Floricanto, 2003.

Moraga, Cherríe. *Loving in the War Years: Lo que nunca pasó por sus labios.* Expanded 2nd. ed. Cambridge, MA: South End Press, 2000.

Morawetz, Nancy. "Understanding the Impact of the 1996 Deportation Laws and the Limited Scope of Proposed Reforms." *Harvard Law Review* 113 (2000): 1936–1962.

Moreiras, Alberto. *The Exhaustion of Difference: The Politics of Latin American Cultural Studies*. Durham, NC: Duke University Press, 2001.

———. "The Fatality of (My) Subalternism: A Response to John Beverley." *CR: The New Centennial Review* 12, no. 2 (Fall 2012): 217–246.

Moreno, Luisa. "Non-Citizen Americans of the South West." In *Proceedings of the Fourth Annual Conference of the American Committee for Protection of Foreign Born*, 46–52. Washington, DC: American Committee for Protection of Foreign Born, 1940.

Muñoz, Carlos. *Youth, Identity, Power: The Chicano Movement*. Rev. and expanded ed. New York: Verso, 2007.

Nail, Thomas. "Alain Badiou and the Sans-Papiers." *Angelaki* 20, no. 4 (2015): 109–129.

Neocosmos, Michael. "The Nation and Its Politics: Fanon, Emancipatory Nationalism, and Political Sequences." In *Living Fanon: Global Perspectives*, edited by Nigel C. Gibson, 187–199. New York: Palgrave Macmillan, 2011.

Nevins, Joseph. *Operation Gatekeeper: The Rise of the "Illegal Alien" and the Making of the U.S.-Mexico Boundary*. New York: Routledge, 2002.

Ngai, Mae. *Impossible Subjects: Illegal Aliens and the Making of Modern America*. Princeton, NJ: Princeton University Press, 2004.

Nye, Robert A. *The Origins of Crowd Psychology: Gustave LeBon and the Crisis of Mass Democracy in the Third Republic*. Beverly Hills, CA: Sage, 1975.

Oboler, Suzanne, ed. *Latinos and Citizenship: The Dilemma of Belonging*. New York: Palgrave Macmillan, 2006.

Ochoa O'Leary, Anna, Andrea J. Romero, Nolan L. Cabrera, and Michelle Rascón. "Assault on Ethnic Studies." In *Arizona Firestorm: Global Immigration Realities, National Media, and Provincial Politics*, edited by Otto Santa Ana and Celeste González de Bustamante, 97–120. New York: Rowman and Littlefield, 2012.

Olivas, Michael A., ed. *"Colored Men" and "Hombres Aquí"*: Hernandez v. Texas and the Emergence of Mexican-American Lawyering. Houston: Arte Público, 2006.

Ong, Aihwa. *Flexible Citizenship: The Cultural Logics of Transnationality*. Durham, NC: Duke University Press, 1999.

Orozco, Richard. "Racism and Power: Arizona Politicians' Use of the Discourse of Anti-Americanism against Mexican American Studies." *Hispanic Journal of Behavioral Sciences* 34, no. 1 (2012): 43–60.

Pallares, Amalia, and Nilda Flores-González. "Introduction." In *¡Marcha! Latino Chicago and the Immigrant Rights Movement*, xv–xxix. Urbana: University of Illinois Press, 2010.

Passel, Jeffrey S., D'Vera Cohn, and Ana Gonzalez-Barrera. "Population Decline of Unauthorized Immigrants Stalls, May Have Reversed." Pew Research Center, Hispanic Trends, September 23, 2013. http://www.pewhispanic.org /2013/09/23/population-decline-of-unauthorized-immigrants-stalls-may -have-reversed/.

Pick, Daniel. "Freud's *Group Psychology* and the History of the Crowd." *History Workshop Journal*, no. 40 (1995): 39–61.

Pithouse, Richard. "Fidelity to Fanon." In *Living Fanon: Global Perspectives*, edited by Nigel C. Gibson, 225–234. New York: Palgrave Macmillan, 2011.

Poblete, Juan. "Introduction." In *Critical Latin American and Latino Studies*, ix–xli. Minneapolis: University of Minnesota Press, 2003.

Popper, Deborah Epstein, Robert E. Lang, and Frank J. Popper. "From Maps to Myth: The Census, Turner, and the Idea of the Frontier." *Journal of American and Comparative Cultures* 23, no. 1 (2000): 91–102.

Prashad, Vijay. "Ethnic Studies Inside Out." *Journal of Asian American Studies* 9, no. 2 (June 2006): 157–176.

———. "How the Hindus Became Jews: American Racism after 9/11." *The South Atlantic Quarterly* 104, no. 3 (Summer 2005): 583–606.

Preston, William. *Aliens and Dissenters: Federal Suppression of Radicals, 1903–1933*. 2nd ed. Urbana: University of Illinois Press, 1994.

Pulido, Laura. *Black, Brown, Yellow, and Left: Radical Activism in Los Angeles*. Los Angeles: University of California Press, 2006.

———. "A Day without Immigrants: The Racial and Class Politics of Immigrant Exclusion." *Antipode* 39, no. 1 (2007): 1–7.

Ramírez, Arthur. "Reseñas: Book Review of *The Autobiography of a Brown Buffalo* and *The Revolt of the Cockroach People*." *Revista Chicano-Riqueña* 3, no. 3 (1975): 46–53.

Ramírez, Catherine S. "Learning and Unlearning from Ethnic Studies." *American Quarterly* 66, no. 4 (December 2014): 1057–1069.

Rancière, Jacques. *Disagreement: Politics and Philosophy*. Translated by Julie Rose. Minneapolis: University of Minnesota Press, 1999.

Redding, Arthur. "Frontier Mythographies: Savagery and Civilization in Frederick Jackson Turner and John Ford." *Literature Film Quarterly* 35, no. 4 (2007): 313–322.

Rocco, Raymond A. *Transforming Citizenship: Democracy, Membership, and Belonging in Latino Communities*. East Lansing: Michigan State University Press, 2014.

Rodríguez, Richard T. "Carnal Knowledge: Chicano Gay Men and the Dialectics of Being." In *Gay Latino Studies: A Critical Reader*, edited by Michael Hames-García and Ernesto Javier Martínez, 113–140. Durham, NC: Duke University Press, 2011.

Rosaldo, Renato. "Cultural Citizenship, Inequality, and Multiculturalism." In *Latino Cultural Citizenship: Claiming Identity, Space, and Rights*, edited by William V. Flores and Rina Benmayor, 27–38. Boston: Beacon, 1997.

Rosales, F. Arturo. *Chicano! The History of the Mexican American Civil Rights Movement.* 2nd ed. Houston: Arte Público, 1997.

Rousseau, Jean-Jacques. "On the Social Contract." In *The Basic Political Writings*, translated by Donald A. Cress, 139–227. Indianapolis, IN: Hackett, 1987.

Ruda, Frank. "Remembering the Impossible: For a Meta-Critical Anamnesis of Communism." In *The Idea of Communism*, vol. 2, edited by Slavoj Žižek, 137–168. New York: Verso, 2013.

Ruiz, Vicki L. "Una Mujer sin Fronteras: Luisa Moreno and Latina Labor Activism." *Pacific Historical Review* 73, no. 1 (February 2004): 1–20.

Saldaña-Portillo, María Josefina. *The Revolutionary Imagination in the Americas and the Age of Development.* Durham, NC: Duke University Press, 2003.

———. "'Wavering on the Horizon of Social Being': The Treaty of Guadalupe-Hidalgo and the Legacy of Its Racial Character in Americo Paredes's *George Washington Gómez*." *Radical History Review* 89 (Spring 2004): 135–164.

Saldívar, Ramón. *Chicano Narrative: The Dialectics of Difference.* Madison: University of Wisconsin Press, 1990.

Saldívar-Hull, Sonia. *Feminism on the Border: Chicana Gender Politics and Literature.* Los Angeles: University of California Press, 2000.

Salecl, Renata. "Introduction." In *Sexuation*, 1–9. Durham, NC: Duke University Press, 2000.

Santa Ana, Otto, Sandra L. Treviño, Michael J. Bailey, Kristen Bodossian, and Antonio de Necochea. "A May to Remember: Adversarial Images of Immigrants in U.S. Newspapers during the 2006 Policy Debate." *Du Bois Review* 4, no. 1 (2007): 207–232.

Sassen, Saskia. "U.S. Immigration Policy toward Mexico in a Global Economy." *Journal of International Affairs* 43, no. 1 (1990): 369–383.

Schmidt Camacho, Alicia. *Migrant Imaginaries: Latino Cultural Politics in the U.S.-Mexico Borderlands.* New York: New York University Press, 2008.

Sekyi-Otu, Ato. *Fanon's Dialectic of Experience.* Cambridge, MA: Harvard University Press, 1996.

Shafir, Gershon, ed. *The Citizenship Debates: A Reader.* Minneapolis: University of Minnesota Press, 1998.

Sharpley-Whiting, T. Denean. "Fanon's Feminist Consciousness and Algerian Women's Liberation: Colonialism, Nationalism, and Fundamentalism." In *Rethinking Fanon: The Continuing Dialogue*, edited by Nigel C. Gibson, 329–353. New York: Humanity Books, 1999.

Simon, Jonathan. *Governing through Crime: How the War on Crime Transformed American Democracy and Created a Culture of Fear*. Oxford, UK: Oxford University Press, 2007.

Smith, James Morton. *Freedom's Fetters: The Alien and Sedition Laws and American Civil Liberties*. Ithaca, NY: Cornell University Press, 1956.

Sohi, Seema. *Echoes of Mutiny: Race, Surveillance and Indian Anticolonialism in North America*. New York: Oxford University Press, 2014.

Soto, Sandra K., and Miranda Joseph. "Neoliberalism and the Battle over Ethnic Studies in Arizona." *Thought and Action* (Fall 2010): 45–56.

Stavrakakis, Yannis. "Antinomies of Formalism: Laclau's Theory of Populism and the Lessons from Religious Populism in Greece." *Journal of Political Ideologies* 9, no. 3 (October 2004): 253–267.

———. "Enjoying the Nation: A Success Story?" In *The Lacanian Left: Psychoanalysis, Theory, Politics*, 189–210. Edinburgh, UK: Edinburgh University Press, 2007.

Stevens, Jacqueline. "Thin ICE." *Nation*. June 5, 2008.

Swanger, Joanna. *Radical Social Change in the United States: Badiou's Apostle and the Post-factual Moment*. Cham, Switzerland: Palgrave Macmillan, 2017.

Tatum, Charles M. *Chicano and Chicana Literature: Otra voz del pueblo*. Tucson: University of Arizona Press, 2006.

Taylor, Keeanga-Yamahtta. *From #BlackLivesMatter to Black Liberation*. Chicago: Haymarket Books, 2016.

Torgerson, Dial. "Start of a Revolution? 'Brown Power' Unity Seen behind School Disorders." *Los Angeles Times*. March 17, 1968.

Torres, Rodolfo D., Louis F. Mirón, and Jonathan Xavier Inda, eds. *Race, Identity, and Citizenship: A Reader*. Malden, MA: Blackwell, 1999.

Turner, Frederick Jackson. *The Frontier in American History*. New York: Holt, Rinehart, and Winston, 1962.

Varsanyi, Monica W. "'Getting Out the Vote' in Los Angeles: The Mobilization of Undocumented Migrants in Electoral Politics." In *Latinos and Citizenship: The Dilemma of Belonging*, edited by Suzanne Oboler, 219–246. New York: Palgrave Macmillan, 2006.

Viego, Antonio. *Dead Subjects: Toward a Politics of Loss in Latino Studies*. Durham, NC: Duke University Press, 2007.

Villanueva, Silvia Toscano. "Teaching as a Healing Craft: Decolonizing the Classroom and Creating Spaces of Hopeful Resistance through Chicano-Indigenous Pedagogical Praxis." *Urban Review* 45, no. 1 (March 2013): 23–40.

Walker, Gavin. "On Marxism's Field of Operation: Badiou and the Critique of Political Economy." *Historical Materialism* 20, no. 2 (2012): 39–74.

Wang, Ted, and Robert C. Winn. "Groundswell Meets Groundwork: Building on the Mobilizations to Empower Immigrant Communities." In *Rallying for*

Immigrant Rights: The Fight for Inclusion in 21st Century America, edited by Kim Voss and Irene Bloemraad, 44–59. Berkeley: University of California Press, 2011.

Weber, David J. *Myth and the History of the Hispanic Southwest.* Albuquerque: University of New Mexico Press, 2002.

Weissbrodt, David, and Laura Danielson. *Immigration Law and Procedure in a Nutshell.* 6th ed. St. Paul, MN: West, 2011.

Wiecek, William M. "The Legal Foundations of Domestic Anticommunism: The Background of *Dennis v. United States." Supreme Court Review* (2001): 375–434.

Wilderson, Frank B., III. "The Prison Slave as Hegemony's (Silent) Scandal." *Social Justice* 30, no. 2 (2003): 18–27.

Williams, Gareth. *The Other Side of the Popular: Neoliberalism and Subalternity in Latin America.* Durham, NC: Duke University Press, 2002.

———. "The Subalternist Turn in Latin American Postcolonial Studies, or, Thinking in the Wake of What Went Down Yesterday (November 8, 2016)." *Política Común* 10 (2016): http://dx.doi.org/10.3998/pc.12322227.0010.016.

Williams, Robert A., Jr. *Like a Loaded Weapon: The Rehnquist Court, Indian Rights, and the Legal History of Racism in America.* Minneapolis: University of Minnesota Press, 2005.

Young, Elliott. *Alien Nation: Chinese Migration in the Americas from the Coolie Era through World War II.* Chapel Hill: University of North Carolina Press, 2014.

Young, Iris Marion. "Polity and Group Difference: A Critique of the Ideal of Universal Citizenship." In *The Citizenship Debates: A Reader*, edited by Gershon Shafir, 263–290. Minneapolis: University of Minnesota Press, 1998.

Žižek, Slavoj. *In Defense of Lost Causes.* New York: Verso, 2008.

———. "Introduction: Robespierre, or, The 'Divine Violence' of Terror." In *Virtue and Terror*, translated by John Howe, vii–xxxix. New York: Verso, 2007.

———. *The Parallax View.* Cambridge, MA: MIT Press, 2009.

———. *The Sublime Object of Ideology.* 2nd ed. New York: Verso, 2008.

Zupančič, Alenka. "The Case of the Perforated Sheet." In *Sexuation*, edited by Renata Salecl, 282–296. Durham, NC: Duke University Press, 2000.

———. *The Odd One In: On Comedy.* Cambridge, MA: MIT Press, 2008.

———. "When Surplus Enjoyment Meets Surplus Value." In *Jacques Lacan and the Other Side of Psychoanalysis*, edited by Justin Clemens and Russell Grigg, 155–178. Durham, NC: Duke University Press, 2006.

INDEX

Note: Numbers in italics refer to figures.